CANAL — PLAN AND PROFILE
FROM
...RCES BOARD — PLATE I.

...ANUARY 30, 1942

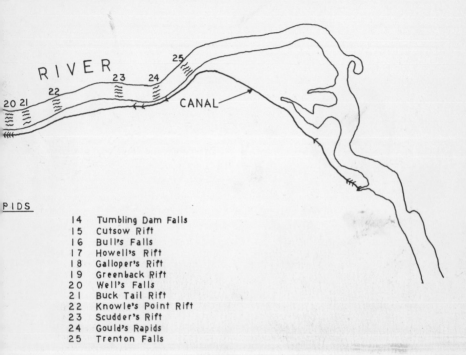

RIVER

20 21 22 23 24 25

CANAL

...PIDS

14	Tumbling Dam Falls
15	Cutsow Rift
16	Bull's Falls
17	Howell's Rift
18	Galloper's Rift
19	Greenback Rift
20	Well's Falls
21	Buck Tail Rift
22	Knowle's Point Rift
23	Scudder's Rift
24	Gould's Rapids
25	Trenton Falls

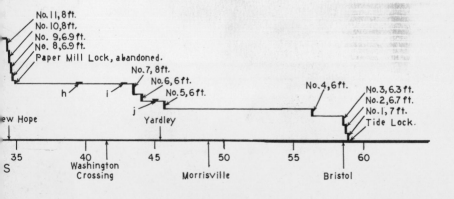

No. 11, 8 ft.
No. 10, 8 ft.
No. 9, 6.9 ft.
No. 8, 6.9 ft.
Paper Mill Lock, abandoned.
No. 7, 8 ft.
No. 6, 6 ft.
No. 5, 6 ft.
No. 4, 6 ft.
No. 3, 6.3 ft.
No. 2, 6.7 ft.
No. 1, 7 ft.
Tide Lock.

h   i

j

...ew Hope   Yardley

35   40   45   50   55   60
S
Washington   Morrisville   Bristol
Crossing

With kind regards

C. P. Yoder

DELAWARE CANAL JOURNAL

A

Definitive History

of the Canal

and the

River Valley

Through which it Flows

by

C. P. "BILL" YODER

Published by

Canal Press Incorporated

Bethlehem, Pennsylvania

1972

LIBRARY OF CONGRESS CATALOG CARD NUMBER: 72-93835

First Printing   Printed by Lehigh Litho, Inc.
November 1972   Bethlehem, Pennsylvania

To

BETTY

in

Loving Memory

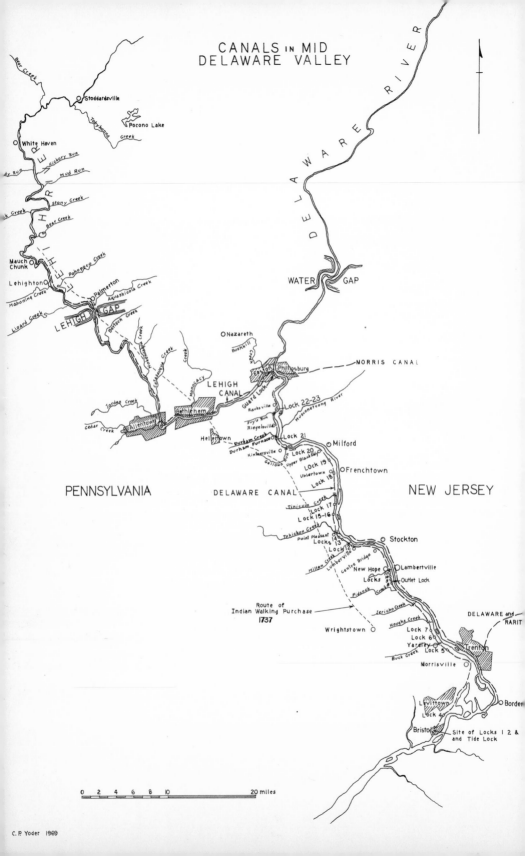

CANALS IN MID
DELAWARE VALLEY

DELAWARE RIVER

Bear Creek

Stoddardsville

Pocono Lake

Tobyhanna Creek

White Haven

Hickory Run

Mud Run

Stony Creek

Bear Creek

WATER GAP

Mauch Chunk

Lehighton

Pohopoco Creek

Mahoning Creek

Palmerton

Aquashicola Creek

Lizard Creek

LEHIGH GAP

Pohatcong Creek

Nazareth

Bushkill

MORRIS CANAL

Easton

Phillipsburg

Guard Lock

Jordan Creek

LEHIGH CANAL

Monocacy

Raubsville

Lock 22-23

Bethlehem

Fry's Run

Musconetcong River

Cedar Creek

Allentown

Riegelsville

Hellertown

Durham Creek

Lock 21

Durham Furnace

Milford

PENNSYLVANIA

Kintnersville

Lock 20

Gallows

Upper Black

LOck 19

Uhlertown

Frenchtown

Lock 18

DELAWARE CANAL

NEW JERSEY

Tinicum Creek

Lock 17

Lock 15-16

Tohickon Creek

Point Pleasant

Lock 14

Locks 13

Lock 12

Stockton

Milton Creek

Lumberville

Centre Bridge

New Hope

Lambertville

Locks

Outlet Lock

Pidcock

Route of
Indian Walking Purchase
1737

Jericho Creek

DELAWARE and
RARIT

Wrightstown

Hough's Creek

Lock 7

Lock 6

Yardley

Lock 5

Buck Creek

Trenton

Morrisville

Levittown

Lock 4

Borden

Bristol

Site of Locks 1 2 &
and Tide Lock

0 2 4 6 8 10   20 miles

C. P. Yoder 1969

CONTENTS

Foreword

It was during the summer of 1966 that I made my discovery of the Delaware Canal. Officially, the name of this waterway is the Delaware Division of the Pennsylvania Canal, a rather imposing and cumbersome title. But since the old boatmen, other residents of the valley and the historical markers installed by the Pennsylvania Historical and Museum Commission all use the shorter term, I will follow their example.

From my earliest recollections until graduation from high school I had lived among canals. I grew up near the Cayuga and Seneca Canal in New York State, and its banks and the waterway itself were my playground. Later, I lived for several months on the old Erie Canal. Then, after a lapse of nearly sixty years, my early interest in canals was rekindled when I moved to eastern Pennsylvania and made my discovery of this waterway and the Delaware Valley.

Naturally, my first interest was to learn as much as possible about the Delaware Canal and its history. Yet from casual inquiry I was unable to find books or other readily available information to satisfy that curiosity. Finally a visit to the library of The Bucks County Historical Society in Doylestown, Pennsylvania, produced my first encouragement. This library is a rich source of the area's history, and my experience here led me to continue the search at other libraries, historical societies and the files of old newspapers. The libraries of

Lafayette College, Lehigh and Cornell Universities, and especially, the Pennsylvania State Archives produced a wealth of historic material. I was also delighted to become acquainted with many of the people still living in eastern Pennsylvania who had worked on the Delaware Canal or had been closely associated with it during the latter years of active service. Without exception, they were most gracious in sharing with me their knowledge and their experiences.

At about that time, the summer of 1966, the Pennsylvania Canal Society was organized. One purpose of this society is "to make available to the public materials on canals, their operation and history." It has been my good fortune to have the time and opportunity to assemble from original and other sources much of the history of the Delaware Canal and the valley through which it passes. My belief that others may share my interest and enthusiasm is my justification for compiling this volume. To the reader who may find an inordinate amount of quotation, let me say that this feature is deliberate and based on the belief that the original writer, with his sometimes quaint but always articulate language, could much better convey a sense of the times and the circumstances than any paraphrase of mine.

Even a modest work such as this would be impossible without the helpful cooperation of many people in a position to supply valuable help, information and advice. My special gratitude goes to Mr. and Mrs. J. Edwin Porter for supplying the spark that ignited my renewed interest in old canals; to Emily and Hayward Madden, those inveterate researchers of canal lore who continually contributed choice gleanings from their research; and to Harry L. Rinker, president of the Pennsylvania Canal Society, for prodding my interest into productive channels and for critically reviewing the manuscript.

My grateful thanks also go to Mrs. Cora B. Decker, Librarian, and Mrs. Elizabeth Moore, Assistant Librarian, of The Bucks County Historical Society; to William H. Work, Archivist, and Miss Martha L. Simonetti, Associate Archivist, of the Pennsylvania State Archives; to Miss Ruth Leh, Librarian, Nazareth Memorial Library; to the library assistants at the Cornell and Lehigh University and Lafayette College libraries; to Russel S. Paetzell, the first superintendent of Roosevelt State Park and to his successor James M. Bailey; and to William F. Taylor, first president of the Delaware Valley Protective Association.

Finally, my sincere gratitude to a very special group of canal people who were closely associated with the Delaware Canal during its active years. By contributing reminiscences, photographs and, in particular, numerous taped interviews, they have greatly enhanced the history of this waterway. Where these individuals are quoted in the text, the material used is from taped interviews, the originals of which are in the possession of the author and Harry L. Rinker. It is a privilege to express my appreciation to Grant G. Emery and Mrs. Chester Mann of Phillipsburg, New Jersey, and the following residents of Pennsylvania:

George Amey, Walnutport
Mrs. Martha Best, Walnutport
Richard DeWalt, Catasauqua
George Fox, Allentown
Arlington Greenzweig, Walnutport
Miss Flora K. Henry, Point Pleasant
Carl Kilpatrick, Bethlehem
Clinton H. Kreitz, Raubsville
Joseph A. Lum, Easton
William A. Minder, Lodi
Joseph W. Reed, Sr., Freemansburg
Theodore A. Sherman, Zionsville
Frank Sigafoos, Upper Black Eddy
Horace Sigafoos, Erwinna
Charles Soloman, Easton
Mrs. Esther Weaver, Uhlertown
Mark F. Wismer, Easton

With the advent of modern transportation, the old canals, with one exception, have passed into obscurity. The Delaware Canal still remains. Located as it is, along the western bank of the Delaware River, passing through a section of outstanding scenic beauty and an area rich in historic lore, this canal is annually inspected by an ever increasing number of interested visitors. To make a tour of the Delaware Canal is to relive history.

It is the intent of this book to locate the main features of interest along the canal, to recall its construction and operation and the people who made those activities possible, and to remind the visitor of the rich historical heritage of this portion of the Delaware Valley.

Chapter 1

The Delaware River Before Canals

*On Saturday night last there was a riot at Snufftown (Williams-
port) across the Lehigh from our borough. Mr. Downing, keeper of
the hotel in that town, had an Irish dance—some of the lumbermen
from up the river, of whom we had a great number in town, went over
to see the fashion, and after the most of them had come away the
balance and the Irish got to loggerheads; clubs, spades, stones and
other missiles were used in great profusion, and some of the lumbermen were seriously injured.*

The Whig, Easton, Pa., April 13, 1830

The Delaware is a perverse river. Nobody knows just where it
begins; and, where it ends was a popular subject of debate, particularly
among the early raftsmen. Some maintained the river ended when
tidewater was reached near Bristol while others argued it continued
far down into what is now recognized as Delaware Bay, between the
New Jersey and Delaware shores. Unlike its neighbors, the majestic
Hudson on the east with its Tear-of-the-Clouds, high up in the
shadow of the Adirondacks' Mt. Marcy, or the sprawling Susquehanna
on the west with its placid Otsego Lake in eastern New York, the
Delaware has its beginning in some obscure stream or spring on the
western slopes of the Catskill Mountains. Any settler on the upper
West Branch of the Delaware may declare "that the river starts from
his own spring-house or from his barnyard pool"[1] while a partisan of
the East Branch may be equally emphatic that its origin is in one of
the tributaries of that branch. But from the junction of these branches
at Hancock, New York, on the Pennsylvania boundary, there is no
question of the identity of the historic Delaware throughout its winding course southward for some three hundred miles until it merges
at an indefinite point with the estuary of Delaware Bay. From a few
miles above Hancock to Port Jervis the Delaware forms the boundary
between New York and Pennsylvania, while from the latter city to
its mouth the river forms the boundary between New Jersey and
Pennsylvania.

The Delaware was not always a river. For aeons it was trapped
as a huge lake north of the Blue Mountain barrier. Once this barrier
was breached, during the retreat of the ice age, the river had a comparatively free course to the sea, leaving behind the famous Delaware
Water Gap with its nearly perpendicular bluffs rising over 1300 feet

on either side. In the horse-and-buggy days the Water Gap was the spectacular wonder of the east, attracting thousands of visitors who lingered at fashionable resorts to enjoy its scenic beauty. Today, the motorist speeding along the turnpike that runs through the Gap appears content to obtain a fleeting glimpse of this famous landmark. But the Delaware is also generous in distributing its natural beauty throughout its course, making the Delaware Valley one of the most spectacular in the east.

Innumerable streams and rivers contribute to the waters of the Delaware. Among the latter the Lackawaxen River, entering the Delaware near Minisink Ford, the Neversink River entering near Port Jervis and the Lehigh River entering at Easton, have made important contributions to the industrial development of the Delaware Valley.

From prehistoric times the Delaware has been a natural route of transportation, first by the dug-out and bark canoes of the Indians and later, for over a hundred and fifty years, by the great fleets of log and lumber rafts that were guided down the waterway on the spring freshets by the intrepid raftsmen.

As the population and industry of Philadelphia and other down river communities expanded through the late colonial and early state-hood period, the demand for lumber as building material for business structures, homes and wharves increased correspondingly. Although several hundred miles away, the great virgin forests of northeastern Pennsylvania and adjacent New York State were the most attractive source of supply. At that time the only logical means of transporting logs and timber from this region was the Delaware River. But the river's winding course and treacherous rapids had proven barriers to the use of rafts.

According to Dr. Wheaton J. Lane of Princeton University,[2] the credit for navigating the first raft down the river, from above Port Jervis to Philadelphia, belongs to Daniel Skinner and an unnamed assistant. This feat of navigating the river for nearly 200 miles was performed about 1750.[3] The success of this venture was widely acclaimed in Philadelphia; both men were given the freedom of the city, and Skinner was awarded the title of "Lord High Admiral of the Delaware." Dr. Lane states that the raft consisted of six pine logs 70 feet long, to be used as masts of ships then building at Philadelphia.

For over 150 years following Skinner's adventure, great numbers of log and timber rafts were guided down the Delaware River. Accord-ing to Hazard's Register, (Vol. III, p. 384), over a thousand rafts passed down the river on the spring freshet of 1828, many of them of huge size, measuring as much as 60 feet wide and 200 feet long. On occasion fifteen to twenty rafts could be counted in view at one time.

The rafting era reached its greatest height in the decade from 1875 to 1885. Blake Calkings, an old raftsman of long experience, stated that the year 1875 was the greatest single year for rafting in his memory. During a trip down the river in early May of that year he asked the record keeper at Lackawaxen Dam—called Lackawack by the rivermen—how many rafts had gone down so far that spring. He was told "that 3,140 rafts had been recorded up to that day."[4] From that decade rafting began to decline and by the turn of the century it had pretty much disappeared from the river. "The Mitchell boys of Callicoon claimed the distinction of taking the last raft ever floated down the Delaware River to the down river market. It was run from Dillontown . . . to Bordentown in 1913."[5] On the upper river a few rafts were in evidence up to 1921 or 1922.

Four types of rafts were used on the Delaware River[6]: (1) The toggle timber, or piling, raft: made from round poles 12 inches to 14 inches in diameter and of various lengths. They were used mainly for building wharves at cities along the lower river. (2) Square timber raft: For this raft large logs were squared by means of axes. In later years when sawmills were established, this work was done at the mill. This material was used in the construction of wharves. (3) Sawed lumber raft: for transporting sawed lumber, usually in 3 inch thick planks. (4) The log raft: made of logs as they came from the forest or, in some cases, with the bark peeled off.

All of the rafts with the exception of the sawed lumber raft, for which a special cribbing had to be constructed, were assembled in a uniform manner. The log raft may be used to illustrate the method of construction. A number of logs as nearly as possible of the same diameter were collected, side by side, in the river, the number used depending on the width of the raft. These logs were held together by "lash poles" which were small saplings about 4 inches in diameter. The lash poles were placed across the raft at right angles to the logs and spaced at 3 to 4 feet intervals along the length of the raft. On each side of and close to the lash pole, 1¼ inch diameter by 6 inch deep holes were bored in each log. Triangular pieces of elm, slightly larger than the diameter of the hole, were next split from a block 14 to 16 inches long. One side of each piece was then shaved down with a draw shave. The individual pieces were bent around the lash pole, the ends being inserted into the holes in the log. By striking with a mallet first one side and then the other side of the loop, or

Courtesy, Walter Longley
Large log raft on Delaware River.

bow as raftsmen called it, the ends were driven down until the bow
was tightly against the lash pole. To further secure the bow, ash
wedges were driven into each hole adjacent to the shaved portion.
It was found in later years that a great deal of work could be saved
and equal results could be obtained by substituting old horseshoes
for the elm bows.

Across each end of the raft parallel to the lash poles, 16 inch
high blocks were fastened to the logs by means of large wooden pegs.
A 2 inch diameter, hard wood pin for supporting the oar stem, then
was inserted through a hole in the block into the timber below. The
oar was a massive affair, consisting of a 40 foot long basswood stem,
8 inches in diameter at the butt, tapering to 2 inches at the stem end.
At the butt end a two inch wide slot was cut to receive the 12 inch
wide oar blade. Finding the point of balance of the oar was one of
the important details. This was accomplished by sliding the oar along
the supporting block until the stem end could be pressed down with
one finger. At this point a hole was bored through the stem to receive
the supporting pin. The hole was tapered to a larger diameter at the
top of the stem to permit raising and lowering the oar without binding.
Proper balance of the oar was necessary to reduce fatigue in its
manipulation during the long passage down the river.

From RAFTING ON THE DELAWARE
Closeup view showing method of fastening the lash poles to the logs.

An essential feature of most rafts was the "shirt pole." This pole was made from a small sapling which included short extensions beyond the crotch of the tree. Near the center of the raft a hole to support the pole was bored in one of the logs. The purpose of the pole was to hold extra clothing to keep it from becoming drenched with water when the raft went over a dam or through rough rapids. The inevitable whiskey jug usually was found at the base of the pole.

From RAFTING ON THE DELAWARE
A single log raft, 30 feet by 160 feet, on the Delaware River near Hancock, N.Y.

Much of the fine timber of the region was found along the north and south branches and other tributaries of the Delaware River. These streams were winding and filled with treacherous rapids. Even during flood conditions navigation was dangerous and extremely difficult. Here, a smaller version of the main river raft, called a "colt," was used. While conforming to the usual construction of larger rafts, its dimensions were not over 22 feet wide by 80 feet long. When these colts reached the main stream, four or more were connected together to form a river raft.

The crew of a raft consisted of the "steersman," who was an expert river pilot as well as commander of the raft, and one or more "forehands." The steersman was always located at the rear oar while the forehand manned the front oar. The great river rafts, which might be 50 to 60 feet wide and 210 feet long, often had two or more oars at the front end. The function of these oars was to push the head end of the raft to the right or left at the command of the steersman, "Go Pennsylvania!" or "Go Jersey!" In the upper reaches of the river, where sharp turns were common or where islands were numerous, pushing the head end to right or left was almost a continuous activity. In the difficult parts of the river steering was done on "points." These might include a certain tree, a prominent feature in a ledge of rock, a house, barn or other landmark. It was incumbent upon an experienced steersman to know every point on the river.

The rugged life of the raftsmen required men of great strength and endurance, disdainful alike of weather and the dangers of navigating the river. Most of these men were descendants of the pioneer settlers of the region. With little or no education, many still had keenness of perception and sharpness of judgment and most were ready for a fight at the slightest provocation. Since the best rafting season was during the spring freshet, right after the breakup of ice in the river, the weather was usually cold with sometimes rain or snow. The men were usually cold and drenched by the elements or the river. Their chief bulwark against these hardships was the whiskey jug. But it was not only the elements that caused a drain on the jug. Regardless of time or conditions, the average raftsman just liked the idea. Many oarsmen agreed that they were fortunate when they went down the river with a good pilot who was a bit tipsy. He was more apt to be lenient with the men and, in tight situations, would take daring chances that resulted in success, whereas under sober conditions he might act conservatively and court disaster.[7]

At the more dangerous locations an extra man often was taken on to assist during the passage. "Eugene Lakin, considered one of the

best axemen on the river, often assisted raftsmen in pulling around
Pease Island turn, for which he received the customary dollar bill.
Eugene was always telling that he intended to quit the job because
he gained no monetary advantage therefrom. 'I get on the raft at the
head of the island; pull my hardest around the bend; get off on the
rocks and walk back to the head of the island—and what do I gain?
I'm pretty drunk when I get on, but after pulling around the bend
and walking back, I am sober again and it costs me my whole green-
back to get as drunk as I was when I started. So what's the use of all
the hard work, I can't get any more tipsy.' But he never carried out
his intentions."[8]

One of the most dreaded obstacles along the upper Delaware was
the 7 foot Lackawaxen dam, a short distance below the outlet of the
Lackawaxen River. This dam was constructed to provide a slack
water crossing of the Delaware River from the Delaware and Hudson
Canal. The use of this restrictive area by both rafts and canalboats
was a source of friction and occasional collisions. After the slack
water crossing was replaced by an aqueduct, another hazard was
imposed on the raftsmen. In constructing the aqueduct three piers,
only 300 feet below the dam, were installed in the river. If a raft had
any difficulty going over the dam, only these 300 feet were available
to correct its course in order to pass safely by the piers. In spite of
this restriction few accidents occurred here.

Another dangerous condition confronted the raftsmen at Easton.
Just below the outlet of the Lehigh River two railroad bridges with
their supporting piers cross the Delaware River. Under freshet con-

From RAFTING ON THE DELAWARE
*A log raft on the Delaware River. Delaware and Hudson Canal aqueduct
built by Roebling, in background.*

ditions the water disgourged by the Lehigh produced abnormal currents that taxed the skill of the raftsmen to escape contact with the piers. At Durham during the rafting season, it was almost a daily occurrence to see broken rafts floating down the river as a result of collisions with bridge piers at Easton. Residents along the river found profitable business in salvaging the scattered timber and logs. Often, however, the owners appeared to lay claim to the salvaged material, particularly if they had taken the precaution to stamp their initials or mark on the timber.[9]

The Delaware River from Black's Eddy to Trenton is rough and rocky, with a drop of 12 feet through the rapids at Wells Falls and a drop of over 9 feet at Trenton Falls. Upper river raftsmen invariably employed a Wells steersman to pilot their rafts through these waters. These "Wellses," as the rivermen called them, were older men who knew every rock and channel in that part of the river. They knew exactly how to steer the raft in any heights of water or any condition of wind. After delivering a raft safely at Trenton, the Wellse collected his 8 dollar fee and hurried back up the river to get another raft.[10]

By the time a raft reached the longer eddies of the lower river, the raftsmen's whiskey supply frequently was exhausted. But they knew where liquor could be obtained. As they approached a favorite inn, they called to the inn-keeper who would gladly row out with an assortment of bottles. B. F. Fackenthal, Jr., recounts that he "often witnessed the inn-keeper, whose establishment was in New Jersey, opposite the Durham furnace, row out to meet the rafts. To [my] mind they never seemed to be in a hurry, and by the time each had been served with his favorite tipple, the raft with the inn-keeper and his bateau had drifted down stream fully three-quarters of a mile. By the time he rowed back another set of thirsty raftsmen would signal and yell at him, whereupon the operation was repeated, and thus kept up all day long during the rafting season."[11]

Residents along these long eddies often rowed out to the rafts with home baked pies, cakes and other pastries. A story which has been handed down so long that the names of the participants are forgotten, involved two young boys who rowed out with freshly baked mince pies. The raftsmen purchased and ate several of the pies before paying the older lad. Whereupon the younger boy started to cry, "I want my money!"

"Why, it's your ma's money, ain't it?" asked the steersman.

"Want my money," the boy screamed. " 'Twas my puppy them pies was made of! 'n I want my money."[12]

When the railroads penetrated the lumbering regions in the middle of the nineteenth century the tanning industry, which was to have an important impact on that section of the country, followed in their wake. Great quantities of hemlock bark were required in the tanning of leather; and, the adjacent forests supplied this material. Many raftsmen joined the woodsmen in felling trees and "peeling" the hemlock bark to sell to the tanneries.[13] The peeled logs were then hauled to the streams by yokes of oxen and made into rafts for transport down the river. Thus, the coming of the tanneries produced a second source of income for the raftsmen. By that time the great stands of pine had become pretty well depleted and hemlock became the leading substitute. Old raftsmen have said that from the advent of the tanneries until the end of the rafting era, hemlock comprised 80 per cent of the rafts sent down the river.[14]

During the fall of 1883 the *Walton Chronical* of Walton, New York, published a series of articles by an old raftsman, Josiah Pine, III, which give a detailed history of lumbering, building and assembling rafts, rafting and navigating the Delaware River from above Hancock, New York, to Philadelphia. Pine's recollections include a detailed log of a passage down the river, listing the streams, islands, rapids and other obstacles that were encountered and how navigation of the river was successfully accomplished.[15]

Thaddeus S. Kenderdine was an active participant in this great rafting era. Born at Lumberton in 1836, he grew up amidst the activities of his father's grist and sawmills which he was later to inherit. During his years of purchasing logs and timber from the raftsmen he became acquainted with their activities and idiosyncrasies. In his time, Kenderdine recalled, there were sawmills at Morrisville, Yardleyville, Taylorsville, Brownsburg, at both Hendrick's and Eagle islands just above Centre Bridge, at Lumberton, Erwinna, the Narrows, Monroe, Quinn's Falls, Riegelsville, Carpenterville and Easton. In a paper presented at a 1911 meeting of The Bucks County Historical Society, Kenderdine recorded some of his recollections of this era.

"Sometimes the logs were run through to city markets, but they generally stopped at selling eddies such as Titusville, Lower Black Eddy, Upper Black Eddy and Easton, to where buyers from below came and where bargaining and dickering began. . . . The spaces between the logs had to be agreed on mutually, as these must, when subtracted, determine the width of the raft. This arranged, the number of feet was worked out by a peculiar rule, apparently by guesswork multiples, found in no 'lightning calculators,' but which went.

This was to take three cross measurements of the raft to get the average width. From this was deducted the spaces, and by dividing the width in inches by the number of logs, the average diameter was arrived at. Then the courses were divided in lengths, making, say, 126 logs 16 feet long and 21.4 inches across. The rule was to square this diameter, multiply this by the length and this again by twice the average diameter. This would make 320 feet for each log and a fraction, then multiply this by the double diameter and you had the contents of the raft. This may not have been as good a rule as the golden one or that which worked both ways satisfactorily, but it obtained along our river until it was as fixed as the laws of the Medes and Persians. After some dickering as to the throwing in of the ropes and the delivery of the raft, the seller was paid in cash or notes, for checks were unfamiliar then, and he went on his way home.

"At some of the river water powers, such as at the Narrows and at Riegelsville, log rafts were run and cut into bill timber, rerafted and sold to retail yards below. This branch of the business was risky from the logs stored in the river being knocked loose by other rafts in time of freshets or from canal boatmen stealing the ropes which held them. To avoid this wires were woven in the strands of rope so they could not be cut, or the old-fashioned halliards (lash-poles) were used for fastening the floats to the trees along the towpath. This letting loose of logs caused serious losses from the difficulty of proving property when caught and the amount of salvage claimed when proven. Sometimes a raft would get away in the effort of landing at the unloading wharf.

"There were lively times during spring rafting freshets. I can see one float after another going down the river, the men looking like dressed up ghosts as they silently swung their brobdingnagian oars, and as if going to some mysterious country from which there was no returning. In some instances, although but few, the raftsman would have some of his family aboard. When our particular float was swung in it was when all preparations were made for its unloading; a dozen men or so, a pair of horses and three wagons. The boards run clean until those below the watery surface appear, when they need scrubbing from the roily current which had soaked among them. Then four men with splint brooms are needed to scrub the boards with the water they float in, while two others drag them away and slide them onto the wagon backed against the raft, each calling out in a loud voice the Roman numerals on them to the professional counter. . . .

"The men on the raft had a cold, wet job of it. Besides these were the unloaders and the driver. . . . The opposite shores of Jersey were mainly depended upon for the help, for as fishermen and "stone-hackers" they were used to dampness, as well as to assimilating the liquid for its cure. They were as a class hardy but ignorant. Their wages were $1 per day of sun to sun, after whose close some of them rowed across the river and walked a mile or more to their homes. After the boards had drained off which took a week or two, came the piling. . . . It generally took a year for water-soaked lumber to dry."[16]

While river transportation was a great step forward as compared to the primitive transport by land, there was a continuing demand for greater speed and convenience in moving goods and people. The great canal building era of the early nineteenth century was the result.

Collection of Henry S. Engart
Log raft upstream of the Lumberville covered bridge.

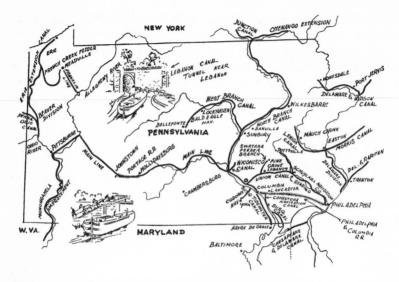

From HISTORIC PENNSYLVANIA LEAFLET NO. 1
The canals of Pennsylvania.

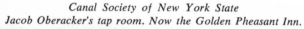

Canal Society of New York State
Jacob Oberacker's tap room. Now the Golden Pheasant Inn.

Chapter 2

Building The Canal

Pennsylvania Canal: DELAWARE DIVISION, April 8, 1829

Proposals will be received at William Shouse's Inn, in Easton, until 4 o'clock in the afternoon of Wednesday the 20th of May next, for the construction of the remaining sections of the aforesaid Division viz; From the termination of Section 106 to Easton, about 6 miles, divided into sections of half a mile each . . .   *Th. G. Kennedy*
Superintendent

Easton Centinel, Easton, Pa., April 10, 1829

It is of interest to recall that during the early history of our country, from colonial times to as recently as 1825, the only means of transportation beyond the seaboard were the natural waterways, trails and more or less impassable roads. Following the Revolutionary War a surplus of population along the east coast and reports of fertile lands beyond the coastal mountains encouraged the migration of great hordes of people to the interior. The prevailing means of travel were so primitive and inadequate that a great clamor arose for some solution to the transportation problem.

One solution was canals, or artificial waterways, which had for centuries been used in Asia and Europe; and, a few sporadic experiments had been made in New England and the South. William Penn and George Washington[1] were among the first to recognize the need for artificial waterways to facilitate the movement of supplies and people to the interior of the country. But it was not until the Erie Canal, across New York State from Albany to Buffalo, was completed in 1825 that the real potential of this means of transportation was demonstrated. Hardly had the Erie Canal been completed before its capacity was strained to satisfy the demands of passengers and freight. It is difficult at this period of the twentieth century to comprehend the universal enthusiasm with which this accomplishment was received. Immediately a canal epidemic spread across the country attacking legislatures and individuals of vision alike. Within two decades, a vast network of canals was in operation from the Atlantic seaboard to as far west as Illinois, carrying masses of settlers and supplies to the midwest and returning products of forests, mines and farms to the cities of the east. During this period approximately four thousand miles of canals were constructed.

Pennsylvania was in the forefront of canal building, not only to protect the prestige of the port of Philadelphia but also to enhance the economy of its mines and industries. The producers of anthracite, or stone coal as it was originally called, demanded cheap transportation for their bulk product to eastern markets such as New York and Philadelphia, while the people of Pittsburgh and the west were demanding better means of transportation for manufactured goods, supplies and farm products. The Pennsylvania Canal system also vied with the Erie Canal in delivering immigrants to the midwest. By the end of the canal building era, Pennsylvania with its more than twelve hundred miles of canals, had outstripped any other state in the Union. See Table VII.

Five important canals made significant contributions to the history of the upper Delaware Valley: the Delaware and Hudson Canal, built with private capital and constructed primarily to transport coal from the Honesdale area in eastern Pennsylvania to Eddyville and Kingston on the Hudson River, from which point river transportation was available to New York City; the privately financed Morris Canal across New Jersey from Phillipsburg to Jersey City, also mainly a coal carrier; The Delaware and Raritan Canal, another New Jersey privately financed project, connecting Bordentown on the Delaware with New Brunswick on the Raritan River, with a feeder extending approximately twenty miles north along the east side of the Delaware River from Trenton, to supply water to the canal summit; the Lehigh Canal, from White Haven to Easton, constructed and operated throughout its life by the Lehigh Coal and Navigation Company to transport coal to seaboard markets; and the Delaware Division of the Pennsylvania Canal.

On October 27, 1827, the first shovelful of dirt was dug at Bristol, Pennsylvania, inaugurating the beginning of the Delaware Canal. This occurrence was a little over ten years after a similar ceremony was enacted on Juy 4, 1817, at Rome, New York, which marked the start of the New York State Erie Canal and the great canal-building era of the mid-nineteenth century.

A bill sponsored by Col. Peter Ihire, state senator from Easton, was passed April 9, 1827, authorizing construction of the Delaware Canal by the Commonwealth of Pennsylvania. A survey of a canal line along the Delaware River from Easton to tidewater near Bristol, and also on to Philadelphia, was commenced by July 9 of that year. On September 12 the engineer, Henry G. Sargent, reported to the Canal Commissioners that the section from Easton to Bristol, a distance of 59¾ miles could be constructed for an estimated $11,443 per mile and the section from Bristol to Philadelphia, a distance of 17½ miles, would cost an estimated $11,474 per mile. In the interest of convenience and economy the Commission was "unanimously of opinion that to terminate for the present at Bristol, keeping such a level as to allow a future extension to Philadelphia, was preferable to any other plan." Thomas G. Kennedy, the newly appointed super-intendent of the division, was instructed to advertise immediately for construction bids, and by October 13 excavation contracts for the whole distance were concluded.[2]

During this same period a survey was conducted for an extension of the canal from Easton to near Port Jervis, a distance of about 67 miles with a fall of 262 feet.[3] Construction of this division, however, as well as of the extension to Philadelphia, was never authorized.

The main purpose of the Delaware Canal was to serve as an extension of the Lehigh Canal, which was conceived and promoted by Josiah White, that great entrepreneur of the era, together with his associates Erskine Hazard and George F. A. Hauto, to transport anthracite coal from their mines near Mauch Chunk to seaboard markets. These three men organized the Lehigh Coal and Navigation Company which, for nearly 150 years, contributed greatly to the economic development of the Lehigh Valley. According to William B. Foster, Jr., "But for this article of freight, the canal [Delaware], doubtless, would not have been made, or if made, the income from it would but little more than pay for its maintenance."[4]

Before a definite terminal point near Bristol could be established, much contention developed on the part of the people living between Morrisville and Bristol as to the proper place for the terminus of the canal. Those living in the neighborhood of Tullytown advocated Scott's Creek near that town as the best place for the canal's con-nection with the river. The citizens of Bristol naturally contended for Bristol Boro. In the course of several meetings with the commissioners, the counsellor for Bristol "employed two men who followed the water to secretly make soundings of the river to ascertain the depth at both points. . . They swore there was not sufficient depth of water at Scott's Creek at any time of tide to float vessels carrying 200 tons while at Bristol there was sufficient to float vessels carrying 500 tons. That settled the question. The commissioners declared in favor of Bristol."[5]

With the terminus decided upon, the people of Bristol were ready for their celebration. Doran Green reported, "The day was beautiful and unusually warm for the time of year. At eleven o'clock, some 500 men under the command of William T. Swift, who had been appointed marshal . . ., marched to the ground near [future] Lock No. 3. At noon a prayer was made by the rector of the Protestant Episcopal Church after which an address was delivered by Peter A. Brown, a prominent member of the Philadelphia bar. George Harrison of Hulmeville and Peter Ihire of Easton appeared, one with a wheelbarrow, the other, with a pick and shovel. Ihrie commenced to dig a trench and throw the dirt in the barrow. Harrison then wheeled it a short distance and dumped it in a heap. The marshal then made a speech congratulating the citizens of Bucks County on the opening of the grandest enterprise of the age. The band played 'Hail Columbia' and the people gave three cheers that made the welkin ring."[6]

Once the canal was started, work progressed rapidly. By the middle of 1829 it was reported to the Canal Commissioners "that since the 13th of October 1827, 106 sections of about half a mile each, making nearly 53½ miles of canal, together with the basin at Bristol, and all mechanical work of every description, with the exception of houses for the accommodation of lock keepers, have been contracted for. Thirty-seven of these sections have been completed in a handsome and satisfactory manner and the remainder, as far as section 87 are progressing with steadiness and energy. . . . [In total, 118 excavation contracts were let.]

"The mechanical work that has been let at different times through the summer and the necessity of procuring suitable timber for each part thereof from the country up the Delaware, rendered it indispensible that the contractors should have in their power to avail themselves of the spring freshet in the river for that purpose. It was, therefore, distinctly stipulated at the time of making the contracts that all the materials should be procured this fall and winter so that the work might be commenced on the line as early next spring as the season would admit of. About six miles, with the mechanical work on it only remain to extend the line from Bristol to Easton."[7]

Among the last contracts to be let were those for the dam and the outlet and guard locks at Easton. Apparently, up to that time it was undecided how water should be supplied to the Delaware Canal, whether by means of a dam across the Delaware River or by damming the Lehigh River. Not to be deprived of communication with the Morris Canal, the Lehigh Coal and Navigation Company already had built a dam and outlet lock to permit transfer of boats across the Delaware River. In a letter from Bethlehem, Pa., dated December 2, 1828, Canvass White wrote, "Josiah White came here last evening and goes with me this morning to see the Easton Dam and to determine what shall be done with it."[8]

On June 5, 1829, the Coal Company submitted to the State a proposal for supplying water to the Delaware Canal which resulted in a contract, dated June 18, 1829, between the two parties for the construction of "a feeder Dam for the said Division across the River Lehigh, near its junction with the Delaware, together with an outlet Lock of twenty-two feet in width connected with said Dam, for the sum of Sixteen thousand dollars. . . . The whole of said work to be constructed under the immediate direction and control of the Engineer on the said Division and completed to his entire satisfaction, on or before the first day of January [1830] next."[9]

A contract for the guard lock at Easton, together with waste weirs No. 19 and 20 was awarded to Thomas and Richard English, under date of May 2, 1829, with the stipulation "that the whole of the work hereby contracted for shall be completed on or before the first day of January 1830."[10] Payment under this contract was on the basis of price per cubic yard and cubic foot of excavation and masonry respectively, and for the wood and iron work complete, Eleven hundred and seventy five dollars.

In the Lehigh Coal and Navigation Company's annual report, dated January 11, 1830, it is stated, "The Managers have spoken of their work as finished; this was strictly the case until the middle of last year, when it was deemed expedient by the canal commissioners, to direct an additional dam to be thrown across the Lehigh at its mouth, below the Company's present outlet lock, consequently making a new outlet lock necessary. This was done with a view to procure a feeder for the Delaware arm of the Pennsylvania Canal, from our jurisdiction on the Lehigh, in place of procuring it, as previously intended, from the waters of the Delaware by damming that river below Easton."

The lack of experience of the farmers and local townspeople who obtained many of the canal contracts, and the constant demands for more speed, undoubtedly contributed to some of the faulty work that periodically developed. On May 8, 1830, it was reported: "There are nine aqueducts, three of which must be rebuilt, part of one of them having already fallen down and the three are so badly founded and so unskillfully pile planked and puddled that they will soon (probably) fall, unless they are taken down. The remainder of the aqueducts are alike defective in pile planking and puddling so that this part of the work must be done over again before the water is let into the canal or great damage will be done to the works. . . . Mr. Kennedy, the intelligent superintendent of the division, appears very confident that this canal will be ready to receive the water in August."[11]

By the end of 1830, when James S. Stevenson, president of the Canal Commissioners made his report, dated December 21, conditions appeared favorable for early operation of the canal. Referring to the Delaware Division he said, "The water has been admitted into this division but only 25 miles are yet navigable. Part of the work first constructed has proved defective and requires extensive repairs." He then gave the following details regarding the physical features of the canal.

"On this division the width of the canal at bottom is 25 feet, at top water line 40 feet, and its depth of water, 5 feet. In its course there are 23 lift locks, ranging from 6 to 10 feet lift, also 2 outlet and 2 guard locks. The canal and locks are arranged for boats of 67 tons burden. Eighteen lock keepers are necessary in this division.

"The lift locks are 11 feet wide and 95 feet long, clear in the chamber. They are constructed of rubble masonry layed in cement on timber bottoms with longitudinal sills and upright posts faced with planks spiked to the timbers. The tide lock at Bristol, guard lock at Easton and the outlet lock into the River Delaware from the pool at Easton are 22 feet by 100 feet long, clear in the chamber. The guard lock at New Hope is 18 feet by 100 feet and affords a communication with the River Delaware.

Courtesy, Marion Greenzweig
A standard lift lock, 11 feet wide by 95 feet long. Lock No. 18 at Uhlertown.

"Nine aqueducts, the shortest 25 feet, the longest 178 feet between the abutments. The abutments and piers are of rubble masonry, the superstructure of wood trunks 20 feet wide, towpath bridge forming part of the superstructure. Twenty culverts, rubble masonry layed in cement. Nineteen waste weirs with slide gates, woodwork with protective masonry. Sixteen lock houses built. Tide basin of 5½ acres constructed in the Delaware and the pier at Bristol nearly finished. Forty-seven road bridges, stone abutments, superstructure of wood. Forty-nine farm bridges, three turnpike and three foot bridges."[12]

Stevenson's optimistic report gave promise of early operation of the canal. However, the vagaries of the Delaware River, through periodic floods, and the gravelly soil in the northern section of the canal, which caused so much leakage that it was difficult to maintain the proper water level, presented obstacles that were yet to be solved.

Then, there was Josiah White, whose irritation mounted at the constant delays that prevented delivery of his coal to eastern markets. According to White, "The constructors on the Delaware was [sic] permitted to fill up the canal to bottom with bad material & when reported to be finished, would not hold water. It was then put under my charge to make it a good job, which I was only able to effect by overhauling a large part of it."[13] The January 9, 1832, annual report of the Coal Company records: "It was not until the 11th month, just before setting in of winter, that the upper part was made strong enough to hold water sufficient to supply the lower part; since then it held 4 to 4½ feet for considerable time, and so as to enable us to send a boat of 25 tons of coal to within four miles of New Hope."

In spite of this success, the Company report for 1832 was not too optimistic. "In our last Report we anticipated the full use of that canal during the past season [1832], but, the occurence of a very unusual ice freshet in the spring, frustrated our hopes, by destroying a considerable portion of the exposed part of the upper section of the canal, which was proved to have been constructed in a very unskilled manner. The repair of this damage occupied much time, and, when effected, the water had become too low to saturate the porous soil over which the canal passed, and fill it to a sufficient depth for navigation. Several feeders were constructed to supply the deficiency, and, it was not until the 23rd of July last [1832], that the first boats arrived at Bristol, each loaded with 20 tons of coal. From this time till the end of the season, there was a gradual improvement in the state of the canal. Small breaches, however, occurred in, parts of it, which, together with want of experience in the Lockkeepers, in regulating the water on the different levels, occasioned

Duvel & Sons lith. Philad.

On stone by A. Newsam

Josiah White

very vexatious delays to our boatmen. The loading of the boats was gradually increased to 25, 30, 35, 40, 45, and finally to 50 tons, when the navigation was closed for the season by a breach near Easton, on the 2nd day of December. We have thus had but a partial use of the Delaware Canal, for a few weeks, near the close of the season, and, during a portion of that time, many of our boatmen refused to go along the line on account of the Cholera, which carried off a number of the individuals who were engaged in the repairs. The days of difficulty, we now hope, are passed by. The canal is, we understand, repaired; the porous soil has become nearly saturated, and, abundant supply of water secured, and the banks will be sufficiently consolidated, the next season, to admit water for boats carrying 60 to 70 tons. The company is only now placed where it ought to have been in July 1829, when the Lehigh canal was finished, it having been commenced in the same season with the State Canal on the Delaware, which has not half so much lockage, and but half the capacity of the Lehigh Canal. To the incomplete state of the Delaware Canal alone, are to be attributed our being so long deprived of the interest on our investment, and the commonwealth, of a handsome remuneration for her expenditures on the canal.

"These untoward circumstances, obliged us again to have recourse to the old mode of navigation, by arks, at an increased expense and risk. . . . During the suspension of the navigation of the State Canal, and the low water in the Delaware river, it was thought prudent to keep the mines regularly at work, and to employ the canal boats, on the Lehigh, in transporting the coal to South Easton at the head of the State Canal. By this arrangement we were enabled to get to market a much larger quantity of coal than otherwise would have been practicable—the canal boats being principally employed, after the opening of the State Canal, in bringing down the coal which had accumulated at South Easton; and, while the depth of water in the Delaware channels permitted, coal was transported direct from Mauch Chunk to Philadelphia by means of arks."[14]

Josiah White was never an advocate of a canal along the Delaware River. In his opinion the development of a series of channels and slack water in the river, similar to his development of the Lehigh, would permit handling much heavier cargoes than could be accomplished by canal.

White commented, "It has been frequently said of latter years, that the Delaware Canal was made for the accommodation of our Coal from Lehigh &c & that we were consequently under great obligation to the State for making it &c & that they made the Locks 11 feet wide for our accommodation, whereas we wished them 22 feet the same dimensions as our own, but if they would not make them of our size, as the alternative we advised them of half our width, so that 2 boats going through our Lock at a time, one of them would fit theirs & go one at a time.

"But our view was not to *Canal* along the Delaware, but to make *channels & Slack Water,* which is shown by this Dft & Petition, which we got signed & sent to Harrisburg in the years 1823-24 & used all our influence to get a Law passed accordingly.

"With this plan we supposed it might take 6 to 12 locks on the Delaware and the rest mere channels. We expected to get 4 feet water in low time & 5 at other times, & that it would carry Steam or boats of 150 tons & for which we had made 4 locks in advance on the Lehigh 30 feet wide & 130 feet long so as to have a steam boat navign of 150 tons burden to Mauch Chunk. . . .

"The Law for Improving the Delaware by *Canal,* was brought by Coll Erie [Ihire] of Easton, who was then a Senator. We believe brought about to oppose our Co procuring the Law for makg the River a Slackwater navigation, as that Borough was always opposed to us."[15]

In spite of the corrective measures, the problems of the waterway persisted; and, it was not until 1834 that the canal was declared satisfactory for regular navigation, with boats loaded up to 70 tons. At that time the cost per mile had more than doubled the original estimates. By the end of 1834 the total cost of the canal, exclusive of land damages which were continually mounting, was reported to be $1,430,000.[16]

Chapter 3
Tour Guide To The Canal

The Packet boat SWAN, intended as an accommodation boat to run between Bethlehem and Mauch Chunk, on the Lehigh Canal, arrived at the Point in this borough, on Tuesday morning last. Her arrival was announced by the firing of a field piece and the acclamations of a number of citizens, who repaired thither to view this (in our part of the country) novelty. The SWAN is a fine boat, and was purchased from Messrs M'Calla & Co. of Philadelphia, by a few enterprising young men of Bethlehem, and seems well adapted to ensure convenience and comfort to passengers. We wish them success.

Easton Centinel, Easton, Pa., June 12, 1829

Canals, like people, have personalities all their own. No two are alike, either in physical features or historical background. While much has been written about our canals, there is a great deal more to be recorded in an effort to preserve for posterity the rich heritage that canals have contributed to the history and development of our country.

The Delaware Canal as it exists today is unique in being the only surviving canal of the nineteenth century building era to remain intact and containing water throughout most of its length with locks, aqueducts and other engineering features about as they existed during its period of operation. By good fortune the canal is paralleled by a scenic highway, permitting access by automobile to its principal features. This happy coincidence can convert a day's outing into an enlightening historic adventure—provided one knows where to look. It is the purpose of this chapter to supply a tour guide to the various points of interest along the canal.

EASTON–SCOTT PARK

A logical starting point for our tour is Scott Park, located between Ferry Street and the Lehigh River at the latter's confluence with the Delaware River in Easton,[1] Pennsylvania. This area is frequently called the Point, or the Forks of the Delaware, probably because in early times the Lehigh River was known as the West Branch of the Delaware. Here, David Martin's ferry connecting with the Jersey shore was established in 1739, and continued in operation until 1806 when the first bridge crossing the Delaware in this area was constructed. This three-span covered bridge was one of Timothy Palmer's famous wooden structures which weathered storm and flood for 91

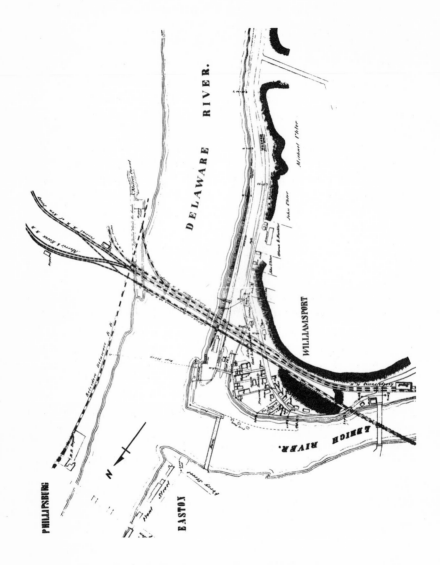

Pennsylvania State Archives: McNair's map
Plate I. *Beginning of the Delaware Canal at Easton, Pa., showing 1830 dam, outlet lock and rope ferry for conveying boats to the Morris Canal together with Guard Lock No. 24 and weigh lock.*

years until it was replaced by a steel bridge in 1896.[2] The ferry was an important link on the main route westward and during the Revolutionary War was useful in transporting troops and supplies.

From this vantage point one has a good view of the Delaware River. Easton dam, now located somewhat upstream from its original site, and completely rebuilt in 1967, was installed to provide slack water for the terminus of the Lehigh Canal as well as a source of water for the Delaware Canal. At the far end of the dam, the stone masonry work of the guard and weigh locks at the entrance to the Delaware Canal, the next stop on our tour, may be seen.

Route 611 south, which extends along Ferry Street, will guide us to the lock location. After crossing Third Street bridge, the route turns left at the traffic light. Ahead several railroad bridges span the highway. Just before reaching the second bridge a driveway to the left leads to the extensive parking facilities of the Canal Museum at the Forks of the Delaware. The building which houses this museum was an old structure of canal vintage that has been remodeled and enlarged by the Hugh Moore Parkway. In addition to the museum, maintained by the Pennsylvania Canal Society, the building also contains the administrative office of the Parkway.

Collection of Harry L. Rinker
Canal Museum at the Forks of the Delaware

Collection of Henry S. Engart
Light boat entering the guard lock of the Delaware Canal at Easton, 1931.

Collection of the Northampton County Historical and Genealogical Society
Snufftown or Williamsport as it appeared ca. 1890. A thriving community,
including two hotels, grew up at the junction of the Delaware and Lehigh
canals.

Situated as it is at the junction of the Lehigh and Delaware canals, the facilities of this building provide a focal point for visitors to the recreational projects of this area. Roosevelt State Park, which includes the Delaware Canal, extends southward for a distance of approximately sixty miles. Hugh Moore Parkway, a recreational and historic restoration project of the City of Easton, extends westward along the Lehigh River for about seven miles. This project, when completed, will include a restored section of the Lehigh Canal containing three locks in operating condition. The museum will be of interest to canal enthusiasts not only for its artifacts and historical material but also in providing helpful information to those interested in touring the two canals and the recreational features of the Hugh Moore Parkway and Roosevelt State Park.

Proceeding beyond the museum to the bank of the river the visitor can observe the impressive masonry of the guard lock, sometimes called Lock No. 24, the weigh lock and Easton dam. These may, however, be seen in better perspective from a short distance up the river bank. The bridge over the guard and weigh locks affords an excellent view of the main engineering features of these structures. The guard lock, which underwent extensive repairs during 1970, is now 18 feet wide instead of 22 feet, its original width. The decrease in width was necessary in order to strengthen the walls of the lock chamber. The massive miter gates are now in operating condition. They are opened and closed by mechanism installed in the "doghouses" located on each wall opposite the gates. The function of this lock is to protect the canal from high water in the river. Normally, both pairs of gates would be open, permitting free passage of a boat through the lock. However, when the Lehigh River was high or in flood stage, the gates were closed. A boat desiring entrance to the canal would be locked through in the same manner as through a lift lock. Having cleared the guard lock, the boatman was then on his way down the Delaware Canal.

Looking down stream, the towing path over which the mules traveled, is on the left bank of the canal. The right bank is called the berm or, in canal jargon, the heelpath. The view in the opposite direction shows the approach to the guard lock from the Lehigh River. It is here that boats from the Lehigh Canal were transferred to the Delaware Canal.

The open channel on the land side of the guard lock is called a feeder or by-pass and, by means of hand operated valves at the head of the feeder, is used to control the depth of water in the canal below the lock when its gates are closed. Similar feeders will be seen at most of the other locks along the canal. On the river side of the guard lock are the remains of the weigh lock, the use of which was discontinued, probably about 1858, when the Delaware Canal passed to the control of the Lehigh Coal and Navigation Company. Of more modern construction are the control gates at the head of this lock, installed to permit its use as an emergency feeder.

Collection of Henry S. Engart
Remains of the outlet lock to Delaware River. The arch in background is the entrance to the Morris Canal.

If one crosses the bridge over the lock and proceeds diagonally to the right, over the embankment and into the ravine beyond, he will discover the remains of the outlet lock that was installed here to transfer Lehigh Canal boats to the Morris Canal. The existing stonework of the lock is readily recognized near the second bridge pier encountered. The original location of the dam in the Lehigh River provided slack water to this point. Upon proceeding to the river bank one can see on the opposite shore adjacent to the railroad bridge a stone wall and archway. This archway was the entrance to the Morris Canal. Boats were conveyed across the river by means of a cable ferry.

To aid visitors unfamiliar with the area along the Delaware River to locate points of interest, mileage designations are given at each point of interest, beginning at Lock No. 24. The first figure shows the cumulative miles along the route and the second figure shows the miles between successive points of interest. Distances apply to the main highway only.

Total	Between
0.8	0.8

Proceeding along Route 611 for 0.8 mile, one encounters a group of three historical markers. These markers are typical of many installed by the Pennsylvania Historical and Museum Commission to call attention to special features along the canal. A small parking area on the left side of the road permits a stop to enjoy the lovely view upriver. The Delaware Canal, in the foreground, with its towpath, meanders along as peacefully as in the old canal days.

At this location may be seen one of the types of control that was installed in an effort to prevent flood waters from devastating lower sections of the canal. About 100 yards south of the three historical markers, a clearing at the side of the road gives access to the first of eight stop gates. Since numbering started at the southern end of the canal, this gate is No. 8. Originally a pair of miter gates were installed between the two parallel masonry walls. These gates were normally open unless high water required that they be closed to protect the lower portion of the canal. At such times navigation was suspended until water conditions returned to normal. The remainder of the channel is closed by a set of sluice gates.

Collection of author
Stop gate No. 8 in Delaware Canal 0.8 mile below Guard Lock No. 24.

Total	Between	
4.9	4.1	RAUBSVILLE

A scenic drive along the winding course of the canal and river brings one to the quaint village of Raubsville. At the northern approach to the village a long overflow may be seen on the towpath side of the canal. This overflow was another means of protecting the canal against high water. When the water exceeded a safe level, the excess flowed over the reinforced embankment into the river.

At the southern outskirts of Raubsville, a large brick building may be seen on the left side of Route 611. This building originally housed the steam plant that supplied electric power to the Doylestown and Easton Street Railway whose tracks paralleled the canal as far as Kintnersville.

During the first quarter of the twentieth century, Easton and Doylestown, Pennsylvania were connected by an interurban trolley line. According to General Davis, "the first spike of the Doylestown-Easton Trolley Railroad was driven on Saturday morning June 22,

Courtesy, David Ennis

An overflow for controlling the maximum height of water in the canal. (The mules walked over the depression in the towpath while the driver used the narrow bridge.)

1901 in the presence of a number of persons who took a deep interest in the proceedings."[3] This ceremony, which occurred at Doylestown, preceded by several years the opening of the entire line to traffic. It was not until the summer of 1904 that through service to Easton was established.

Incorporated February 3, 1897, as The Doylestown and Easton Street Railway, the company was continually beset by financial difficulties and changes of management until August 1921, when the line was finally reorganized as the Philadelphia and Easton Transit Company. By that time the construction of hard top highways and the competition of automobiles presented insurmountable obstacles. The line was abandoned November 25, 1926.

A steam power plant was constructed at Raubsville to supply electric service to the trolley line. According to a brochure in the library of The Bucks County Historical Society[4] the power plant consisted of six 250 H.P. boilers, two 750 H.P. cross compound engines, two 400 KW Stanley direct connected generators, together with switchboards and transformers. Three phase, alternating current was transmitted to substations at Danboro and Harrow which supplied direct current to the trolley line. Upon completion of the hydroplant at Ground Hog lock, power was obtained from that source; and, the steam plant was utilized only for standby. Its service was required when high water in the river and canal temporarily made the hydroplant inoperative. But, according to George Fox, "power from the steam plant was poor. Seemed they couldn't generate enough power to pull the cars up the hills and the lights would go dim."

The Easton terminal of the trolley line was at the southeast corner of 3rd St. and Route 611. Passengers to and from Easton had to walk across the 3rd Street bridge. When the line was installed, Route 611 was a dirt road. Near the end of the trolley's existence, Easton paved the road to the city limits. To prevent having to pay part of the paving costs the company abandoned its track within the city limits, thus forcing its passengers to walk an additional half mile.

The trip from Easton to Doylestown must have been a leisurely, although a very scenic ride through the Delaware Valley. Two hours were required to traverse the 32 miles between the two cities. The route was divided into eleven zones, with a fare of 8¢ per zone; thus the fare from Easton to Doylestown was 88¢, plus 7¢ tax, or a total of 95¢.

From Easton to Kintnersville the trolley followed the line of the canal, after which it ran inland along the main highway to Doylestown. At Raubsville a car barn was located west of the power plant, with a spur extending to a dock on the nearby canal for interchange of freight. Beyond Riegelsville the tracks ran between the highway and the canal with very little space available for either. It was in this area that an experiment was made to tow canalboats with a trolley car. Two items in the *Allentown Morning Call* recount this event.

> September 27, 1906—Philadelphia and Easton trolley, as an experiment will tow five canal boats from Uniontown to Lehnensburg, a distance of one mile. If successful, a trolley line will be built alongside the canal.

> September 29, 1906—On Wednesday, September 26, Car No. 6 pulled four canal boat loads of coal—90 to 100 tons. Strain on the trolley car was terrific, with movement at only four miles per hour.

No further reference was made to this experiment so it undoubtedly was considered a failure.

During a conversation with George Fox, he said, "I worked on the Doylestown-Easton from 1920 to 1924 as a conductor, with additional time on the milk car and the freight car that hauled general freight to the stores along the line. Headway was every hour and Saturdays, Sundays and holidays every half hour. During my time the trolley hauled cement for use on the new road—which was the beginning of the end of our line.

"There used to be a spring just below Easton on the Richards farm that was fresh and cold. We would sometimes stop there for a drink. Some of the passengers would be thirsty too and get off for a drink. There was a cup there and all hands would take a drink.

"At W. Kuebler Sons brewery the beer was loaded right on the canalboats. The trolley also distributed beer along the line. Sometimes there would be a bottle or two short—the fellows said it got too hot and blew the caps off. Sometimes on the milk car we used to drink milk right out of the can.

"There was also a mail car for a time. You would put a letter on at Riegelsville and in five minutes it would be down to Kintnersville. For a time there was a mail clerk, but I guess the government found it too expensive. Mail would be picked up at Doylestown for Easton and intermediate stops. At each stop they would be out to pick up their mail bags.

"Our maximum speed was not over 40 miles per hour. Where the line paralleled the road we used to race with the automobiles. Downhill we would really travel, but the track was pretty shaky and if we went too fast, the trolley pole would fly off. Where the line ran along the mountains, sometimes we would run into stones that rolled down, but we never left the rails.

"Sometimes in the winter, we would have trouble with snow. I remember one time there were two or three days that we had the passengers snow bound. We had to put them up along the line. We had a snow plow but sometimes that couldn't get through and we would have to get farmers along the way to dig us out. They would work night and day, and how the fellows used to drink—to keep warm. Sometimes the banks would be as high as the plow.

"There were no serious floods when I was on the line, but at the Kintnersville turnoff I have seen the water nearly up to the roadbed."

Collection of Ralph Michaels
Trolley car below Ground Hog lock on the Doylestown and Easton line which paralleled the canal to Kintnersville.

Total	Between	
5.5	0.6	GROUND HOG LOCK NO. 22-23

One of the most attractive areas along the canal is located at Ground Hog, or Raubsville, lock. Ample parking facilities permit a leisurely inspection of this area. Lock No. 22-23 is the first and largest lift lock encountered on the canal. Originally two locks were located at this site; but during later modernization they were replaced by this double lock, so-called because its width permitted two boats, side

Collection of author
Double lock No. 22-23. The first house (right) is the lock keeper's home.

by side, to be "locked through" at one time. The miter gates that were installed at the lower end of the lock chamber have disintegrated and have been removed. The drop gate at the head of the chamber is intact. The small building adjacent to the drop gate is the wicket house, or shanty, as usually referred to by boatmen, which still contains the mechanism for operating the wickets and the drop gate. Not in view when water is in the canal is a second drop gate above the main gate. This gate normally is open. Its function was to permit repairs to the lock without draining the water from the upper level, so that there was always a continuous flow of water to operate a hydro power plant at this location.

A better perspective of the size of this lock and its lift of 17.3 feet, the highest on the canal, may be gained from the towpath below the lock. The building between the lock and the river was constructed in 1900 to house a hydro-electric plant, which was in operation until 1954.

One of the collateral assets that the Lehigh Coal and Navigation Company obtained through ownership of the Lehigh and Delaware canals was the excellent water power potential that existed along these streams. Almost from its beginning the Company encouraged the development of industries that could use this water power, thereby increasing industrial expansion and additional traffic on its canals.

Sometime before the Civil War a group of industries, including a sawmill, a distillery and later a papermill were established to utilize the excellent water power existing at Ground Hog lock on the Delaware Canal. By the beginning of the twentieth century only the papermill continued in operation. During the year 1900 a company was organized and incorporated under the laws of New Jersey for the purpose of generating electric power, utilizing some of the water power available at Ground Hog lock under lease from the Lehigh Coal and Navigation Company. Between 1900 and 1902 this company, called the Lehigh Power Company, installed a hydroelectric plant adjacent to Lock 22-23 between the canal and the Delaware River. Before the installation was completed the severe river floods of 1901-1903, which put the Delaware Canal out of business for nearly two years, did great damage to the hydroplant. In 1904 the Lehigh Power Company was purchased at a foreclosure sale by James H. Morris who, in turn, sold the property to B. F. Fackenthal, Jr., and Lee S. Clymer, both of Riegelsville, Pennsylvania.

Collection of author.
View from picnic grounds showing Ground Hog lock (left) and the building that housed the hydroelectric plant (right).

The new owners, under the incorporated name of Clymer Power Company, proceeded to restore the damaged plant which consisted of a 33 inch McCormack turbine, using a 33 foot head of water that was discharged into the Delaware River and a 45 inch McCormack turbine using an 18 foot head of water that was discharged into the canal. Each turbine was connected to an alternating current generator. During a final reorganization of the company in 1908 its corporate name was slightly changed to *The* Clymer Power Company.

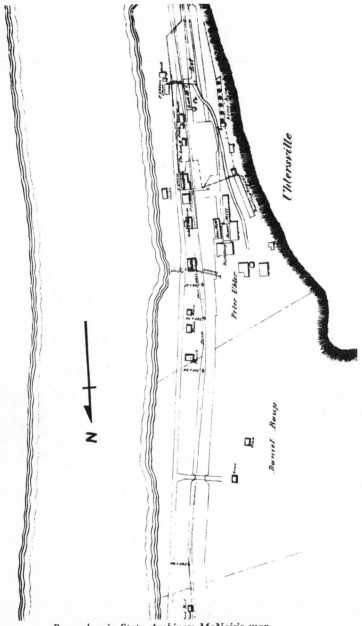

Pennsylvania State Archives: McNair's map.

Plate II. This settlement at Lock No. 22-23, called Uhlersville, included a distillery, sawmill and papermill.

This company had but two customers, the Philadelphia and Easton Transit Company and the Raubsville Paper Company, although in 1909 an electric line was extended along the towpath to Easton to supply surplus power to the Easton Gas and Electric Company.

In 1926 the stock of The Clymer Power Company was acquired by Pennsylvania Power and Light Company which continued to operate the plant for the benefit of the two customers until they went out of business about 1927. On May 28, 1928, the generating facilities were merged with the Pennsylvania Power and Light system and the plant was designated Raubsville Hydroelectric Station. Subsequent improvements produced an ultimate capacity of 1440 kilowatts, partly by installing logs on top of the dam at Easton to raise the water level in the canal. The station continued operation until August 14, 1954, when the plant was abandoned and the equipment salvaged. On December 8, 1954, the remaining property, consisting of the building and two acres of land extending 700 feet along the canal, was conveyed to Pennsylvania Department of Forests and Waters for one dollar.[5]

The Raubsville Paper Company, which was located between the highway and the canal just north of Lock 22-23, had an interesting but erratic career. Built by Peter Uhler as a distillery, operations continued through the Civil War, after which Uhler converted the plant into a paper mill for the manufacture of paper board out of straw. In 1890 the property was purchased by Adolph Segel, "who changed the machinery and manufactured waxed tissue paper, but his operation was not a financial success, and was the beginning of a checkered career for the plant, which changed hands quite often, shut down many times, sold out by the sheriff at least twice, making different kinds of paper under each reorganization, and again became financially embarrassed in 1928, when it was again shut down. In 1930 this paper mill was destroyed by fire."[6]

Below Ground Hog Lock an extensive recreational area is maintained, including picnic tables, grills, drinking water from a pump and toilet facilities. Numerous other picnic sites are located along the line of the canal.

The placid quiet now existing here belies the range of activities that were prevalent during the latter half of the nineteenth century. At that time the present highway from the lock to Raubsville did not exist. Travellers going north crossed the bridge at the lock and continued to Raubsville by a road between the canal and river.

Courtesy, Clinton H. Kreitz
Raubsville Paper Co. located on west side of canal just above Ground Hog lock.

Adjacent to the papermill was the residence of Peter Uhler and a group of dwellings for workmen. Further south, opposite the lock, a group of limekilns were located. On the opposite side of the canal, in addition to the lock keeper's house, still standing, were a hotel and Michael Uhler's home. From these brothers the area took the name of Uhlersville. Subsequently, the brothers were to move further down the canal and contribute their name to Uhlertown.

There is no better way to absorb the unique atmosphere of a canal than to stroll along its towpath; and no more picturesque setting than that stretch of towpath below Lock No. 22-23. Alvin F. Harlow could have had this section in mind when he painted his word picture of the old Delaware Canal.[7]

> An old canal like this has long since lost its appearance of artificiality and seems like a natural stream—a stream which has lost its youthful impetuosity and drifted into the tranquility of age. There are no longer any raw gashes in earth and stone—the banks are covered with verdure down to the brim. Violets and dandelions bloom along the towpath, and rhododendrons and ferns dip their feet in water on the other side. Trees arch overhead from either side until at times their wind-blown bough tops caress each other. Even . . . the locks and aqueducts are so weathered and so covered with moss that one can easily fancy they have been there always.

Total	Between
6.5	1.0

FRY'S RUN AQUEDUCT

The canal crosses Fry's Run (Kleinhaus Creek) over the first of ten aqueducts along the canal. This is also the shortest aqueduct being about 25 feet long. During the winter of 1967 the aqueduct was rebuilt by the Department of Forests and Waters restoring it to its original width.

On the opposite side of Route 611 are the remains of an old stone bridge that originally carried the highway over the stream.

Total	Between
7.2	0.7

STOP GATE NO. 7

Another stop gate is installed in the canal at the northern boundary of Bucks County, back of the small restaurant on the left side of the highway. A short walk through the underbrush brings one to the well preserved and operative stop gate. As opposed to the miter gates at the previous location, a drop gate is installed here, which is normally open. In case of emergency the gate can be closed by the mechanism on the stone abutment. About 200 feet upstream a waste weir is installed to discharge excess canal water into the river.

Total	Between
8.2	1.0

RIEGELSVILLE

In 1804, Riegelsville, originally known as Shank's Ferry, was named after Benjamin Riegel, a farmer who purchased a large tract of land now comprising the southern part of the borough. The Riegel

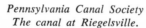

Pennsylvania Canal Society
The canal at Riegelsville.

family operated grist and sawmills on the New Jersey side of the river to take advantage of the fine water power on Musconetcong River. In 1867, John L. Riegel and Son was organized to operate a papermill on the site of the gristmill. Later expansions resulted in the incorporation of the Warren Manufacturing Company in 1873. These operations now are known as Riegel Paper Corporation, comprising three paper mills in Riegelsville, New Jersey and vicinity, and one at Milford, New Jersey.

When the Warren Manufacturing Company was organized, one of the incorporators was John Brown, manager of the Lehigh and Delaware canals who brought valuable experience in building dams and power canals. One of these canals still exists, extending inland from Riegelsville, New Jersey, along the north shore of Musconetcong River for about a mile.

While their industrial activities were located on the New Jersey side of the river, most of the Riegels lived in Riegelsville, Pennsylvania. There John L. Riegel built a large home and in 1886 founded the Riegelsville Academy.[8]

Another resident of Riegelsville, Pennsylvania, was Dr. B. F. Fackenthal, Jr., long time executive of Durham Iron Works, one time president of The Bucks County Historical Society and a noted historian of the Delaware Valley.

Total	Between	
9.3	1.1	**DURHAM FURNACE**

The little settlement of Durham Furnace, at the mouth of Durham Creek, is a far cry from the bustling days when this area was a great iron producing center. Here are located the aqueduct over Durham Creek and Durham Lock No. 21. The former is one of the steel chutes that substitutes for the demolished aqueduct, and the latter was excellently rebuilt in 1966. Plans are formulated for rebuilding the aqueduct to its original dimensions whenever funds are available.

The last of the Durham iron furnaces were located in the approximate area now occupied by the Whippany Paper Board Company. On the north side of Durham Creek, about opposite the paper company, the remains of the once famous Durham Cave are still in evidence. Below the cave, on the shore of the Delaware River, the first Durham boat was made. A significant historic event of the area was an important council with the Indians, held at the original Durham furnace, to discuss the Indian Walking Purchase.

A picturesque drive up Route 212 takes one to Durham Village, the site of the first iron furnace. At 1.1 miles from Route 611 a

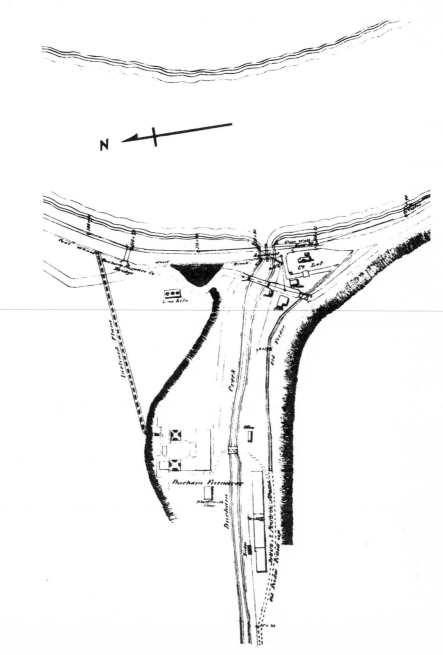

N

Pennsylvania State Archives: McNair's map
Plate III. Durham Furnace near the mouth of Durham Creek.

diagonal road to the right leads to the village, another half mile distant. Here is located Riegel's Mill built by William Long in 1820 on the site of the original buildings. On the hillside adjacent to the mill the arch of the first furnace is still preserved. History records that in 1793 two distilleries were located at Durham Village.

There is probably no other portion of the Delaware Valley with such a variety of historic lore or that contributed as much to its early economic growth as this section of Durham township.

Collection of James Lee
Durham Creek aqueduct and Lock No. 21 in background.

Total	Between	
11.0	1.7	KINTNERSVILLE

At the junction with Route 32, Gallows Run is crossed by a bridge that replaced one of the old wooden covered bridges so characteristic of this part of the country. Route 611, on its way to Doylestown, bears to the right and passes through Kintnersville, settled by German immigrants around 1740. Continuing on Route 32, one enters the area dominated by the palisades of Nockamixon, those high cliffs that extend for several miles and provide some of the most spectacular scenery to be found in the Delaware Valley. Topographic maps of the area indicate that the cliffs have a height of up to 500 feet.

Total	Between	
11.4	0.4	**GALLOWS RUN AQUEDUCT**

Shortly after entering Route 32, which is usually called the River Road, the aqueduct over Gallows Run may be seen at the point where the canal returns to closely parallel the highway and vie with the latter for space between the cliffs and the river. While the road is narrow and winding, there is available space for parking beyond the aqueduct in case a close inspection is desired. The excellent condition of the aqueduct is due to rebuilding the timber portion during the winter of 1966-67.

Total	Between	
11.8	0.4	**NARROWSVILLE LOCK NO. 20**

Narrowsville Lock No. 20 and the surrounding area would hardly be recognized by an old boatman returning after a lapse of thirty or forty years. The lock is being rebuilt to a width of eleven feet. It replaces a structure that was a double lock, 22 feet wide, having been converted from the original single lock during the modernization era of the 1850's. When completed, the vertical concrete walls will be faced with stone and miter gates will be installed at the lower end of the lock chamber. The open feeder that ran between the lock and the highway now flows through a buried tube. This is a safety precaution due to the feeder's close proximity to the highway embankment and the possibility of the embankment collapsing under present day traffic.

It is fortunate for history and canal buffs that photographs of this area during the period of canal operation are in existence. The lock was constructed adjacent to a large gristmill erected by Samuel Rufe on the river bank some years before the canal was built. Waterpower for operating the mill was obtained by means of a wing dam extending into the river below Linn's Falls which has a drop of over seven feet. There was also a large house between the highway and the bluff, directly opposite the lock. Several other houses were also in the vicinity, including one still standing a short distance upstream from the lock. This house, in later years, was occupied by the lock keeper.

As a boon to the early canal builders, Canvass White, a young engineer on the Erie Canal, developed and patented a new type of cement, called hydraulic cement. This cement had the unusual property for that period of hardening under water. Due to its unusual feature, contractors involved in canal construction were able to build the durable stone structures required for locks, aqueducts and bridges.

Collection of author
Narrowsville Lock No. 21 after major repairs (1968).

Oil painting by author
Narrowsville Lock No. 21 and surrounding area during the active canal period.

At the time the Delaware Canal was being built, limestone of the required quality was located in quarries on the New Jersey side of the river about three miles above the Narrowsville mill. After the limestone was burned in ordinary limekilns at the site, the clinker was loaded on Durham boats and floated down the Delaware to the grist-mill where it was ground to the proper fineness on the ordinary buhrstones of the mill.

That most of the hydraulic cement used on the Delaware Canal was ground at the Narrowsville plant is apparent from a report submitted to the Commissioners on November 20, 1829, by H. G. Sargent, general engineer of the Delaware Division: "Lock No. 20 (the Narrowsville lock) would have been erected this season only that it is located directly in front of and occupies a part of the ground on which a gristmill now stands, where most of the hydraulic cement used on the line is manufactured."

Another gristmill in the area known to have supplied hydraulic cement for the canal was the mill owned by Asher Ely, located on Primrose Run which empties into the Delaware River at Phillips Mill about 20 miles below. Account books of this gristmill, still in exis-tence, record that from 1829 to 1833 hydraulic cement was shipped to contractors engaged in building locks, culverts, aqueducts and other masonry on the canal. Hydraulic cement sold at 20 to 21 cents per bushel while ordinary lime sold at 15 cents per bushel.[9]

After completing its stint of producing hydraulic cement, the Narrowsville mill continued to grind grain until about the turn of the century. As a small boy, George Fox, who later became a conductor on the Easton-Doylestown trolley, lived in the house opposite the lock. "The mill was shut down before 1909", he said, "but the millstones and some of the machinery was still there. We used to play around the mill and run the truck back and forth across the bridge on the steel rails."

Having withstood the river floods for over a century, the building fell into decay after milling was discontinued and was torn down after the canal was returned to the state.

The high point in the cliffs just south of Lock 20 is called Top Rock. Like so many promontories, this one too has a legend. This one involves an Indian buck and his blind wife. Tired of looking after her, he took her to Top Rock one early morning and suggested a stroll towards the sunrise. This she did, to her destruction.

Total   Between
12.7   0.9   NARROWS HOTEL

The large building hugging the cliffs about a mile below Narrows lock, known in canal days as Narrows Hotel, was a popular stopping place for boatmen. In recent times it has operated as a restaurant, called Indian Rock Inn. The basin south of the hotel afforded accommodation for a number of boats. Just north of the hotel were extensive mule stables and to the south, a barn and blacksmith shop. The mules could be taken to the stables and blacksmith shop over the "camel back" bridge then in existence. While the sale of liquor on Sunday was prohibited by law, boatmen had no difficulty getting it here. A blicky[10] of beer cost five cents.

Total   Between
14.7   2.0

At the northern outskirts of Upper Black Eddy the highway crosses the canal over a bridge that, while displaying the old camel back design, is reinforced for heavy, present day traffic. At this point the canal travels inland for about seven miles, following the contour along the hills to the west. There is, however, a southerly slope to the terrain, requiring two locks in this distance.

Total   Between
15.5   0.8   UPPER BLACK EDDY

(At the bridge) Upper Black Eddy is so named to distinguish it from another community further down the river also named for the Black family that early inhabited this area. This village is located on the longest eddy of the Delaware River. During the rafting era the eddy was a favorite overnight stopping place for the raftsmen who guided the huge log and lumber rafts that floated downstream during spring high water and other river freshets. The river bridge connects with the New Jersey town of Milford which is the site of a Riegel Paper Corporation plant, located along the river at the southern end of the village. Prior to 1900 Upper Black Eddy frequently was referred to as Bridgeton, the name of the township in which it is located.

The only remaining general store on the Delaware Canal still serves this village. It may be reached by turning right on the first road south of the Route 32 bridge over the canal. Located along the towpath just south of the camel back bridge over the canal, the store has a long history of service to the canal trade and the surrounding community. Prior to 1900 it was owned by Mike McIntee, followed by William Singley whose sons Howard and John continue its operation.

Collection of author
Singley's store at Upper Black Eddy. The last active canal store.

The retreat of the ice age from the Delaware Valley deposited huge quantities of cobblestones, of more or less uniform size, along the bed and shores of the Delaware River. After completion of the Delaware Canal a lucrative business developed from collecting and shipping these stones by canalboats to Philadelphia for paving that city's streets. Shipments were made from nearly all points along the canal from Easton to Yardley.

Collection of cobblestones, or "boothers" as they were locally called, occurred during the summer months when the river water was low and warm. Flat boats, or scows, of from 12 to 18 feet in length were anchored in shoal water; and, pickers standing on the river bottom used specially constructed forks to toss the stones into the boat. Another tool, called a "boother rake", consisted of twelve prongs attached to a long handle. This rake was used to drag the boothers from the deep to shallow water, where they could be handled with the forks.

The loaded boats were poled to the shore where their contents were transferred to carts or wagons, drawn to the canal bank and loaded on canalboats. Fitzgerald records that teams of mules or yokes of oxen were used to haul the wagons. Some shippers took advantage of the outlet locks at Easton and New Hope to eliminate extra handling. Here the canalboats were locked into the river and loaded directly from the river bottom.

Prior to 1850, great quantities of cobblestones for street paving were shipped to Philadelphia. After that date, and until macadam made both obsolete, smooth dressed blocks were favored. Many of the latter, called at the quarries Belgian blocks, were supplied by the Lumberton Granite Company. As the traffic in cobblestones declined the slack was taken up by increased demands for Belgian blocks, thus maintaining heavy traffic in these products for many years over the Delaware Canal.

Among the shippers of cobblestones mentioned by Fitzgerald were: Anderson Colvin, Philip Reese and the Stecke brothers of Raubsville, the latter making weekly trips with eight boats. "William Warner of Riegelsville shipped three boats weekly. John Hoffman of the same place was also a shipper. Aaron F. Harwick of Upper Black Eddy owned five boats, making weekly trips. . . . George Sigafoos of Lodi kept two boats going for some time."[11] Other shippers were Joseph and Elias Samsel of Erwinna, Moses Bird of Point Pleasant and Jeremiah, Thomas, John and Peter Lawless of New Hope. The Philadelphia "wharves to which consignments were made were: Mead Alley, Shackamaxon, Christian and Reed Streets. Among the contractors to whom consignments were made was John M. Mack, founder of The Mack Paving Company."

The toll paid to the canal company by shippers of cobblestones was one mill for one thousand pounds per mile with an additional toll of two cents per mile for the boat.

Total	Between	
16.8	1.3	LODI LOCK NO. 19

Lodi Lock No. 19 takes its name from the small community that sprang up along the canal and River Road during the canal building days. The lock is reached by a narrow road, branching to the right from Route 32, that easily may be missed unless the mileage is checked when passing through Upper Black Eddy. Less than a quarter mile distant the road crosses the canal over a fill under which the canal water passes through a large culvert. In the active canal days a camel back bridge was installed at this location. Just north of the crossing Gray's Creek flows into the canal. Opposite the creek on the towpath side, a waste weir equipped with a Tainter gate is installed. This waste weir is used to protect the canal against high water when a freshet occurs in the creek.

Lock No. 19 is located a short distance south of the crossing and may be reached by the towpath. A feeder paralleling the lock is, like all other feeders, for the purpose of controlling the height of water in the level below the lock. Adjacent to the lock is the original

Courtesy, Robert Harmon
Lodi Lock No. 19. The lock tender's house (right) is now the office of the canal superintendent.

lock keeper's house, now used as the field office for Roosevelt State Park. The surrounding buildings house equipment used by the canal maintenance crew.

Total 18.8	Between 2.0	UHLERTOWN

About a hundred feet south of the river bridge to Frenchtown, New Jersey, a road to the right leads to Uhlertown and Lock No. 18, frequently called Uhlertown lock. In some of the early records made prior to the advent of Uhlertown, the lock was called Frenchtown lock. This little hamlet, which consisted of only the lock keeper's house while the canal was under construction,[12] is universally conceded by visitors to be the most unique and picturesque location on the canal. From the time a few buildings had accumulated, according to Mac Reynolds,[13] "this place long bore the name Mexico, perhaps bestowed by one of the canal builders of lively imagination in 1832." It was not until the advent of Michael Uhler, who transferred his activities from the upper river to this area in the early 1850's and was appointed postmaster in 1871, that its present name was acquired.

Being a man of remarkable business ability and energy, Uhler's arrival started a boom in this small community. In addition to owning extensive farm lands from which grain and hay were supplied to the

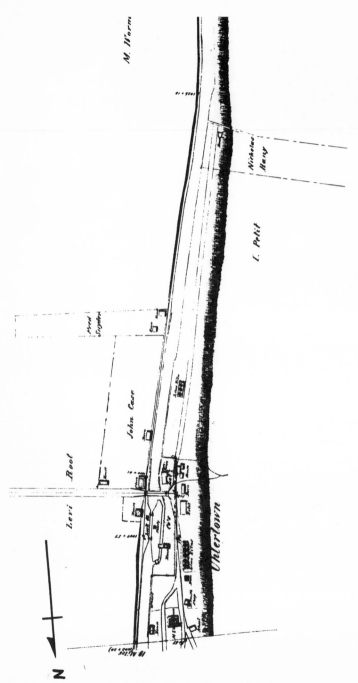

Pennsylvania State Archives: McNair's map
Plate IV. Uhlertown. When this map was made the school building, gristmill
and the boat yard had not yet been constructed.

UHLERTOWN   BUCK'S   CO.   PA.

Courtesy, Allen Saalburg
An intinerant artist's sketch of Uhlertown.

1. Michael Uhler's home   5. Uhlertown mill   9. Lumber and wood yard
2. Store and post-office   6. Boat yard   10. School and Redmen's hall
3. Uhlertown hotel   7. Limekiln   11. Lock keeper's house
4. Uhlertown hall   8. Hay press   12. Lock

canal trade and metropolitan markets, he organized and operated a boat building yard, ran a line of excellenty equipped canalboats called the Michael Uhler Line, built and operated a gristmill and limekilns, a country store, saddler shop, post office and coal yards.

As no limestone exists in the area surrounding Uhlertown, it is reported that Uhler transported this material from Limeport, a place name no longer existing but, according to Richardson's "Solebury Township", was located just north of Phillips Mill. Here, about a belt of limestone rock, a thriving community and many limekilns existed during most of the nineteenth century. A wharf along the Delaware Canal was much used for shipping lime and other products of the vicinity.

The first sight to attract the attention of a visitor approaching Uhlertown is the entrance to the covered bridge with a record of continuous use since its construction in 1832. This is the only covered bridge on the canal. As an excellent example of early bridge building technique, the structure invites closer inspection, particularly the wooden, lattice type, truss construction fabricated entirely by the use of wooden pegs. The view from the towpath, showing the bridge and single Lock No. 18, further upstream, has long been an enticing subject for artists and photographers.

Most of the buildings shown in the artist's sketch are still intact, although a number have been converted to other uses. As one approaches the bridge, the brick building on the right housed a school room on the first floor and the Redmen's meeting hall on the second. The building on the right of the bridge entrance was the residence of Jonas Sigafoos who operated a general store in an extension of the building paralleling the lock, beyond which was a stable for canal mules. At the left of the bridge entrance, the present home was originally a warehouse for the gristmill which was located on the opposite bank of the canal. It is locally stated that at the conclusion of canal operation the mill was torn down to reduce taxes. Water for operating the mill machinery was conveyed by a flume from the canal level above the lock to the mill. Now, a feeder replaces the flume, imparting to the quiet surroundings the pleasant music of the purling stream. The once active boat yard, located along the canal bank below the mill, built and repaired canalboats. The only remaining building associated with the boat yard has been converted into a residence.

The Uhlertown Hotel, built about 1840, is little changed from its active days as a popular hostelry of the canal era. The door near the southern end of the building through which one now enters the dining

Oil painting by author
Uhlertown Lock No. 18 and covered bridge. At right is the lock tender's house and behind it the Uhlertown hotel.

Courtesy, Ernest "Nitro" Schultz
Uhlertown, with (left) gristmill, (center) covered bridge and (right) warehouse. Lock No. 18 in background.

Sigafoos canal store adjacent to Lock No. 18. Boat in foreground is entering lock.

Uhlertown Hotel. Door at left leads to barroom.

room of this attractive private residence, originally gave access to the hotel barroom.

During the early part of the twentieth century the area about Uhlertown provided locations for some of Pearl White's popular movie serial, "The Perils of Pauline". Esther Weaver recalls that her father, then employed at the boatyard, made flower boxes to adorn the canalboat used by the actors. No doubt they also enjoyed the hospitality of the hotel's bar after a day of film shooting.

Adjacent to the hotel, the Uhlertown Hall, later converted into an artist's studio, was the scene of many gay dances and other entertainment for the residents of the area. Grant Emery who, as a boy, attended school in the brick building remembers many of these gay scenes. "The music", he said, "was usually supplied by an accordion or two, a violin and, sometimes, an harmonica. Occasionally someone came in with a banjo. They were all local people. Square dances were the rule, with the Virginia reel being preferred. Once in a while somebody would call for a waltz—or a cakewalk which was very, very popular. These affairs were usually on Saturday nights or holidays. The 4th of July was a big day with all kinds of refreshments—down at the bar".

Opposite the studio, on the canal bank, is the lock keeper's house. Next along the road are the remains of a limekiln and a small building that housed the saddler's shop.

At the fork in the road stands the imposing home that Michael Uhler built in 1854 in which he lived until his death in 1896 at the age of 74. A distinctive feature of the building is the ornate, New Orleans type, metal work that supports the porch roof. This house is now owned and occupied by Jackson Mathews.

The building on the canal bank, opposite the residence, housed the post office and the general store. Hoisting equipment still in the loft was used for raising materials to the second floor or lowering them into boats moored beside the building. The extensive barns, much larger than at present, were a beehive of activity during harvesting seasons. A hay press installed on the second floor of the barn obtained power for its operation by means of an ingenious rope, or steel, cable system extending to the gristmill nearly a quarter mile distant. This cable was supported by pulleys mounted on a series of high supports. During the haying season this press often ran day and night, much to the irritation of local residents, one of whom said the pulleys squeaked so badly that it was difficult to get a good night's sleep. As this was the only press in the vicinity, local farmers brought their hay there to be baled, after which it was shipped by canalboats

Courtesy, Allen Saalburg

Michael Uhler's home later owned by William Overpeck and more recently by Jackson Mathews. The framework (right) supported the cable that operated the hay press in the barn.

to markets up and down the canal. Grant Emery recalls that wagons loaded with hay often were lined up nearly to the main road.

As this little hamlet has ripened into old age, it continues to retain the charm of its canal days. The local residents are extremely proud of their unique community and are determined to prevent any encroachments that will mar its historic beauty.

Total	Between	
20.2	1.4	**TINICUM PARK**

A large tract of land contributed by the Stover family, who owned extensive property bordering River Road, was developed and named Tinicum Park by Bucks County. In addition to various recreational activities, the Tinicum Art Festival has been held here in early July for the past twenty years.

Total	Between	
20.5	0.3	**ERWINNA**

Beyond the park a road to the right leads to Erwinna, a canal town that had a flourishing boat building and repair yard and was also the headquarters of the canal superintendent and engineer while the waterway was under construction. F. Francis Rapp operated the boat yard from 1858 to 1882.[14]

The large, three story house at the junction of Erwinna and River roads catered to summer boarders when this was a popular vacation area. Here, members of the Barrymore family were guests for several summers.

Total	Between	
20.8	0.3	**STOVER MILL**

Stover Mill, between the highway and the river, ground grain for the local farmers for over a century. Water power for operating the mill machinery was obtained by means of a wing dam extending into the river. After electricity became available, the water wheel was replaced by an electric motor. The building now is occupied by the Tinicum Civic Association which sponsors art exhibits open to the public on week-ends during the summer. The second and third floors of the mill still contain wooden milling equipment and conveyor tubes.

Total	Between
21.3	0.5

Just south of the Golden Pheasant Inn the River Road again crosses the Delaware Canal which, from here, continues between the highway and the river to New Hope. Just before reaching the inn, the high embankment of the towpath is seen at the right. Here the canal is ten to twelve feet above the highway.

Courtesy, Flora K. Henry
Aqueduct over Tinicum Creek, with camel back bridge in background.

Total	Between	
21.6	0.3	TINICUM CREEK AQUEDUCT

Tinicum Creek aqueduct may be seen at the left while crossing the highway bridge over the creek.

Total	Between	
22.6	1.0	TREASURE ISLAND LOCK NO. 17

Treasure Island Lock No. 17 and its paralleling feeder are nestled close under the road embankment. The high bluff to the west crowds the highway and canal close to the river. The lock takes its name from the adjacent island, long the site of one of the oldest Boy Scout camps in America. During the camping season the river and canal are alive with canoeing and other water sports. It was to Marshall Island, just north of Treasure Island, that Edward Marshall, of Walking Purchase fame, established his last home in which he died in 1789.

Total	Between	
23.6	1.0	SMITHTOWN LOCK NO. 15-16

Smithtown Lock No. 15-16 which is a double lock and second deepest on the canal takes its name from the community in which it is located.

In 1802 Joseph Smith moved into the area now bearing his name. There he established a shop for making plows equipped with his recently invented cast iron moldboard, a major improvement over the previously used wooden moldboards. A patent for his invention was issued May 19, 1800, in the name of his brother, Robert. The Smith patent precedes by 19 years one granted to Jethro Wood, and by 37 years one granted to John Deere. Most of the buildings occupied by Joseph Smith were in the path of the Delaware Canal and were destroyed at the time this waterway was built.[15]

Access to this portion of the canal is gained by a private road which crosses the canal over a camel back bridge just below the lock. Beyond the towpath the property is privately owned and not open to the public. While the fall gate at the head of the lock has been replaced by a dam, the miter gates at the lower end are in place and retain the rods and handles used to open and close the wickets located near the bottom of the gates. The "dog-house" containing the mechanism for opening the miter gate and the wicket shanty at the head of the lock have long since disappeared. A gate at the head of the feeder controls the flow of water to the lower level of the canal. Due to the drop of 12 feet between levels, the water rushes through the channel with the cadence of a mountain stream.

Courtesy, Flora K. Henry
Smithtown double Lock No. 15-16 with dog-house (foreground) and lock shanty (background) containing the mechanism for operating the drop gate and wickets.

Courtesy, Flora K. Henry
Flora Henry and her dog Buster.

The building adjacent to the lock is the lock keeper's house, to which Flora Henry came as a child of five, when her father, Jacob Henry, was appointed lock keeper in 1915. In recalling this period she said, "When I was about 14 years old I could handle the lock just like a man could". From that time she assisted her father with the lock until his death in 1931, after which she remained as lock keeper until the Delaware Canal ceased operation as a commercial waterway in October of that year. To protect her from what Flora Henry called "nasty boatmen", her father gave her a dog, Buster, which became her guardian and companion during her stay at the lock. Among other duties of the lock keeper was to maintain the proper height of water in the lower level. "There was a mark on the bank", Flora Henry said. "If the water dropped below that point, I would go to the feeder gate and raise it a notch or two. After the water reached the mark, I would lower the gate to its original position".

The old water wheel at the end of the feeder adds a pictuesque charm to the surroundings. This wheel, connected to an electric generator in the adjoining building, was installed in 1932 by Joseph Aaron, an ex-circus performer. Aaron purchased the property below the lock, including an old building which had been an inn from stage coach days. A building along the highway above the inn was originally a stable for canal mules. The old inn, which Aaron used as a woodworking shop, is now an attractive dwelling house. He converted the stable into an apartment on the second floor and a restaurant on the first floor, which he operated as *The Cat and Fiddle*. This building is recognized by a large coffee pot atop one of the chimneys. The generator at the feeder supplied electricity to both buildings.

Total	Between	
26.0	2.4	POINT PLEASANT

As one descends the hill into Point Pleasant he is confronted by a maze of roads, streams and bridges, not to mention the numerous quaint buildings of uncertain architecture, interspersed here and there with old stone structures characteristic of "the valley". The concrete bridge which carries the River Road over Tohickon Creek replaced a single-span covered wooden bridge. Another bridge just to the right spans the mouth of Geddes Run where it joins Tohickon Creek.

In earlier days the portion of the community south of Tohickon Creek was called Black's Eddy. Later the name was changed to Lower Black Eddy to distinguish it from the village further up the river. Still later the name Point Pleasant was given to the whole area, its charming scenic surroundings suggesting the name.

Tohickon Creek aqueduct rebuilt in 1948.

Aqueduct over Tohickon Creek, equipped with overflow to control height of water in that level. The man stands on mule driver's footbridge.

Upon crossing Tohickon Creek a parking area, from which the aqueduct over Tohickon Creek may be inspected, is available behind the Community Fire House. This aqueduct, which is the longest on the canal, periodically collapsed or was carried away by floods. In 1948 the present substantial concrete structure was erected. While its trunk dimensions are too small to pass a canalboat, its present function is to supply sufficient water for downstream requirements. For the visitor interested in hiking, a pleasant walk of about one half mile along the towpath brings one to locks Nos. 14 and 13.

Total	Between	
26.5	0.5	**POINT PLEASANT LOCKS NO. 13 AND 14**

Continuing by automobile from Point Pleasant, Locks No. 14 and 13, frequently called the Point Pleasant locks, may also be reached by stopping at Mountainside Restaurant, which they are opposite. The restaurant, which is a continuation of a long line of taverns, occupies one of the oldest buildings in the valley, reputed to have been built in 1689. In the days of rafting the tavern was a favorite stopping place for Philadelphia lumber buyers who came up the river to bargain with the raft captains.

The locks, which are only about 700 feet apart, present a charming picture in this secluded area. Due to their proximity, only one lock keeper was required. His house was adjacent to Lock No. 14. In 1947, these locks, together with No. 12 at Lumberville, were rebuilt, including gates and all operating features. Unfortunately the ponderous mechanisms installed on the gates for operating the wickets or, in this case, the slide valves, are not characteristic of Delaware Canal construction. This equipment came from the much larger, discarded gates of the Schuylkill Canal, where the locks were 18 feet wide.

Total	Between	
27.1	0.6	**ENTRANCE OF FEEDER TO DELAWARE AND RARITAN CANAL**

A short distance above the river dam north of Lumberville, the entrance to the feeder of the Delaware and Raritan Canal may be seen on the New Jersey shore, approximately ¾ mile north of Raven Rock, New Jersey. A good view of the feeder entrance can be had in the area where the towpath bank is protected by a concrete wall. The V dam in the river was installed to increase the height of water at the feeder entrance.

Courtesy, Frank Swope
Boat, headed upstream, leaving Point Pleasant Lock No. 14.

Collection of author
Lock No. 13 (foreground) and No. 14 (background), both rebuilt in 1947 utilizing salvaged wicket mechanism from the Schuylkill Canal.

Total	Between	
27.8	0.7	LUMBERVILLE

Lock No. 12, together with its feeder, usually called Lumberville lock, is just to the left of River Road. This attractive location, equipped with picnic tables, is a popular stopping place for visitors. Just above the lock an aqueduct conveys the canal over Paunaucussing Creek, sometimes called Milton Creek. The residents above the aqueduct make good use of the canal by incorporating it as background to their attractive lawns and gardens.

Lumberville, as the name implies, started as a lumber and sawmill town. When the first sawmills were built by Col. George Wall, the place was known as Walls Saw Mills & Walls Landing. After the business changed hands, the purchaser gave the present name to the village. In 1869 William Tinsman purchased the lumber business, which has continued in the family through four generations to the present time.[16] A toll bridge which had spanned the river for many years was condemned and replaced by the present footbridge in 1949. While this latter bridge leads to no place in particular, it does afford pedestrians an excellent scenic view up and down the river. The stone building at the bridge entrance was the home and office of the bridge toll collector.

Just south of this building is the famous Black Bass Hotel which has existed as a hostelry since 1745. The canal builders found the hotel a source of relaxation and amusement, sometimes carried to such an extreme that on one Saturday night a fire broke out that could have led to disaster except for the courage of one man who broke into the cellar and carried to safety a large quantity of blasting powder stored there by the canal builders. Among the hotel's famous guests was President Grover Cleveland who, on more than one occasion, slipped away from his cares of office to indulge in his favorite sport, fishing.

Total	Between	
28.8	1.0	HARD TIMES—LUMBERTON

In the area where River Road crosses Cuttalossa Creek, a few ancient buildings mark the site of a once flourishing community. Reputed to have had more names than any other hamlet in Bucks County, they started with Rose's Ferry, from the man who started the first one about 1720. Then followed a succession of ferry owners, each giving his name to the crossing. During a business decline in 1819, the community was called Hard Times, a name that continued until 1834 when John E. Kenderdine bought the entire property, constructed grist and sawmills along the creek and gave the name Lumberton to the community. Of late years, this name has practically disappeared from common usage.

About 1758 William Skelton built a gristmill along the creek in the area now occupied by the Delaware Canal. At the same time he constructed the building on the west side of Cuttalossa Road at its junction with River Road. This building was long operated as a tavern, first called Hard Times and later the Sign of the Camel. It recently was owned and occupied by William F. Taylor, artist and first president of Delaware Valley Protective Association.

According to local legend, one of the early atrocities of the Doane gang of bandits of the area occurred in this house. Believing that Skelton had a large quantity of money stashed in the tavern, they broke in at night, ransacked the premises, but found only a small amount of gold. To appease their frustration and to satisfy their warped sense of humor, the bandits decided that Skelton must do a dance. When the old man demurred, one of the bandits, noticing a large iron bake pan hanging by the fireplace, put it on the hot coals. When properly heated, the pan was placed on the floor and the old gentleman was compelled to dance on it. The pan "was not hot enough to burn him severely, but still sufficiently so to keep him moving pretty actively, while their mirth became boisterous in the extreme."[17]

Across Cuttalossa Road from the tavern, a more recently constructed building has housed the Cuttalossa Inn for quite a number of years. On the opposite side of the creek from the Inn, the remaining stone walls of one of Kenderdine's mills form the setting for an outdoor bar and dining terrace maintained by the Inn. The waters of the creek supplied power for a number of mills, including grist and saw mills and a handle factory which, over the years, were owned by a variety of individuals.

The creek road, considered one of the most beautiful drives in the county, has attracted many home owners to the area. Among its distinguished early residents was General Zebulon M. Pike, for whom Pike's Peak was named. As a boy he lived here in a house that has long since disappeared. When asked the location of the house, one owner of the tavern said, "it was over that way", pointing in the direction of the dam in the creek. The charm and beauty of the Cuttalossa have been recorded in the poetry of Thaddeus S. Kenderdine. A bit of this charm is captured in his stanza:

> While Cuttalossa's waters
> Roll murmuring on their way,
> 'Twixt hazel clumps and alders,
> 'Neath old oaks gnarled and gray,
> While just across the valley
> From the old, old grist-mill come
> The water-wheel's low patter,
> The millstone's drowsy hum.[18]

The Delaware Quarries, below Cuttalossa Road, present an interesting picture, not at all unsightly, due to the skillful management of Joseph Busick, their owner. Here, for those interested in the subject, a bit of geology is on display. The first quarry in this area, called the Lumberton Granite Company, was located further up the river, just west of the old Hard Times tavern. The present appearance of this location illustrates how nature, assisted by the ingenuity of man, can correct the landscape scars produced by commercial exploitation. According to John Richardson[19] the quarry furnished building stone for many Philadelphia homes and, no doubt, for the locks of the Delaware Canal. One item of production was the so-called Belgian blocks, cut stone used for paving streets. At peak operations approximately 200 stonecutters were employed. The products of the quarry were transported to markets by canalboats, for which dockage space was built along the canal.

In 1883 the company erected a tramway over the canal and river to carry stone to a siding of the Pennsylvania Rail Road on the New Jersey side of the river. The tramway consisted of a heavy steel cable on which a large grooved wheel ran, from which a box type platform for carrying stone was suspended. The wheel was propelled by an endless cable operated by a stationary steam engine at the quarry.

Total	Between	
31.1	2.3	**CENTRE BRIDGE**

After bearing the names of several ferry operators, this community acquired its present name, Centre Bridge, when the first covered toll bridge was built in 1814. The name signifies the hamlet's location half way between Lumberville and New Hope. The last covered bridge was struck by lightning and burned in 1923, after which the present steel structure was built. This bridge connects with Stockton, New Jersey, where the famous Colligan's Inn is located. An inn has existed in Centre Bridge adjacent to the bridge entrance since the days of the first ferry. After at least two previous buildings had been destroyed by fire, the present building housing the Centre Bridge Inn was built in 1961. Due to the presence of a dining terrace bordering the canal bank, the inn is a frequent rendezvous for parties chartering one of Pete Pascuzzo's mule drawn canalboats.

Total **Between**
32.6   **1.5**   **PHILLIPS MILL**

Upon approaching Phillips Mill the highway crosses Primrose Creek. To the left of the highway may be seen some interesting stone masonry forming the entrance to one of the largest culverts on the canal, through which the creek passes under the Delaware Canal.

Phillips Mill, located along a sharp "S" turn in the highway, consists of several buildings of pre-Revolutionary vintage. In 1756, Aaron Phillips built a gristmill on Primrose Creek, later named Phillips Creek. The mill, just to the right at the first turn, was operated by four generations of Phillipses. After the mill ceased operations, it was rescued from falling into decay by the Phillips Mill Community Association. Here, art exhibits and other community avtivities are held.

The impressive stone building on the left side of the highway was the home of Aaron Phillips. Back of the house is a stone building that was used as a cooper shop for making barrel staves, hoops and tops for the gristmill. About the turn of the century, the famous artist, William L. Lathrop, purchased the property and lived there for the rest of his life. The old cooper shop he converted into a studio.

Total **Between**
33.6   **1.0**   **NEW HOPE**

At the northern approach to New Hope, the highway again crosses the canal over a camel back bridge. From this point the canal flows through the main portion of the village, supplying not only a popular tourist attraction but also an important financial asset to the community.

Total **Between**
34.4   **0.8**   **BRIDGE AND MAIN STREETS**

(At the traffic light). New Hope takes its name from the leading industry that was erected after a destructive fire in 1790. That year the flour, linseed oil and lumber mills of Benjamin Parry were destroyed. With determination and renewed hope for the future, Parry at once rebuilt his mills and called them New Hope Mills. Prior to that time the village was named for the various ferries that operated on the river, the best remembered being Coryell's Ferry.

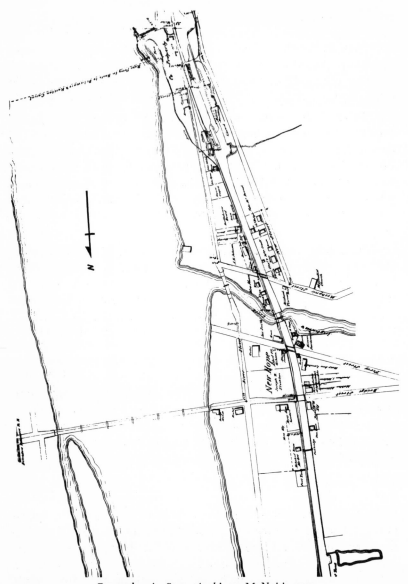

Pennsylvania State Archives: McNair's map

Plate V. New Hope, showing Locks Nos. 11 and 10 and the outlet lock to the Delaware River.

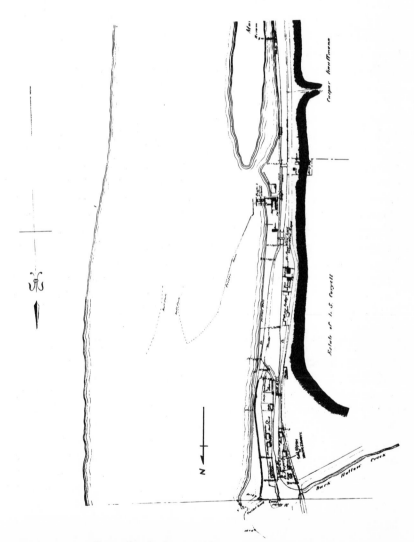

Pennsylvania State Archives: McNair's map
Plate VI. New Hope, showing Locks Nos. 9 and 8, the stop gate in the feeder
to the outlet lock, the lock near Union Mill and the lifting wheels in the
Delaware River.

It was this ferry that carried many of Washington's Continentals prior to and following the Battle of Trenton.

Due to the fine water power along Ingham Creek, New Hope, during the nineteenth century, developed into the foremost industrial town in Bucks County. By the turn of the century as the old industries began to decline, New Hope became the center of a distinguished art colony. The attractions of fine studios, antique and gift shops, the Bucks County Playhouse, together with the allure of the old canal, bring thousands of visitors to this area each year.

In spite of the influx of summer visitors, New Hope retains its colonial quaintness due principally to its many old historic structures. Prior to construction of the Delaware Canal, the community consisted mainly of the two block area between Main Street and the river, from Bridge to Mechanic Streets. To some village sceptics, the canal was merely that ditch dug up there along the hillside west of town. In this colonial area are most of the historic reminders of pre-Revolutionary days: the Logan Inn at the corner of Main and Ferry Streets, a successor of inns from before 1732; on the opposite corner the Parry Mansion, built in 1784, now housing the New Hope Historical Society, and its stone barn across Main Street; back of the barn, the Parry gristmill, built after the fire of 1790 and now the home of the Bucks County Playhouse; the Coryell Ferry toll house on Ferry Street, now the village library; the Town Hall at the corner of Main and Mechanic Streets, built in 1790 and since that time the seat of local government; and further along, at 105 Main Street, the Coryell home built in the mid 1700's.

The towpath, access to which is obtained by a flight of steps at the Ferry Street bridge, is a convenient means of inspecting the various mechanical structures of the canal. Just south of the bridge one crosses the aqueduct over Ingham Creek, also known as Aquetong Creek. This aqueduct was rebuilt during the winter of 1968. Peter Pascuzzo uses the basin further downstream, as the terminus for his fleet of mule drawn, pleasure boats, which he has operated since 1954. No visit to New Hope is complete without taking this picturesque ride on the canal in one of these unique boats. Regular schedules are maintained from early May until the end of October, and individual boats may be chartered for private parties. This scenic ride is enjoyed by thousands of visitors each season.

Lock No. 11 at the end of the basin is the first of four double locks, spaced at intervals of about 500 feet. Adjacent to the lock is the original lock keeper's house. Lock No. 10 was replaced by a dam when the latest highway bridge was constructed over the canal.

Courtesy, Robert Harmon
Boat entering Lock No. 11 at New Hope. Building (left), still standing, was lock tender's house.

Collection of Henry S. Engart
Boats in level between locks No. 10 and No. 9 at New Hope. The loaded boat (left) is leaving Lock No. 10.

On the towpath below Lock No. 10 is a lock keeper's house, now the home and studio of artist Robert J. McClellan.[20] Dark Hollow Creek flows into the basin between Lock Nos. 10 and 9, opposite which an overflow and waste weir control the height of water in the basin when the creek is in flood. In this general area, along the berm bank, were lumber yards, facilities for making boat repairs and accommodations for the work boats used by the canal maintenance crews. On the towpath, opposite Lock No. 9, is the toll collector's office, now the home of Madam Odette Myrtil, proprietor of Chez Odette at Lock No. 8. This inn served for many generations as a rendezvous for raftsmen and, later, for canal boatmen. Known for many years as the River House, it catered to overnight guests, the inner man and what supplies he might need. One of the last proprietors

Courtesy, David Ennis
Locking upbound boat through Lock No. 8. Lock No. 9 in background.

Collection of Henry S. Engart
Loaded boat in basin below Lock No. 8. The feeder (right) leads to New Hope outlet lock.

Collection of author
The outlet lock at New Hope as it appears today.

of canal days was Big Mag Featherstone. Many boatmen still living can attest to her facility in handling obstreperous guests.

Boats leaving Lock No. 8 bound for the Delaware and Raritan Canal made a sharp left turn in the basin below the lock and proceeded through the short feeder to the outlet lock at the river bank, from which they were lowered into the river and conveyed by cable ferry to the opposite shore. The present dam in the feeder replaces a pair of miter gates which were normally open. When closed, they prevented flooding of the lower canal during high water in the river. Boats continuing down the canal entered the nine mile level, one of the longest on the waterway. The only obstruction in this course was the Paper Mill lock, the remains of which are seen in front of the Union Mills Paper Company. This lock was installed when the canal was constructed to serve as a guard lock. At that time a feeder extended into the Delaware River to supply water to the lower portion of the canal. However, during low water in the river, this feeder did not serve its purpose; and, the waterwheel at the wing dam was substituted to supply the water. After the outlet lock was installed, the guard lock, or the Paper Mill lock as it was then called, was used to maintain the proper water level in the basin below Lock No. 8. Boats going downstream were locked through, with a drop of about two feet.

The A. W. Kennedy map of the Delaware Canal, circa 1828-30, shows that Locks No. 8 and No. 9 were constructed as combined locks, i.e., the two locks were adjoining so that a boat passed directly from one lock chamber into the other chamber, with the lower gates of Lock No. 9 serving as the upper gates of Lock No. 8. That combined locks existed at this location for many years, probably until the four locks at New Hope were changed to double locks, is indicated by a contract awarded January 9, 1840, for repairs to the combined lock at New Hope.[21] The contract identifies the locks as No. 9 and No. 10 which, as sometimes happened, may have been an error in writing the contract.

Total   **Between**
36.8   **2.4**   **UPPER WASHINGTON CROSSING STATE PARK**

Continuing our tour from the traffic light at New Hope, the highway crosses Pidcock Creek in "upper park", the northern portion of Washington Crossing State Park. The main park is four miles further down the river. This park was established by the Commonwealth of Pennsylvania[22] to commemorate the turning point of the American Revolution, that memorable Christmas night in 1776 when General Washington and his courageous army of 2400 men crossed the ice clogged Delaware to inflict a stunning defeat on the British army at the Battle of Trenton and revive the waning hopes of the American patriots.

At the left of the road stands the Thompson-Neely "House of Decision", so named because of the important military conferences held there in preparation for the impending battle. A road back of the house crosses the nearby canal and leads to a tree shaded glade between canal and river, the resting place of a number of unknown soldiers who died of sickness and exposure and were buried here on Christmas day. The only marked grave is that of Capt. James Moore who died that day at the Thompson-Neely house.

In this area Pidcock Creek flows into the Delaware Canal. Along the towpath opposite the creek, a long overflow is installed to carry off excess water when freshets occur in the creek. About one quarter mile below the creek the last stop gate on the canal is installed to protect the downstream portion from flood waters.

Bowman's Hill dominates the landscape at the right of the road. On this summit the Continental soldiers erected a signal tower to watch the movements of British troops on the opposite side of the river. The site is now topped by a 110 foot tower which rewards the hardy visitor who climbs its steps with a gorgeous panorama of the surrounding country.

On the slopes below Bowman's Hill an extensive wildflower preserve, interspersed by a number of trails, displays a great variety of plants, shrubs and trees native to Pennsylvania. Nearby is the recently constructed Nature Education Center where lectures are scheduled for interested groups. Just to the west of the Education Center is the site of a copper mine, reputed to be the oldest in the country. While the entrance to the mine shaft is closed, the tunnel is said to extend about 200 feet into the hillside.[23]

A gristmill, built by one of the owners of the Thompson-Neely property, is located along Pidcock Creek near the highway bridge. At the building just south of the bridge bird banding programs, open to the public, were conducted until recently. It is anticipated that this popular program will be resumed sometime in the future.

Total	Between	
39.2	2.4	**JERICHO CREEK AQUEDUCT**

To the left of the highway bridge over the canal, an aqueduct crosses Jericho Creek, sometimes called Stony Run. The combination of camel back bridge, aqueduct, creek and adjacent river presents a scenic expanse which is a favorite haunt for towpath walkers.

Total	Between	
41.5	2.3	**WASHINGTON CROSSING STATE PARK**

Washington Crossing State Park at the intersection of River Road
(Route 32) and Route 532 presents a panorama of spacious simplicity
to commemorate this milestone of our historic heritage. The Taylor
house at the road intersection is the headquarters of the Washington
Crossing Park Commission where park literature and other information may be obtained. On the opposite side of the road is located the
Old Ferry Inn, on the site of the original McKonkey's Ferry House.

Collection of author
Washington Crossing Memorial Building where a copy of Leutze's painting
Washington Crossing the Delaware is on display.

The focal point of the park is the Washington Crossing Memorial
Building. Here, for over 18 years, the famous Emanuel Leutze painting, Washington Crossing the Delaware, on loan from the Metropolitan Museum of Art, was on display. During 1969 the Metropolitan
requested the return of this painting to highlight an exhibit in celebration of its 100th anniversary. Before its departure Robert B.
Williams, a Washington, D.C., artist, was commissioned to paint a
full-size duplicate of the original. As a memorial to her late husband,
L. John Hutton, Mrs. Ann Hawkes Hutton presented the new painting
as a gift to the Washington Crossing Foundation. The transfer
occurred January 17, 1970. Through this generous gift visitors to the

Memorial Building henceforth may enjoy the inspiration of this famous subject and hear a new taped explanation of the event narrated by Chet Huntley.

A path from the Memorial Building leads to a small monument on the river bank, marking the area where the Colonial troops embarked in the Durham boats, brought down river from their hiding place back of Malta Island near New Hope. A comparable marker on the New Jersey Shore indicates where the troops landed. On display near the Memorial Building is a 40 foot replica of a Durham boat. The Delaware Canal skirts the western boundary of the park. For boating enthusiasts, a canoe livery is located near where Route 532 crosses the canal.

Before leaving this scene associated with one of the great victories of the Revolutionary War, it may be of interest to recall a seldom remembered incident that might have disastrously affected the outcome of the Battle of Trenton and perhaps the American struggle for independence.

For a number of years during and following the War of Independence, various families in Bucks County and adjoining areas in New Jersey were victims of a marauding gang of outlaws who conducted their depredations with the avowed intent of punishing those espousing the cause of freedom. This gang, known far and wide as the Doane Outlaws, consisted of six members of the Doane family and a cousin, and was headed by Moses Doane who, in the course of time, became an important spy for the British army. From hideouts in various caves along the streams flowing into the Delaware, the bandits made frequent forays, robbing, torturing, but seldom murdering their victims.

When, on Christmas day, Moses Doane observed the unusual activity in the American camp, which he accurately surmised to be in preparation for an attack on Trenton, he hastily crossed the river and made his way to the British headquarters which he reached late on Christmas night. His demand to see Colonel Rahl, commander of the Hessian forces, being denied, he hastily prepared a note for the colonel. That gentleman, being filled with Christmas cheer and engaged in a game of cards, was annoyed at the interruption and thrust the unread note in his pocket. The next day, after the battle, the note was found on the colonel's dead body:

> "Washington is coming on you down the river, he will be here afore long".
>
> Doan[24]

If the visitor to the Delaware Canal believes his tour is completed upon reaching Washington Crossing State Park, such is not the case. Two aqueducts and four locks remain to be explored. Though their locations are somewhat difficult to discover, their rustic setting, together with the attractive drive along the Delaware River, justifies continuing the tour. Even an exploration of the canal beyond Morrisville, where its very existence is challenged by a rapidly expanding metropolitan complex of industry, railroads and highways, affords a visitor some idea of the problems involved in retaining the canal's identity in this environment.

HOUGHS CREEK AQUEDUCT

To conveniently reach this aqueduct, locally known as Taylorsville aqueduct, turn right at Washington Crossing on Route 532. After crossing the Delaware Canal at the western boundary of Washington Crossing State Park, turn left at the first intersecting road. This road parallels the canal to the aqueduct, a total of 1.4 miles from Washington Crossing. The aqueduct was rebuilt during 1969.

To reach the remaining points of interest along the canal it is desirable to return to Washington Crossing and continue south on Route 32.

Total	Between	
44	2.5	BORDEN'S LOCK NO. 7

The narrow road to the right, which appears to be no more than a private driveway, may be easily missed unless the distance from Washington Crossing is checked accurately. Upon reaching the canal this single lock can be seen about 150 feet upstream, directly behind a large white house to which the short roadway leads.

Total	Between	
44.3	0.3	LEAR'S LOCK NO. 6

Just before reaching the Scudders Falls bridge over Route 32 and the Delaware River, turn right on Woodside Road. When the canal is reached a walk of 0.4 mile south on the towpath brings one to single Lock No. 6. The remodeled lock keeper's house is located on the berm bank opposite the head of the lock.

Total	Between	
45.4	1.1	YARDLEY AND BUCK CREEK AQUEDUCT

At East Afton Avenue turn right and proceed a short distance west to the canal bridge. The aqueduct is just north of the bridge and may be reached by the towpath. The picturesque Yardley Mill may

Pennsylvania State Archives
Borden's Lock No. 7 north of Yardley.

be seen on the opposite bank near the aqueduct. This mill was operated by waterpower from the canal.

Total	Between	
45.9	0.5	YARDLEY LOCK NO. 5

At Letchworth Avenue turn right, cross the canal and proceed to Canal Street where a left turn is made. This street dead ends after about a block. A 200 foot walk brings one to single Lock No. 5. The remodeled lock keeper's house is located on the berm bank beyond the feeder.

Total	Between	
48.9	3.0	MORRISVILLE

Route 32 crosses Trenton Avenue adjacent to the canal bridge over which the avenue passes. Beyond the bridge the canal turns abruptly to the southwest and continues through what, in the days of canal operation, was rich bottom land. This section now has succumbed to industrial and suburban development, requiring the use of many culverts to carry the canal under obstructions, the longest of which is the culvert under the parking area of the Levittown Shopping Center. One interested in inspecting this seven mile section of the canal from Morrisville to Lock No. 4 should walk along the towpath, with due caution in crossing the numerous highways and railroads under which the canal passes through culverts.

Total	Between	
57.6	**7.8**	**EDGELY LOCK NO. 4**

To reach Lock No. 4 by car proceed from Morrisville along Route 32 for 1.1 miles where a turn to the right brings one on old Route 13. After 1.7 miles, this road merges with new Route 13. Continuing south on new Route 13 for 5 miles one comes to Edgely Road where a right turn should be made, bringing one to the canal. Lock No. 4, the last remaining structure at this end of the canal, is reached by travelling south along the towpath for approximately one half mile.

From Lock No. 4 the canal continues for another 1.7 miles and ends abruptly at Washington Street in Bristol. Adams Hollow Creek, which intersects the canal at this point, provides an outlet for the canal water to the Delaware River. It is somewhat ironic that this final obstruction to the continuation of the canal should bear the name of one of the enthusiastic early advocates of canals.

The approximately one mile of abandoned canal in Bristol contained three lift locks and terminated in a large tidal basin about five acres in area at the end of which a tide lock gave access to the Delaware River. All evidence of these structures and the tide basin now have disappeared.

Canal enthusiasts wishing to trace the course of the abandoned portion of the Delaware Canal will find that reference to Plate VII will be of service in this undertaking.

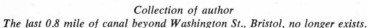

Collection of author
The last 0.8 mile of canal beyond Washington St., Bristol, no longer exists.

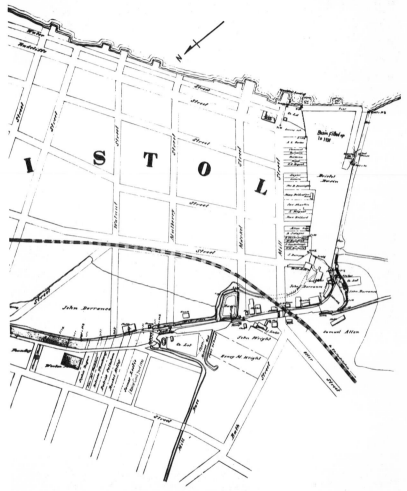

Pennsylvania State Archives: McNair's map
Plate VII. Section of Bristol showing locks Nos. 3, 2, 1, Bristol basin and the tide lock.

Collection of Robert G. Fuhr
Lock No. 3 at Bristol.

Collection of Robert G. Fuhr
A portion of Bristol basin, now a parking area paralleling Mill St.

Collection of Robert G. Fuhr
The tide lock at Bristol. In the background are boats in the basin.

Chapter 4
Locks, Aqueducts and Other Engineering Features

INTERNAL IMPROVEMENTS

Sealed proposals will be received at the public house of Mr. Horn in Easton until sunset on Tuesday the 23rd of April, for constructing a Weigh Lock on the Delaware Division . . . near the guard Lock at Easton.

> *Simpson Torbert*
> *Superintendent*
> *Easton Centinel,* Easton, Pa., April 12, 1833

A canal, unlike a river, consists of a succession of level waterways. A river, in progressing from its source to mouth, always flows from a higher elevation to a lower one by a series of falls, rapids and comparatively level sections, and with a more or less rapid flow of water depending upon the season of the year. During spring freshets or after severe storms a river can become a raging torrent, overflowing its banks and inundating surrounding areas, while in dry seasons it may be a placid stream. In pioneer days downstream navigation of such rivers was often possible and much traffic was conducted by arks, rafts and bateaux. Upstream travel was difficult if not impossible, except by canoes or specially constructed craft such as Durham boats. To overcome this situation, canals were resorted to. In hilly or mountainous terrain the canal was usually located in a river valley, often adjacent to the river itself.

From Easton to tidewater at Bristol, a distance of 60 miles, the terrain drops 165 feet. This drop in elevation produces a series of 25 rapids in the Delaware River. In the same distance the Delaware Canal consists of a series of "'levels" and 23 lift locks.

LOCKS

A variety of names were assigned to locks installed on the Delaware Canal to indicate their specific purpose. They included lift locks, guard locks, outlet locks, tide locks and weigh locks, although the general construction and method of operation was the same in each case.

Lift Lock A lift lock may be considered a hydraulic elevator for raising or lowering a boat from one canal level to another. It consists of a rectangular chamber built into the canal channel, having wooden gates at each end. The original locks installed on the Delaware Canal were 95 feet long, 11 feet wide, with a lift of from 6 feet to 10 feet.

The side walls of the lock chamber frequently were constructed of cut-stone masonry, although the walls of many of the earliest locks were built of rubble stone laid in hydraulic cement, with heavy, vertical beam inserts to which wood planking was spiked. The bottom of the chamber was also lined with heavy planking. This latter type of construction was known as a composite lock.

Collection of Henry S. Engart
Lock No. 19. The close fit of the boat in this 11 feet wide lock is quite apparent. Near the bow may be seen the towing post, the capstan and the nighthawker.

A pair of heavy wooden gates, called miter gates, which turned on vertical hinges, were installed at each end of the lock chamber. When the leaves, or main section, of these gates were closed, they formed a slight angle, or miter, at the center point of contact. Hence the name, miter gates. Miter gates always opened upstream. When the water level above the gates was higher than below, the pressure of the water forced the gates tightly together and prevented leakage of water along the center contact. The gate leaf was mounted in a heavy vertical post, called a quoin post, or heel post, which could be rotated to open or close the gate. The quoin post was supported on a pivot at the bottom and by a heavy metal strap near the top, which was secured to the lock wall. The gates closed against a timber projecting from the bottom of the lock, called a miter sill.[1] Openings, or sluices, were installed near the bottom of each leaf. Passage of water through these sluices was controlled by slide valves in some cases, but generally on the Delaware Canal locks, by rotating valves, called wickets, that were operated by metal rods extending to the top of the gate. Two or three wickets were installed on each gate, depending upon its width.

The miter gates were opened and closed by mechanism installed in a small structure called a "dog-house", located on the side wall adjacent to each gate. A rack bar extending from the center edge of the gate to the "dog-house" was moved in and out by gears connected to a crank. By turning the crank the gate could be opened or closed. When open, the gate fitted into a recess in the chamber wall to prevent interference with moving boats.

No record has been discovered to indicate when the "dog-house" method of operating the miter gates on the Delaware Canal was introduced. There is evidence, however, to suggest that the early miter gates on both the Delaware and Lehigh canals were of the balance beam construction. This name derives from the fact that the top of each gate consisted of a heavy wooden beam about 15 inches square, which extended over the wall of the lock for 10 to 15 feet. The weight of this extension was intended to counter balance the weight of the gate. By placing his shoulders against this beam and his feet on a cleated board, the lock keeper pushed the lock gates open or closed. In reporting on the 1862 flood the Lehigh Coal and Navigation Company recorded that, "In most instances the balance beams . . . were torn away".[2] In a paper titled "Lehigh and Delaware Division Canal Notes," which F. Francis Rapp presented before The Bucks County Historical Society, he said, "The old locks were 11 feet wide and the gates constructed with a heavy turn-style beam unlike the later ones."[3] By 1862 both canals were owned by the Coal Company. It is, therefore, logical to believe that sometime subsequent to that date, when worn-out miter gates were rebuilt, the "dog-house" method of operation was introduced.

In the mid 1850's a number of Delaware Canal locks were rebuilt to a width of 22 feet to correspond in size to those on the Lehigh Canal. At that time a different design of gate, called a drop, or fall gate, was installed at the head end of these locks. The miter gate design, however, was retained at the lower end of the chamber. The drop gate was hinged at the bottom; and, when open, rested at the bottom of the canal channel. Upon closing, the gate pressed securely against recesses in the chamber wall at a slight angle to the vertical in the upstream direction. Metal bars often were installed along the upper edge of the gate. This additional weight acted as a counter-balance, permitting the gate to drop automatically when the water level on each side was the same. Mechanism for operating the drop gate, as well as the wickets installed below the gate hinge, was located in a wicket house adjacent to the gate.

People unfamiliar with the functioning of canals find it difficult to understand the operation of locks. Flora Henry, who superseded her father as lock tender at Smithtown lock, and recalls locking through the last boat in 1931, consented to go to the lock and explain its operation. This explanation, which was tape recorded, is here given in her own words.

"If a boat is coming down, we go to the lock shanty and open the middle wickets to fill the lock and let the fall gate down, which it does automatically. Then close the wickets at the bottom of the canal under the gate. When the boat comes in and is snubbed, we go to the lower end and pull three wickets on the miter gates. Then the lock tender goes to the lock shanty to raise the fall gate, which weighs five tons altogether. After the gate is raised we wait a couple of minutes and come down and pull another wicket; then continue until all six wickets are open. After the water in the lock has lowered to the level below the lock we open the lower gates. If only one boat is being lowered only one gate need to be opened. The boat that is waiting to come up must stay on the berm side and the boat leaving must be careful so it will not get stuck on the towpath side. When the light boat comes in we close the gate. During the time the gates are open the wickets should be closed. The lock tender then goes to the lock shanty and adjusts the fall gate chain so the gate will drop only about halfway instead of going all the way to the bottom, since the boat going north is light, and opens the wickets under the fall gate to fill the lock and bring the boat to the upper level. As soon as the level is the same on each side of the gate, it drops automatically. After the boat has cleared the lock by a few feet we go to the lower gate and open about three wickets. The current this makes causes the fall gate to close by itself."

I asked Flora Henry if it was hard to turn the crank at the "dog-house" that opened the miter gates. "No," she said, "this was an easy turn. The only time there might be a little trouble was if the cog wheel knobs got stuck on the straight rack that connected to the gates. Then I might have to take a little board and loosen it up."

"How was the boat handled in and out of the lock", I asked. "Well, the captain, or whoever was on the boat, would throw out a line with a loop in it which the lock tender, or the driver, would put over a cleat along the side of the lock. The captain would then snub the rope on the boat cleat and stop the boat before it hit the lower gates. As the boat sank in the lock the captain would have to keep loosening the rope. If the boat was coming up through the lock, he would have to do just the opposite, keep tightening the rope as the water raised the boat up.

"When a boat went out or entered the lower end of the lock the driver had to get the rope under the bridge there. There was a rope extending under the bridge from one side to the other with a pulley on it. The driver had to disconnect the towline from the mules, throw the loose rope on the boat and pass the end under the bridge by means of the pulley. He then attached the end to the mule harness and they started out slowly until the rope was tight and the boat started slowly. Then they took their regular pace." The same principle of operation applies to locks with miter gates at each end.

Guard Lock   The Delaware Canal begins at and obtains its main water supply from the Lehigh River at Easton. At this location a

Collection of William H. Shank
Easton Guard Lock after major repairs during 1970-71. The entrance (right) is the feeder, the center entrance is the guard lock and the entrance (left) is to the weigh lock.

guard lock, 100 feet long and 22 feet wide, is installed. This lock, with miter gates at each end, is constructed in a manner similar to a conventional lift lock. The river level as well as the height of water in the first level of the canal is controlled by the height of the Easton dam in the Lehigh River. These levels normally being the same, the gates of the guard lock were kept open, allowing free passage of boats from the river to the canal. During spring freshets and other periods of high water, when a foot or more of water might flow over the dam, the lock gates were closed to guard the canal from damage due to an excess flow of water. During such periods a boat desiring passage into the canal was locked through in a manner similar to a lift lock.

During construction of the Delaware Canal, a second guard lock, 100 feet long by 18 feet wide, was installed in the canal below a feeder from the Delaware River at New Hope.[4] The original purpose of this lock, later called the Paper Mill Lock, was to guard the section of canal below New Hope against damage from high water in the Delaware River. After construction of the outlet lock at New Hope in 1847, the guard lock no longer was required for its original purpose.

Outlet Lock The chief function of an outlet lock was to provide access from a canal into a river, usually at a lower level than the canal. An outlet lock, 100 feet long by 22 feet wide, was installed at the Easton dam to permit transfer of boats from the Lehigh River to the Delaware River and the Morris Canal at Phillipsburg. In reality a lift lock since it transferred boats from one water level to another, the name outlet lock was assigned merely to indicate the principle function of the lock.

In 1847 a similar lock was installed at New Hope to give access from the canal to the Delaware River for transfer of boats to the feeder of the Delaware and Raritan Canal on the east side of the river. At this point a corresponding lock also was installed.

Tide Lock The lock that was installed at the Bristol basin gave access to the Delaware River at tidewater. Because of this fact it was called a tide lock. At low tide, when the river level was below that in the basin, the lock, which was 100 feet long and 22 feet wide, functioned as a lift lock. At times of high tide the river level might be higher than that in the basin, causing a flow of water into the latter. In such cases the lock gates remained open permitting passage of boats to and from the river without locking.

Weigh Lock Adjacent to the guard lock at Easton a weigh lock was installed to measure the weight of boats passing down the canal. While

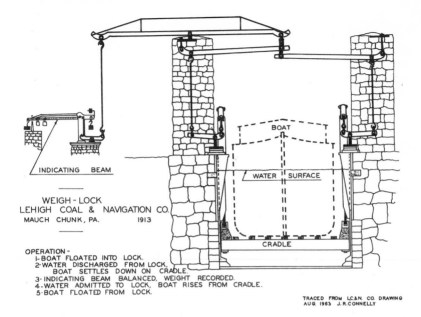

INDICATING BEAM

WEIGH - LOCK
LEHIGH COAL & NAVIGATION CO.
MAUCH CHUNK, PA.   1913

BOAT

WATER   SURFACE

CRADLE

OPERATION -
1- BOAT FLOATED INTO LOCK.
2- WATER DISCHARGED FROM LOCK,
    BOAT SETTLES DOWN ON CRADLE.
3- INDICATING BEAM BALANCED, WEIGHT RECORDED.
4- WATER ADMITTED TO LOCK, BOAT RISES FROM CRADLE.
5- BOAT FLOATED FROM LOCK.

TRACED FROM LC.&N. CO. DRAWING
AUG. 1963   J.R.CONNELLY

Courtesy, John Connelly
Diagram of typical weigh lock.

Collection of George Atwell Richardson
The remains of the Weigh Lock at Mauch Chunk in 1935.

constructed similar to a conventional lock, the floor of this lock consisted of a platform suspended from a system of levers that communicated with the weighing balance in the scale house adjacent to the lock. After a boat entered the lock and the gates were closed, the water was released through an outlet to the river below the dam, permitting the boat to rest on the scale platform. After weighing was completed, water was again admitted to the lock chamber to raise the boat from the scale platform and permit it to pass out of the lock.

No specific information has been discovered to indicate how boats entered and left the weigh lock at Easton. But speculation can perhaps provide the answer. Under normal water conditions in the Lehigh River, the water level at each end of the weigh lock would be the same. While the boat was being weighed the water level within the lock would be lower than that both above and below the gates. This would require that the upper lock gates open upstream and the lower gates open downstream. With normal river conditions the boat to be weighed could enter the lock through the upper gates and, after weighing was completed, could leave through the lower gates. However, when the Lehigh River was higher than normal, producing a difference in level between the river and the canal below the guard lock, another procedure would be necessary. It may be assumed that the boat would lock through the guard lock to get to the level of the canal after which it would back into the weigh lock through the lower gates. Weighing would proceed as explained previously.

At the beginning of navigation each spring, all empty boats were weighed and a record of this weight was kept at the scale house. Upon weighing a loaded boat, its tare, or light weight, was deducted to give the weight for which toll was charged. To prevent unscrupulous boatmen from filling the bilge of the boat with water before the spring weighing, the weigh master would insert a gauge rod through the pump well into the bilge to measure what water there was. If more than a half inch of water existed, the boatman was required to pump out the bilge before the boat was weighed.

When the Commonwealth disposed of its canals in 1858 and the Delaware Canal came under the jurisdiction of Lehigh Coal and Navigation Company, the weighing of boats at Easton was abandoned. A weigh lock near Mauch Chunk was used to obtain the weight of cargoes transported over the Lehigh and Delaware canals. Cargoes passing through the Delaware Canal frequently were checked at the toll house in New Hope. This was accomplished by means of a gauge rod, consisting of a rod with graduations along its length and a right

Collection of author
James Bailey with gauge rod.

angle projection at one end. By placing the projection under the bottom, the draft of the boat was measured, from which the weight of its cargo was calculated.

AQUEDUCT

An aqueduct is a structure made of masonry or wood for conveying a canal over a stream or a deep depression in the ground. It may be likened to a water bridge and is installed where the bed of the stream or depression is considerably below the bottom of the canal.

The aqueducts first installed on the Delaware Canal were made of wood, with the ends resting on stone masonry built into the sides and bottom of the canal. The water channel, or trunk of the aqueduct, was 20 feet wide and the same depth as the canal. A wooden towpath over which the mules passed was built along one side of the superstructure.

Collection of Robert G. Fuhr
Jericho Creek aqueduct.

Originally 9 aqueducts were installed on the canal, all over
streams, and ranging in length from 25 to 178 feet. In the case of
the longer aqueducts, one or more masonry piers were installed to
support the weight of the structure. At a later date the culvert originally installed to pass Fry's Run under the canal was replaced by
an aqueduct, thus accounting for the ten aqueducts at present on
the canal.

CULVERT

The culverts installed under the Delaware Canal for the passage
of small streams consisted of arched masonry or large tubes.
Throughout the length of the canal 20 culverts were installed. This
type of installation was used when the maximum flow of the stream
was too small to justify the more expensive aqueduct.

WASTE WEIR

A waste weir, or sluiceway, is a structure built into the towpath
side of the canal bank as a means of regulating the height of water
in the canal. The vertical waste, or sluice, gates are operated by a
mechanism installed at the top of the structure. The gates are opened
when water in a given canal level rises to a dangerous height, or
when a level has to be drained for maintenance or other reasons.
Nineteen waste weirs were installed along the canal. In several
locations, particularly opposite Gray's Creek north of Lock No. 19,
and opposite Dark Hollow Creek below Lock No. 10, Tainter gates
were installed in the sluiceway. Because of their reinforced construction and rotation about a fulcrum, Tainter gates can more readily
control large volumes of water than conventional sliding gates.

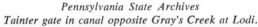
Pennsylvania State Archives
Tainter gate in canal opposite Gray's Creek at Lodi.

OVERFLOW

An overflow is a reinforced depression in the towpath for automatically controlling the water level in the canal. The depression is slightly above normal water level. An increase in the height of water causes the excess to flow over the depression into low ground beyond the canal bank. A wooden footpath was installed for the convenience of the mule drivers. The mules walked across the depression and, when water was flowing, frequently stopped for a drink.

STOP GATES

Stop, or safety, gates were installed at various points in the canal to assist in protecting the waterway from excessively high water. A stop gate is, in reality, a dam across the canal with an opening near the towpath side wide enough for the passage of a boat. While normally open, this passage could be closed in case of emergency, by miter gates or a drop gate. In the other portion of the dam sluice gates were installed. After flood conditions subsided, the sluice gates were operated to equalize the water level on each side of the dam before the gates were opened. A total of eight stop gates were installed in the canal, two during construction of the waterway and the others as experience indicated their need. Towpath hikers frequently confuse these structures with locks.

CABLE FERRY

While not a part of the canal system, the cable ferry was an important adjunct to its operation, particularly at the outlet locks at Easton and New Hope. The cable ferry consisted of a cable, originally of rope but later of steel, supported by high towers on each bank and extending across the Delaware River. When a boat entered the river from the outlet lock, ropes from the bow and stern were attached to pulleys on the cable. By adjusting the length of the ropes the bow of the boat was pointed upstream at an angle of about 45 degrees. The pressure of the river current against the side of the boat forced it across the river. As the opposite bank was approached the stern line was released until the bow of the boat pointed upstream, thus reducing its speed. While crossing the river the boat's speed could be regulated by the angle presented to the flow of the current. If the flow was rapid, the bow of the boat was pointed more upstream than when the current was slow. This method of propulsion also was used by the various ferries that transported people and vehicles across the river.

Joseph Lum who crossed the river many times by means of the cable ferry at New Hope explained that, in his time (circa 1890), the men responsible for taking the boats across used a large scow to assist in the crossing. This scow was attached to the cable and manipulated in the manner previously explained. A boat leaving the outlet lock for the crossing was lashed to the side of the scow and the two were propelled across the river. On occasion, Lum said, two boats made the crossing by being lashed together, side by side. Upon reaching the opposite bank of the river the boat was released from the scow and was floated into the outlet lock of the feeder by poling or by passing a line to the shore.

Pennsylvania State Archives
A vehicular ferry over Delaware River at Masthope, Pa.

Chapter 5
Canalboats

BOAT YARD

The subscriber respectfully informs his friends and the public that he has taken the boat yard formerly occupied by Mr. Jesse Forster in the borough of Easton, immediately above the Lehigh Bridge, where he will at all times be ready to furnish CANAL BOATS and other craft to order, at the shortest notice, at reasonable prices.

He has recently erected machinery on the Railroad principle, which is superior to any other now in use for preparing boats; there being no strain in operation . . .

Thomas Bishop

Easton Sentinel, Easton, Pa., August 14, 1834

CANALBOATS

The boats that plied the American canals of the 19th century were as varied in size and design as the canals on which they were built. The width of the lock was the controlling dimension governing the size of boat that could be used on any given canal. On the Delaware Canal the original locks were 11 feet wide. This dimension established the maximum width of 10½ feet for all boats used on the Delaware and Lehigh canals.

The class names applied to boats were, in general, an indication of their use or the part of the country in which they originated. There were flickers; stiff boats; bullheads; scows; lake boats; store boats; work, or hurry-up boats; packets; line boats; section, or hinge boats, frequently called squeezers, or lemon squeezers on the Morris Canal; chunkers from Mauch Chunk; skukers from the Schuylkill Canal, and numerous others.

By the time the Delaware Canal was open to navigation, there had accumulated in the vicinity of Easton a number of small boats of various designs, probably mostly of the flicker class, together with a sprinkling of Durham boats, to compete for the potential canal business. That these boats were semi-round bottom is indicated by a letter of protest regarding the design of the weigh lock at Easton. This letter, dated October 14, 1883, and signed by 17 boatmen was addressed to the Canal Commissioners of Pennsylvania. According to the letter, "This lock is constructed with a flat scale dish, and is only adapted for receiving, supporting and weighing the flat bottomed boats or Scows such as are used by the Mauch Chunk Company in the transportation of Coal and by an experiment made a short time since with an empty regular Canal boat in the presence of the Collector and the builder of the Scale it was ascertained to the entire satisfaction of all present that it would be utterly destructive of the round bottom regular Canal Boat to place it upon that Scale when loaded."[1]

It was not long before the 'regular canal boat' of the above complaint was to be superceded by a boat design that would become standard, not only on the Delaware Canal, but also on the Lehigh, the Morris and, to a lesser extent, the Delaware and Raritan—the section, or hinge boat. The idea of the section boat, as a logical design for use on the planes of the Morris Canal, was undoubtedly brought to the Lehigh Canal by Canvass White during his tenure as chief engineer of that canal. He was, apparently, the first to advocate this design while serving as consulting engineer for the Portage Railroad. According to Jesse L. Hartman, "The first mention of it came from Canvass White. As early as 1826 he noted the feasibility of moving boats across the Alleghenies. 'I would suggest the idea of making the canal boats in three or four pieces, to be divided transversely, and transported over the Portage without changing the Cargo,' he wrote to the Pennsylvania authorities."[2]

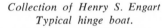

Collection of Henry S. Engart
Typical hinge boat.

The section, or hinge, boat was a clumsy craft, but particularly adapted to the coal trade of the eastern Pennsylvania canals. The boat was 87½ feet long, 10½ feet wide and, in cross section a perfect rectangle, with flat bottom and vertical sides which curved in forward to produce a pointed bow and a slight curve aft to meet the square stern which was 9½ feet wide. At the center the height was 6½ feet, with a sheer to 9 feet 2 inches at the bow and 7 feet 10 inches at the stern. As its name implies, the section boat was made in two halves, as if the finished boat were cut through transversely and the open portions closed by flat vertical bulkheads. At the bulkheads the two sections were joined by metal fittings and pins, permitting vertical movement of the two halves. The maximum space between the two sections was 7 inches. When the pins were removed, the two halves could be handled independently.

The primary function of the section boat design was to permit its use on the inclined planes of the Morris Canal, although there were other advantageous features. Normally, an 87 foot boat could be turned around only in enlarged sections of the canal, called basins, which were established where docking facilities were required or where idle boats could be stored. By withdrawing the pins and separating

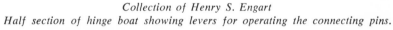

Collection of Henry S. Engart
Half section of hinge boat showing levers for operating the connecting pins.

Collection of Henry S. Engart
Bow half of section boat with hatch covers in place. Showing stove, coal box, water barrel and feed box (on stern section).

Collection of Henry S. Engart
Stern half of section boat with hatch covers in place. Note chain attached to stove pipe to prevent loss if knocked off while passing under bridge.

the two sections, a turn-around could be made in any part of the canal. The hinge boat also provided a means for carrying mixed cargoes, such as chestnut coal in one hold and egg coal in the other. During unloading, less strain was placed on a hinge boat than would occur on a stiff boat.

A minimum of deck space was installed, consisting of 8 feet at the bow, 3 feet on each half at the hinge and 8 feet at the stern. The remainder of the boat was open except for an 18 inch running plank along each side. Since no gunwales or other form of railings were installed along the running planks, the transit from one end to the other could be hazardous, particularly in stormy weather. Most boats were equipped with sectional hatch covers for protecting the cargo and preventing excess water from heavy rains getting into the bilge.

Externally, the deck fittings consisted of a large rope cleat in the bow, two cleats on either side of each half boat and two cleats at the stern. These cleats were used for attaching the towline, for snubbing while passing through a lock and for tieing-up at a wharf or other mooring. Two pump wells were located on each side of the half boats, extending from the deck into the bilge, through which the tube of the hand pump could be passed, for pumping out excess water that might accumulate in the bilge. Early bilge pumps were made of wood but in more recent times they were made of metal, usually galvanized iron. Many boats were equipped with plugged holes in the bottom, usually located near the hinge. When these boats were conveyed over the planes of the Morris Canal, the plugs were removed, allowing the bilge water to drain out during transit.

On the deck at the hinge, a barrel for drinking water and a feed box were located. During the summer the cook stove was frequently moved from the cabin to this location, or the boatman might have a second stove permanently located here. One might wonder why this stove was located so far away from the cabin and the captain, who normally had to tend it. As indicated previously, the deck at the hinge was 16 inches lower than the stern deck. Due to the low clearances under the canal bridges, a boat running light barely made the passage. If the stove was located at the stern, it would be knocked off. Crew and passengers had to crouch low, hence the importance of the warning signal "low bridge", which was a common call on all canals. On some boats, a compartment was constructed under the deck at the hinge with access through a covered hatch. A similar compartment also might be located under the fore deck. These compartments were for storing rope and other boat gear.

The rudder post was mounted, externally, at the stern, with a removable tiller extending inboard for use by the helmsman. Both rudder post and tiller were of heavy construction. The latter, in particular, was subjected to a great deal of sitting and leaning on during the life of the boat, as well as the normal stresses due to steering. Most rudder blades were hinged to the post at the lower corner and held in position by a rope extending from the outer top corner to a rope cleat near the top of the rudder post. When the boat was loaded, most of the rudder blade would be below the water line and thus give the maximum steering effect. A light boat drew very little water, with only a small portion of the rudder blade being immersed. By adjusting the rope, more of the blade could be dropped under water producing much better steering.

The small cabin under the stern deck offered rather cramped quarters for the crew. Surprisingly, the captain's family frequently spent the summer with him and occasionally a baby was born in the tiny cabin. Access to the cabin was by means of a ladder extending from the companionway in the rear deck. Internally, the cabin was not over 8 feet by 10 feet, with head room of about 7 feet. There were two bunks, an upper and a lower, hinged so that when not in use they could be raised against the wall. A locker for storing food was located at the stern. According to Joseph Reed, the bottom of this locker was always below the water line of the boat, thus providing

Collection of Henry S. Engart.
Stern of boat showing hinged rudder blade lowered to improve the steering of a light boat.

reasonable protection for perishable food. When the hinged table which dropped over the locker was not in use, the locker top served as a bench. A cupboard for dishes and kitchen utensils was located on one wall. In the front corner opposite the bunks, that most important item of canal life, the stove was installed. Its location at the foot of the ladder was especially convenient when the helmsman was also the cook. Throughout the years a variety of stoves were used, but toward the end of the boating era the most popular design was a two griddle unit called a "boatman's choice", made by Orr, Painter and Company, Reading, Pennsylvania.

A door in the forward bulkhead of the cabin opened into the cargo hold. This door was a convenience to the captain's wife during stormy weather. If the boat were returning light, she could hang her laundry to dry in the empty hold. Sometimes from necessity, or choice, the captain might decide to winter on his boat. Quite comfortable additional quarters could be obtained by using the adjacent cargo space. To provide adequate head room it was necessary to raise the hatches and install temporary side walls in which suitable windows were inserted.

Since the cabin did not project above the deck, the only source of light for the interior was two small windows in the stern, or through the companionway, if the cover were removed. Lamps mounted on wall brackets, or lanterns, supplied night illumination. One of the necessary accessories for night operation was the "night-hawker", a means of external illumination consisting of an oil lamp with polished reflector, which was placed in a boxlike structure twelve to fourteen inches on a side, enclosed by glass on three sides. A gayly decorated board, called the dasher, usually circular in shape, was installed in the bow, on the front of which the "night-hawker" was hung. A number of boatmen have confirmed that the "night-hawker" gave reasonable illumination along the towpath as far as the mules.

Boats built in most boat yards along the Lehigh and Delaware canals conformed to the above description as shown on a drawing made by the Canal Department of the Lehigh Coal and Navigation Company.[3] The capacity of this design was specified as 100 tons. The principal boat yards along the Delaware Canal were located at Uhlertown, Erwinna and Upper Black Eddy. Here boats were constructed and old ones repaired. A yard at New Hope was only for repairs. Most of the boats on the two canals were made in yards located along the Lehigh.

Courtesy, Esther Weaver
Uhlertown boat yard.

Courtesy, Horace Sigafoos
Boat under construction at Uhlertown boat yard.

Boatmen still living in the Delaware Valley agree that, barring unusual accidents such as floods or other catastrophies, the useful life of a canalboat was from 25 to 30 years. To withstand the rugged service to which the boats were subjected the best of materials were used in their construction. Oak was the preferred material for making frames, or ribs, and select pine ranging in thickness from 2½ inches to 3 inches was used for hull planking. In the cargo area a false bottom was installed by placing lining planks over the ribs. In addition to assuring a smooth surface on which the cargo, usually coal, rested and could be readily shoveled out, the false bottom afforded an air space of about 5 inches between it and the hull planking from which accumulated bilge water could be readily pumped.

The boats owned by the Lehigh Coal and Navigation Company were painted a reddish brown with white trim and on either side at the bow a large white circle, or "O", with a dark center, was painted. Company boats were not given names but were assigned numbers. The standard designation L. C. & Nav. Co. No. 234, or whatever number was assigned, was painted across the stern. Boats owned by individuals or other companies were always named. These names were as varied as the whims of the owners; the only requirement, there must be no duplication of names on the canal.

A useful and necessary accessory for all canalboats was a pole, frequently called a pike pole. One old boatman said there were various types of poles such as bow pole, stern pole, chain dam pole for pulling across the chain dam in the Lehigh River and hook poles, the latter for general use about the boat. It was the hook pole that was most commonly seen. In one end of the pole was inserted a steel rod with a hook along one side. This kind of pole was useful for moving a boat along a wharf, for pushing or changing the location of a boat, when the mules were not available, and for vaulting to and from the towpath, particularly when the driver was being changed.

Another useful addition seen on many boats was a capstan or windlass. This device consisted of a heavy spool shaped cylinder, usually of wood, mounted vertically in a bearing in the fore deck. By means of bars inserted in holes near the top, the capstan could be rotated. If one end of a rope was attached to a fixed anchorage and several turns at the other end wrapped around the cylinder, great force would be exerted on the rope. One use of the capstan was to pull a boat off accumulated silt or other obstructions on the bottom or sides of a canal.

Collection of Joseph W. Reed, Sr.
Capstan installed near bow of boat. Joe Reed, the captain, is leaning on the
dasher.

While hinge boats and stiff boats of the same dimensions contributed, by far, the heaviest traffic on the canal, numerous other designs were also seen. A boat of low freeboard with a cabin extending from bow to stern was used for hauling miscellaneous freight and usually attempted to maintain a faster schedule than the coal boats. The flicker of 20 tons burden and not over nine feet wide was extensively used on the Delaware and Hudson Canal before the locks were increased in size to permit use of larger boats. In the early days flickers were seen on the Delaware Canal, principally as work boats. A more conventional work boat was a square ended, open scow, of low freeboard. This boat, when cleaned up, was a popular choice for picnic parties, as the open space assured plenty of room for the picnickers. Work scows equipped with cabins for living quarters also were used by maintenance crews.

In more recent times, a steam dredge replaced the more laborious method of removing silt by shovel and wheelbarrow. When in use, pontoons were attached to each side of the dredge scow for added stability. When the dredge moved along the canal, these pontoons were removed to permit passage through the locks. The scow was

Collection of Henry S. Engart
Dipper dredge on canal below Lumberville.

Collection of Robert G. Fuhr
Scraper boat for removing silt from the 6 mile level between the Guard Lock and Ground Hog Lock.

equipped with a small engine driven propeller which moved the dredge at a slow pace. If the equipment was to be moved for some distance, mules frequently were used to increase its speed.

Another method of removing silt from the canal was by the use of the scraper boat. This boat was used only on the 6 mile level between Easton and Ground Hog lock, where a strong current existed in the canal. A cable for drawing the boat passed through pulley blocks at the bow and stern and around an engine driven drum. The two ends of the cable were anchored on the shore. Upon dropping the scraper to the bottom of the canal the accumulated silt was drawn, or pushed, to a waste weir. When the gate at the waste weir was opened, the rapid current that rushed through carried the silt into the river.

Passenger service was never popular on the Delaware Canal, probably due to more rapid transportation from Philadelphia to Easton by stagecoach. As a result, the colorful packet boat was not seen on this waterway in spite of early efforts to establish this service.

The ark, while never used on the Delaware Canal, was a common sight on the river before the canal was built. Dr. Fackenthal described arks as "built of sawed timber in a square, boxlike form 16 by 18 feet wide and from 20 to 25 feet long. After discharging their cargo at point of consignment, usually Philadelphia, they were taken apart and the lumber sold, thus requiring a new boat or ark for each cargo of coal."[4] Besides hauling coal, arks also were used for transporting flour, whiskey and similar products. Once started on its journey, the ark was at the mercy of the river current, as this was the only means of propulsion. Steering was accomplished by means of a long oar or sweep.

"Him and his fancy white walls . . ."

Chapter 6
Canal Maintenance and Improvements

A New Dam—We are informed that it has been determined upon by the Board of Canal Commissioners to build a new dam across the Lehigh at Easton, for the purpose of feeding the Delaware Division of the Pennsylvania Canal. The State Engineer, who has for some time past been examining the streams for a good location, has settled upon a place immediately below the present dam. When the new dam therefore is completed, the interval between it and the old one is to be filled up with stone; which will render it proof against the highest freshets, and perhaps make it superior to any other one in the State.

The Whig, Easton, Pa., August 7, 1839

CANAL MAINTENANCE AND IMPROVEMENT

Even before the canal was open for navigation, maintenance and improvements began. The problem that confronted the builders from the time water was admitted was the inability to maintain the proper depth of water in the channel due to the porous nature of the soil, particularly in the upper section of the canal. The work supervised by Josiah White went a long way in correcting the leakage problem; but, the question remained whether the water supplied from the Lehigh River was adequate for the entire length of the canal. While the porous nature of the soil forming the canal bottom and sides was overcome by puddling, additional sources of water also were being introduced. The Lehigh Coal and Navigation Company's annual report, dated January 9, 1832, in commenting on this subject states, "Hence it has been found necessary to introduce other feeders; one for conveying into the channel, the water of Durham Creek, about ten miles below Easton; it is 1890 feet long and twelve feet wide at the bottom; and another near Lumberville, by which the water of Milton Creek is conveyed into the canal; it is 1509 feet long". About the same time the Canal Commissioners reported, "a large waterway has been constructed around the guard lock at [Easton]".[1]

During this same period a most ingenious device was erected at Union Mill, just south of New Hope, for pumping water from the Delaware River into the canal. This was accomplished by constructing a wing dam in the river to supply water to a lifting wheel. On June 9, 1831, an agreement was made with Lewis S. Coryell and three associates for the erection of the dam and water wheel.[2]

Possibly the only description of this installation is contained in a letter dated November 25, 1831, by Lewis S. Coryell, addressed to James Clark, president, Board of Canal Commissioners, in which he said, "I have the honor to Report that in conformity with a resolution of your Board directing a wing Dam to be erected in Well's Falls for the purpose of raising water to Supply the Canal from the combined locks near New Hope to Bristol, I commenced the erection of the dam in July . . .

"The general plan of this mode of feeding the canal having been suggested by a member of your Board it is only necessary for me to remark upon this Subject, that I caused a model to be made agreeable to your plan on a Scale of one inch to the foot in order to test it . . . I therefore propose to erect a water wheel 15 ft. 3 in. diameter with a 25 foot bucket acting under a head & fall of 4 feet to be geared with cast iron wheels into the shaft of the raising wheel of the same dimensions in Such manner as to give the latter a motion of 3⅛ feet per second. This motion from a comparison with the effect produced by the model will when the wheels act with their full force & power raise 6000 cubic ft. per minute 3½ feet above the top water line

Collection of James Lee
Water wheels at New Hope for pumping water into the canal.

of the Dam, the height required to feed the Canal—according to your estimate 2400 cubic ft. per minute in addition to the Supply of water expected from the Lehigh will be Sufficient to Supply this Section of the Canal—but if that from the Lehigh Should disappoint your expectation—The increased capacity of the Machinery beyond that required by your estimate will be sufficient for every demand of water".[3]

The lifting wheel produced the results expected of it and, with periodic maintenance, continued in operation until near the end of the useful life of the canal. One report of a major overhaul was made in 1880 by the Superintendent of Canals to the Coal Company. "The wheels at New Hope, used for raising water into the Canal, having been in use over 20 years, began to show signs of failing, and new shafts of the best southern pine have been put in. The masonry supporting them has also been rebuilt in the most substantial manner, and next winter the arms and buckets will also be renewed, and it is thought they will then be good for the next 20 years."[4]

Mr. Ferdinand R. White, president, Union Mills Paper Mfg. Co., states that the pumping wheels and part of the supporting masonry were carried away by the severe floods of March 11 to 20, 1936, thus ending nearly one hundred years of useful service by this unique device.

A somewhat similar method of pumping water was used on at least one other American canal. Joseph Lum recalls that during a trip through the Chesapeake and Delaware Canal he saw "the same arrangement at Chesapeake City for supplying water to the upper level." According to Ralph D. Gray [5] a steam-operated pump was installed at Chesapeake City in 1837, to raise water from Back Creek to the summit level. In 1852 this original pumping unit was replaced by a steam engine driven lifting, or scoop, wheel. "The wheel, 39 feet in diameter and 10 feet wide, was made of wood and iron and consisted of 12 buckets. As the wheel rotated water scooped into the buckets flowed out lateral discharge openings located near the center of the wheel."[6] A gear on the outer circumference of the wheel engaged a pinion connected to the engine. With a normal engine speed of 24 revolutions per minute, the wheel made 2.46 revolutions and raised a minimum of 200,000 cubic feet of water per hour to the summit level of the canal. When, in 1927, the waterway was made a lock-free ship canal, this pumping unit was no longer required. However, the water wheel and its steam engine may still be seen at Chesapeake City.[7]

In addition to the streams that flow under the canal by means of culverts and aqueducts, about twenty creeks flow directly into the canal channel. These creeks, however, contribute little to the water supply because in summer, when water is most needed, they are practically dry. Their main contribution, which added to the problems of the maintenance men, was to deposit large quantities of silt into the channel during the spring runoff or when heavy storms caused freshets. Prior to the introduction on the line of a steam operated dredge the silt had to be removed during winter maintenance by shovel and wheelbarrow. This material did serve one useful purpose. As the silt was carried along by the slow current of the canal, it deposited on the bottom, worked into the pores of the sandy soil and aided in reducing leakage.

In the 1832 report of the Lehigh Coal and Navigation Company, Josiah White summarized his prediction for the Delaware Canal which "consists of

> 13 river sections of about a half mile each (Easton to Riegels-
> ville) which will require the banks to be loaded with gravel.
> 17 river sections (Riegelsville to Upper Black Eddy) which
> are good and will not require more than ordinary repair
> 88 inland sections, (Upper Black Eddy to Bristol), which will
> never require much repair".[8]

That White's prediction was prophetic is indicated by the distribution of the maintenance force established by the superintendent, W. K. Huffnagle. In his 1848 report he said, "The line is divided into six divisions, the first is 8 miles in length [Easton to Riegelsville] and includes the river works at Easton. This division requires the greatest permanent force on account of its exposure to damage by the river and the gravelling required both on the face of the towing path as well as riprapping on its rear due to damage by spring freshets. A force of 11 men, including watchman which is necessary for the present to keep at night on the most dangerous portions of the division.

"The second division is also 8 miles long [Riegelsville to Upper Black Eddy] and extends also along the Delaware and requires constant care and much gravelling on the top and face of the towing path. Eight men are employed.

"The third division is 9 miles long [Upper Black Eddy to Point Pleasant], is more inland and requires mostly the dressing of the tow path bank. Upon this division but four men are employed.

"The fourth division is 10 miles long [Point Pleasant to New Hope], also a portion inland and not exposed to great damage. Three hands are employed.

"The fifth division is 12 miles long [New Hope to Morrisville] and is also inland throughout a great portion of its length. Three hands are employed.

"The sixth division is 13 miles long [Morrisville to Bristol]. This division is entirely inland and upon it is kept one hand who dresses the banks and, with the foreman, keeps up the mechanical work and attends to the waste weirs at time of high water in the canal.

"In addition to the hands there is a foreman to each division. The foreman receives pay of $1.25 a day and the hands 87½ cents a day".[9]

As the construction work neared its completion, residents along the line of the canal were much interested in other work assignments that involved the day to day operation of the waterway. Among these assignments were the lock keepers. Speculation was set to rest when, by a letter dated November 1, 1830, T. G. Kennedy, superintendent of the canal, announced that the following list of lock keepers had been appointed:

John I. Hibbs	Lock No. 1 and the Tide Lock
Elias Gilkyson	2 and 3
Daniel Kirgen	4
Charles Shoemaker	5
Joseph Suber	6
David Kirgen	7
Samuel Daniels	8 and 9 and the Guard Lock at New Hope
Samuel Stockdan	10 and 11
John Everitt	12
George Solliday	13 and 14
Mahlon Smith	15 and 16
John Speer	17
Ralph Harrison	18
George Fox	19
Wyllys Rogers	20
Charles Wagener	21
Joseph Shepherd	22 and 23

The letter concluded, "There is no appointment made yet for the Guard Lock and Outlet Lock at Easton".[10]

While a great many local people found temporary, or permanent, employment on the canal, there were others who viewed with alarm the mounting cost of canal construction throughout the state and the anticipated taxes with which they would be burdened.

The *Bucks County Intelligencer* of February 3, 1832, recounts a meeting of irate citizens held in Newtown to consider petitioning the Legislature to sell the Delaware Canal. During the meeting the following resolution was adopted.

"Whereas, the public works have involved the State in a debt of 15,000,000 of dollars, without a prospect that the proceeds arising from them will meet the interest in a reasonable time, or furnish the means for its liquidation for an age to come—and thus loading us with oppressive taxation. . . . We therefore deem it expedient to advise the acceptance of any proposition tending to diminish the public debt, and to lessen an onerous tax. The Delaware Division has cost the State nearly a million and a half, and owing to its injudicious location, and the bad materials of which it is composed, it is not likely soon to be in full operation. Upwards of ninety-seven thousand dollars have been expended within the last year in repairs . . .

"Therefore:

"Resolved: That we consider the proposition made by Messrs. Porter and Carey of Northampton, to purchase the Delaware Division of the Pennsylvania Canal, a liberal and fair one, and that it meets our decided approbation.

"Resolved: That a committee of five be appointed to draw up a memorial to the Legislature, recommending its sale . . .

"Resolved: That we disapprove of multiplying Incorporate Companies, but in the present juncture of two evils, we choose the less.

"Resolved: That one person be appointed in each township to receive and circulate the memorials".

Twenty-eight townships were represented at the meeting. Nothing tangible, however, was accomplished by this group of irate tax payers.

Others, singly and in groups, were not averse to offering criticism regarding the supervision and operation of the canal. In a June 3, 1829, letter to the Board of Canal Commissioners, a group of forty-four Bucks County citizens complained:

"That we are fully of the opinion that there has been great abuse committed by the present Superintendent of said division by giving contracts to favorites at an advanced price thereby enabling them to sell to great profit to gentlemen well recommended who had thrown in proposals to do the work for much less money and the purchasers are now doing the work with the full approbation of the Superintendent thereby subjecting the State to the unnecessary expense of many thousand dollars—He has also assumed full power taking away bridges that the engineer had located also giving contracts for lock houses without consulting and contrary to the plans desired by the principal Engineer . . .

"We therefore humbly pray your Honorable Board to remove said Superintendent and appoint a better man it will restore harmony and confidence for which your petitioners will pray."[11]

Even Josiah White, who came out of retirement to contribute his experience to correcting the defects in the Delaware Canal, was not spared the darts of criticism. A group of ten citizens found it necessary to come to his defense in a letter of February 20, 1833, to Governor George Wolf, in which they stated:

"There is a report in circulation here that there will be an effort made with the Canal Commissioners to remove Josiah White, Esq. from the Office of Engineer of the Delaware division of the Pennsylvania Canal. The undersigned feeling much interest in this matter beg leave to suggest that in their opinion such removal would be highly injurious to the best interest of the State and would probably long retard the completion of this useful public work. They believe that Mr. White has very faithfully done his duty in this office and has done more to improve the Canal and has been more assiduous in his efforts for its early completion than any other individual who could have received the appointment or would probably now receive it. They are constrained to add moreover that any opposition to Mr. White originates as they believe in improper motives and with persons whose conduct to speak of it in the mildest terms had been of some injury both to the Canal and to the Commonwealth. They beg to state moreover that although Mr. White has done everything for the benefit of the Canal, yet has had the unusual good fortune to conciliate most of the people residing along the line and in a great measure to allay the irritation heretofore existing against the Canal and those connected with it."[12]

One irritated citizen who looked upon certain canal appointments and regulations with a jaundiced eye aired his feelings through an open letter to the local paper.

"To the Canal Commissioners:

"The next question is, gentlemen, was it necessary for you to place Major Pugh at the toll locks in Bristol where J. J. Hibbs has tended both the tide lock and lock No. 1—until April last for twelve dollars per month, which he was satisfied with, until the first of April his pay, by your order, was increased eight dollars a month—making in all twenty dollars per month.

"Is it not a fact, that by your order the Major has been placed at the tide lock, with a salary of some thirty to forty dollars per month? and is it not a fact that he is a relative of the present collector? and does that make a difference of $32 per month, and of $384 per year to the State?

"Are all the funds of the State to be expended on the Collector's family, Generals, Majors and so on to Corporals? Is there nobody in that part of the state near Bristol, that is capable of collecting tolls or tending locks, (especially locks that open themselves every flood tide). . . .

"All know that the Delaware Division of the Pennsylvania Canal has never paid anything like the expenditure for repairs, etc. Another fact I believe to be gentleman, that you are endeavoring to drive from the Canal the only source from which you have received what little you have received (i.e.) the Durham boats, so called, by taxing them fifty cents to pass the tide lock into the basin, over and above paying for boats and cargoes to navigate the canal. Is it not a fact that these boats have paid nine-tenths of all the money received at Bristol? . . . Drive the Durham boats from the canal & you will have it yourselves, collectors, agents, etc."[13]

IMPROVEMENTS TO LOCKAGE

The narrow locks of the Delaware Canal were, from the start of the waterway, a source of irritation to the operators of the Lehigh Canal with its 22 feet wide locks. In spite of protests by the management of the Lehigh Canal, the Pennsylvania Legislature, no doubt influenced by William Strickland's report[14] on England's canals where small cargoes and small locks were favored, was adamant in specifying 11 feet as the width of locks on the Delaware Canal. This dimension also established the maximum width, and hence the tonnage for a given depth of water, for all coal boats from the Lehigh Canal, destined to continue through the Delaware Canal. In addition to limiting the capacity of the boats, the narrow locks of the Delaware Canal permitted only one boat to pass at a time, while two boats side by side, could pass through all of the locks of the Lehigh and Delaware and Raritan canals. This, in effect, limited the maximum tonnage through the Delaware Canal to 50 percent of the tonnage through the other two waterways.

Prior to 1851, when the Morris Canal was enlarged to accommodate the boats then used on the Lehigh Canal, the Lehigh Coal and Navigation Company transported the major part of its coal for New York markets through the Delaware and Delaware and Raritan canals. This was accomplished by sending boats to Bristol, where tugs towed them through the treacherous tide water of the Delaware River to Bordentown for passage through the Delaware and Raritan Canal to the Raritan River and New York bay. This was a roundabout route, considering that the navigable feeder for the Delaware and Raritan Canal extended up the east side of the Delaware River to opposite Black's Eddy. As early as 1835 the Coal Company called attention to the desirability of installing an outlet lock in the vicinity of Black's Eddy for transfer of boats to the Delaware and Raritan feeder, thus "the expense of the circuitous route via Bristol and Bordentown will be saved on all the coal going eastward by this route."[15]

Not only did the Coal Company want a shorter route to New York City but also faster passage through the Delaware Canal, which latter could be acomplished by increasing the size of the locks. Upon completion of the Lehigh Canal extension to White Haven, the Canal Commissioners realized that the capacity of the Delaware Canal would be further taxed and so indicated in their report of December 12, 1838: "This division is destined to become one of the most profitable portions of the public works, owing to its connection with the improvements of the Lehigh Company. . . . The increasing

Collection of Henry S. Engart
This double lock at New Hope permitted two boats, side by side, to lock through at one time.

demand for coal and iron will render it necessary, at no distant period, to increase the capacity of this division by the construction of additional locks along side the present ones, of dimensions corresponding with those of the Lehigh."[16]

In spite of the apparent advantages to the Commonwealth of increasing the capacity of the Delaware Canal and in providing a shorter route to the New York market, powerful interests in Philadelphia and along the Schuylkill Canal were using every effort to block these improvements. In its annual report of January 8, 1844, the Coal Company observed, "So palpable is the justice and the reasonableness of the claim of the producers on the Lehigh to an outlet lock at Black's Eddy, that it has hitherto been refused chiefly through the influence and the instrumentality of powerful and determined rivals. . . . By the grant of this outlet, so long withheld, fifty-four miles of distance, two hundred and twelve feet of lockage and two days detention would be saved to all boats engaged in the supply of New York, now compelled to take the circuitous route to Bristol, in passing between the Delaware division and the Delaware and Raritan Canal. Interested rivals have hitherto succeeded in exciting an unfounded hostility to this measure by representing it as injurious to Philadelphia and to the Commonwealth."

Taking cognizance of the rival arguments, particularly that business in Philadelphia would be impaired, that the revenue on the canal would be reduced, and at the request of the Pennsylvania Senate, the Canal Comissioners submitted a report, dated February 3, 1846,[17] in which the introductory paragraph summarizes its content.

"The Canal Commissioners have the honor to acknowledge the receipt of a resolution of the Senate, dated April 5, 1845, requesting them to report upon the expediency of constructing an out-let lock at the most convenient point, to connect the Delaware division of the canal, with the feeder of the Delaware and Raritan Canal, and to increase the size of the locks to suit the passage of double Lehigh boats, together with the probable amount of the same, . . . and also to report whether, in their opinion, the effect of the construction of such out-let lock, will be to diminish the resources of the Commonwealth, arising from tolls on said division. . . ."

Three alternatives were presented respecting transfer of boats to the Delaware and Raritan canal: an aqueduct across the Delaware River from the vicinity of Morrisville to Trenton; an outlet lock at Black's Eddy; or an outlet lock at Wells' Falls near New Hope. For reasons explained in the report, the Commissioners favored the Wells' Falls location.

In the Commissioners opinion, "if such connection should be permitted, that all tonnage passing out of or into the Delaware division at this point, should pay the same tolls as if it passed out or entered at Bristol. . . . If the State should permit any portion of it to pass out before reaching Bristol, for the purpose of saving freight to the transporters, it furnishes no reason why she should lose any of her tolls on a work made purposely for the benefit of such trade." As later events will indicate, when this suggestion was put into effect, it was greatly resented by the operators on the two canals.

Commenting on increasing the size of the canal locks, the Commissioners stated, "The coal trade upon the Lehigh has been rapidly increasing for the last two or three years, and should the same ratio be observed in its future increase, it will in the course of two years more exceed the present capacity of the locks upon the Delaware division. . . .

"It would seem therefore important that every facility which can reasonably be afforded by increasing the capacity of this branch of our State improvements should be given. . . . With this in view, we do not doubt the expediency of enlarging the locks . . . so as to correspond in capacity with those upon the Lehigh."

Acting promptly on the Commissioners' report, a contract was awarded August 26, 1847, to Alanson Sumner and Moreau Delano to construct "all that Canal, Lock and fixtures necessary to form the connection between the feeder Level of the Delaware Division . . . and the Delaware River at Wells' Falls, authorized to be constructed by the act of the 20th of April 1846 . . . and to finish the same on or before the thirtieth day of November next . . . And the said Sumner & Delano are to be paid for completing this contract the sum of Eighteen thousand dollars."[18]

That the contractors complied with the terms of the agreement is confirmed by the Coal Company's report dated May 2, 1848. "A connection by means of locks into the bed of the river, has at last been effected between the Delaware division and the navigable feeder of the Delaware and Raritan canal; but the tolls levied by the State upon the former, and by the Delaware and Raritan canal upon the latter, are such as very nearly to neutralize the whole advantage from this connection."

However, the increased tolls did not deter the use of this connection. In 1849 over 100,000 tons of coal were transferred through the outlet lock,[19] and the quantity increased yearly until a peak of 526,000 tons was reached in 1866.[20]

The final moves of the State Legislature to authorize improvements of the Delaware Canal preceded only briefly the beginning of ominous signs that the era of coal transport by canals was approaching an end. By 1855 the Lehigh Valley Rail Road was completed to Easton and Phillipsburg, and the following year the Coal Company stated, "From the Company's canal there will be some diversion, by the Lehigh Valley Rail Road, of the trade from the second coal field."[21] To protect its interests the Coal Company began an extension of its own railroad, the Lehigh and Susquehanna, from Mauch Chunk to Phillipsburg, which was completed in 1868.

In the meantime, while the Coal Company was complaining that, "The capacity of the Delaware division continues to be limited throughout its entire length by the defective and unskillful arrangement of the locks at Uhler's and at New Hope,"[22] the Legislature voted an improvement appropriation to correct these conditions. On August 14, 1852, a contract was awarded to James Burns to replace the two single locks by "a Lift Lock at Eulerville. [Uhlersville]"[23] This lock now is called Ground Hog Lock, No. 22-23. The same year the four single locks at New Hope, which included the combination locks No. 8 and 9, were rebuilt and enlarged to double locks.[24]

Collection of author
Double Lock No. 22-23, installed in 1852.

The belated efforts of the State Legislature to improve the only revenue producing division of the Pennsylvania Canal came in the face of mounting public resentment at the tremendous expenditures which had been made in the name of public works. Commenting on this situation, the Coal Company said, "popular opinion is now setting so strongly in favor of a separation between the State government and the ownership and control of the public improvements . . . that there seems to be grounds for hope that the Delaware division . . . will before long pass into hands by which it will be managed . . . for the promotion of the common good."[25]

While rebuilding several locks was a step in the right direction, it was a far cry from correcting the deterioration of general maintenance along the line of the canal. In summarizing the situation, the Coal Company said, "we are obliged to reiterate the oft repeated statement of insufficient depth of water—of contracted and unsafely constructed aqueducts and locks—of banks and towing paths inadequately supplied with overfalls, imperfectly and partially protected by slope walls and by paving, and so little raised above the surface of the water in the levels as to be liable to be overflowed and breached by every passing summer shower; and of a supply of water at some seasons, dependent upon a rickety and rotten water-wheel."[26]

As its final expenditure for major improvement, the Legislature authorized an appropriation to increase to six feet the depth of the Delaware Canal from Easton to New Hope.[27] This improvement was completed the same year the canal was sold to the Sunbury and Erie Railroad Company, shortly after which it came under the jurisdiction of the Lehigh Coal and Navigation Company.

In spite of the great flood of June 1862, the ravages to The Coal Company's canals were corrected. The Coal Company also continued major repairs to the Delaware Canal. "The two locks at Smithtown being in a delapidated condition, it has been decided to combine the two in a single new lock, with a higher lift."[28] This new lock, now the double Lock No. 15-16, was ready for use by the time navigation opened in 1868. It was undoubtedly during this period that the Narrows Lock, No. 20, was changed to a double lock but information regarding this improvement is not presently available. By 1870 the Coal Company was able to report, "Much has already been done to improve the Delaware division and to protect it from high water, by raising the banks, building stop-gates and renewing locks, and with completion of the new aqueducts and other works now in progress, that canal may be regarded as less liable to injury than at any previous period."[29]

This program of regular maintenance that was instituted after the Delaware Canal came under the management of the Lehigh Coal and Navigation Company kept this waterway in good operating condition throughout most of its remaining active life. Raising and strengthening the canal banks, which had previously been badly neglected, was an important improvement that was completed in 1878.[30] While several serious floods occurred in the interum, the damage to the Delaware Canal was kept to a minimum; and, navigation was not seriously interrupted until the floods of 1901-3.

An improvement to the canal previously mentioned was the installation of the weigh lock at Easton. A weigh lock at this location evidently was not included in the original engineering studies as it is not shown on the A. W. Kennedy map.[31] However, on April 30, 1833, the "President (of the Board of Canal Comissioners) laid before the board a contract made by the superintendent upon the Delaware Division, with Long and Law for building a weigh lock at Easton," which was unanimously approved by the Board.[32].

FLOODS

Any story of the Delaware Canal would be incomplete without reviewing briefly the devastation that the paralleling river periodically inflicted upon the canal. The Delaware River, together with its tributary, the Lehigh, annually was subjected to spring freshets, especially when the melting snows in the drainage areas produced high and rapidly flowing streams. It was these freshets that the rivermen—the pilots of the arks and rafts—took advantage of each year to convey their products to down river markets. The Lehigh and Delaware canals were designed and built to cope with these annual events. But it was the abnormal situations, when heavy snows were rapidly melted by spring rains, or torrential storms caused the rivers to become raging torrents, that brought destruction to the river valleys. Particularly was this true of the Lehigh, where the narrow valley and a drop of about 1000 feet between White Haven and Easton greatly accelerated the torrent, played havoc with the Lehigh Canal, and disgorged great volumes of water and accumulated debris into the Delaware River at Easton.

Hardly had the banks of the Delaware Canal been completed when a severe ice freshet occurred on March 13, 1832, which damaged the banks and caused breaches in the waterway to some distance below New Hope. In a letter dated March 19, 1832, Simpson Torbert, engineer of the lower section, reported to the Canal Commissioners that "the water rose to a height sufficient to overflow the top banks of the canal below New Hope, at Black's Eddy and Lumberville. I am however happy in being able to say that it has not done any material injury on my division and the navigation below New Hope will not be interrupted. Damage has only been done where the banks were made of sand and this you know is a substance which must ultimately give place to a more substantial material. . . . The muddy water from the river has had a very salutory effect in saturating the banks and bottom particularly in the gravelly district extending from Centre Bridge to New Hope. The percolation and leakage was very profuse in this portion of the canal last fall."[33]

The second section of the Lehigh Canal from Mauch Chunk to White Haven had been in operation for only two years when the greatest flood to strike the Lehigh Valley in recorded history occurred on January 8, 1841. The high dams and locks on that section were severely damaged, less damage was done on the lower section between Mauch Chunk and Easton and considerable damage was inflicted on the banks of the Delaware Canal. Navigation was resumed on the lower section by July 10, 1841, and by August on the Delaware Canal. Damage to the upper section of the Lehigh Canal was so severe that navigation was not resumed until the spring of 1844.[34]

W. H. Gausler, who had started work as a mule driver only the year before, vividly recalled this flood. "The canal from White Haven to Easton," he said, "was completely destroyed by a freshet which nearly bankrupted the company. . . . In this freshet all the bridges, with the exception of the chain bridge at Lehigh Gap, were swept down the river and ninety percent of the canal boats at Freemansburg, a small town depending on the earnings, were lost. The boats were all tied to a line, and every man, woman and child was holding on this rope on the night of the 8th when the rope broke and all the boats belonging to the boatmen of the town went down the river. I was at the rope when it broke. It took nearly all summer till boating could be resumed from Penn Haven to Bristol."[35]

In the spring of 1843 high water produced breaches in the Delaware Canal that interrupted navigation for about 60 days. This was the occasion, mentioned elsewhere, for the first strike of boatmen on the canals.

Then followed a succession of freshets to plague the operators of the canals. During the flood of October 12, 1845, the water was higher than any time, excepting the 1841 flood, and interrupted navigation for about twenty days. The year 1850 produced two freshets, the first on July 19, causing a suspension of navigation for three weeks and the second on September 2nd which interrupted boating for about a month. During the year 1852 frequent breaches in the banks of the Delaware Canal caused interruptions for about two months and "furnished grounds for constant complaint on the part of those navigating the canal."[36]

The great flood of June 4, 1862, was more destructive and exceeded in height the flood of 1841. The worst damage was inflicted on the Lehigh Canal although there was considerable damage to the banks of the Delaware. Heavy rains in the Lehigh Valley north of Blue Mountain precipitated the flood.

"The rain . . . commenced falling on the afternoon of the 3rd and continued without interruption for thirty hours. Many of the artificial dams, designed to furnish water power to the numerous saw mills located upon the tributary streams which flow into the river . . . gave way, suddenly precipitating from the pools . . . a vast amount of water into the river, thus increasing the volume, already swelled to an extent rarely, if ever before equalled.

"About the time the flood attained its maximum, the booms erected by the lumbermen in the pools near White Haven gave way, releasing from 200,000 to 300,000 saw logs, which, swept down by the current with resistless force, occasioned great damage to the works along the whole extent of the line. . . . It is quite probable that, without this extraneous influence added to the unusual accumulation of water, many of the dams which gave way might have resisted the pressure, thus averting much of the damage that actually occurred.

"The effect of the logs upon the canal and guard banks, both on the Upper and Lower Sections, was also very damaging, in many places battering down the protection walls, and plowing up the embankments, thus affording to the impetuous current an unobstructed way for the completion of the ruin, by washing away the now unprotected and loosened earthwork. . . . The loss of life and the destruction of private property along the valley was (sic) also immense; it is estimated that between one and two hundred persons perished in this calamity. . . . As near as could be ascertained, from 150 to 200 coal boats were carried away, few of which were ever recovered. In addition to those, nearly all the gravel boats and all the boarding boats belonging to the Company, were destroyed."[37]

Damage to the upper section of the line was so great that the Coal Company decided to abandon this portion of the line. But work was started immediately to restore the portion from Mauch Chunk to Easton. "At the very commencement of the work, great difficulties had to be encountered. . . . All the wheelbarrows, picks, shovels and other implements of repair belonging to the Company, having been swept away, the whole surrounding country, as well as the cities of Philadelphia and New York were laid under contribution to furnish the needed supply of these articles. All communication with the sources of supply, having been for a season cut off by railroad, as well as by canal, and all the bridges on the ordinary highways spanning the streams that flow into the river, having been destroyed, everything needed for the prosecution of the work, including even the food for the laborers, had to be transported by team, in some instances, many miles, over circuitous, rough and almost impassable roads.

"Another difficulty was encountered in the scarcity of laboring men, as well as artisans of all kinds. The call of the President of the United States for 300,000 volunteers, and the draft that immediately followed, occuring about this time, took off a great number of men. . . . The average number of men engaged on the line, during the whole period, until resumption of navigation, was about 2500, and the number of teams about 500. On some important governing points the work was prosecuted night and day—Sundays excepted—by different sets of hands, in order to secure the simultaneous completion of the whole line."[38]

By herculean effort the line from Easton to Mauch Chunk was open to navigation by September 29, 1862. In the meantime, repairs to the Delaware Canal had been completed permitting resumption of coal shipments on October 3rd until navigation closed on December 19.

Again the boy mule driver who witnessed the flood of 1841, now grown to manhood and a respected merchant and owner of a fleet of canalboats, was to feel the devastating effects of this great flood. He recalled that, "On June 6, 1862, I lost by a freshet, my house, lumber yard, coal yard and boats. My family got out of the house at one o'clock in the morning with only their night clothing. All went down the Lehigh River. There was not enough left to build a fire. I was at Key West at the time with the Forty-seventh Regiment and did not hear the news for a month."[39]

The debris swept up by the flood waters was carried far down the Delaware River. Dr. B. F. Fackenthal, Jr., has recorded, "The surface of the water in the Delaware at Riegelsville was covered with lumber, logs, houses, barns, pig sties, hay stacks, bridges, canal and other boats."[40]

During the year 1868, a number of interruptions to navigation, which were characteristic of others to follow, occurred on the Delaware Canal. In the month of May, navigation on the canal for boats passing through the outlet lock at New Hope and destined for the feeder of the Delaware and Raritan Canal was suspended for eight days due to high water in the Delaware River. Over the years this was a frequent interruption when the river water was too high to assure safe passage by the ferry. In June of that year, a freshet in Buck Creek swept away the aqueduct at Yardley.

The freshet of October 4, 1869, produced a larger volume of water than the great flood of 1862 and closed the Delaware Canal for the remainder of the season. Damage to a number of aqueducts was particularly heavy. The Coal Company's annual report records that, "Tinicum and Tohickon aqueducts were entirely washed away, and those at Durham and Gallows Run seriously damaged. The loss of these aqueducts was caused not by the rise of the Delaware River, which was then only twelve feet above ordinary level, but wholly by their affording insufficient water-way to pass the flood from the mountain streams over which they formed the canal crossing.

"Subsequently, the Delaware rose to thirty feet, or two feet above the height in the freshet of 1862. The damage due to the rise in the Delaware was comparatively triffling; and, had it attained its height in advance of the rise of these side streams, the aqueducts would not have been swept away. . . . In rebuilding these works, increased water-way is being provided, so as to secure them from a similar occurrence in the future."[41]

Another storm, October 4, 1877, raised some of the mountain streams flowing into the Delaware River to unprecedented heights. "This storm being confined to a comparatively small area, the rise in the Delaware River was small, thus causing a heavy fall at the mouths of the side streams, and increasing the velocity of their currents to such an extent that they carried everything before them.

"At Gallows Run and Durham Creek, where the rain was heaviest, the aqueducts were completely destroyed; the superstructures being carried bodily into the river, and the stone abutments leveled to their foundations. At each place, also, the bottom of the canal was washed out for several hundred feet by the water in the levels rushing out at the openings thus made. The canal was dammed north of Durham Creek aqueduct so that the winter supply of coal for the Durham Iron Company could be brought down."[42]

The program to raise and strengthen the banks of the Delaware Canal that was started soon after this waterway came under the jurisdiction of the Coal Company, reduced to a great extent the damage inflicted by subsequent high water. In spite of the many breaches and the loss of aqueducts, the lock structures themselves sustained very little damage.

Of the succeeding freshets, that of October 11, 1878, produced a rise of about 30 feet in the river with only slight damage to the canal; the heavy rains of September 23, 1882, caused excessive stream rise between New Hope and Bristol, damaging the aqueducts at Taylorsville and Yardley; the rise in creeks caused by the rains of August 3, 1885, carried away the aqueduct at Lumberville and washed out the culvert at Kenderdine's Mill (Cuttalossa Creek).

The improvements which protected the Delaware Canal from serious damage through the last quarter of the nineteenth century were not able to cope with a series of floods which occurred immediately after the turn of the century. A severe river freshet on December 14, 1901, followed by another on March 2, 1902, badly damaged the canal banks. Before the repairs were completed a third freshet of devastating volume, occurred on October 10, 1903. As a result of these three freshets canal traffic was suspended for nearly two years. No coal shipments were reported for 1902 and only 75,000 tons each, for the two succeeding years.

Collection of William H. Shank
Boats washed onto shore at Delaware Quarries by the flood of 1903.

Grant Emery, at that time a small boy living near Uhlertown, was old enough to drive a mule attached to a two wheel cart. He helped repair the towpath near Lumberville. "There were crews all along the way from Easton to Bristol", he said, "wherever there was damage done by that flood. It was mostly done by canal men and their wagons, carts and mules. I think there was some labor imported. I recall that was my first experience seeing Italian labor. It was quite amusing to see those fellows come with their loaf of bread for lunch, while we carried our dinner pails and, of course, the feed baskets we used on the canal to feed the mules when we stopped for dinner hour."

While the controversy that finally resulted in transfer of the Delaware Canal to the State was underway, the great storm of March 18-19, 1936, occurred. This storm, which was state wide, produced disastrous floods in all of the river valleys in the state; and, the Delaware was not spared. With the decline of business on the Delaware Canal during its last years of operation, normal maintenance was neglected. This neglect undoubtedly accounted for much of the damage that the flood inflicted. Under the conditions then existing— the country in the midst of a depression and World War II approaching—it is remarkable that the canal recovered from this calamity. Recognizing the seriousness of the situation, a group of dedicated citizens of the Delaware Valley banded together and organized the Delaware Valley Protective Association for the primary purpose of rescuing the Delaware Canal from the fate that overtook the other old canals of the country. Having accomplished this objective, the Association continues its active support in preserving the historic and natural beauty of the Delaware Valley.

By far the greatest disaster to befall the Delaware Valley ocurred August 18-19, 1955, when hurricane Diane passed through eastern Pennsylvania. The resulting flood water, which rose to its greatest recorded height, took a heavy toll in human life and property damage. The Delaware Canal, then the major feature of Roosevelt State Park, did not escape this calamity. Commendably, the Department of Forests and Waters acted promptly to repair the damage. At the December 1955 meeting of the Delaware Valley Protection Association Forester Felton was able to report "that seven miles of towpath had been rebuilt; ten miles of silt had been dredged; 6 of 11 destroyed bridges had been replaced with concrete pipes and fill; 4 of 9 damaged waste gates have been repaired; and the river wall repaired in many places."[43] Later, the Department of Forests and Waters reported that $315,000 had been spent in repairing damage to the canal.[44]

Chapter 7

The Coal Trade and
Other Commodities

An ark belonging to the Lehigh Coal and Navigation Company sunk on the 6th instant, in passing the sluice of the dam at this place. The men hung on to the oars, and were taken off by a skiff sent from shore to their rescue. The coal (about 140 tons) was lost.

The Whig, Easton, Pa., June 8, 1830

A large boat load of cabbage has been lying at the canal wharf in Old South Bethlehem, since Saturday last. Lovers of saurkraut have been investing extensively.

Bethlehem Daily Times, Bethlehem, Pa., October 26, 1874

THE COAL TRADE

The coal trade in the Lehigh and Delaware valleys had its beginning when anthracite coal was accidentally discovered, in 1791, on Summit Hill west of what was later to become Mauch Chunk. According to a popular legend of long standing, Philip Ginder, a shiftless hunter, was returning home from an unsuccessful quest for game. As he trudged through a drizzling rain, his foot struck an obstruction in the rock formation, causing a piece to break off. Observing it to be shiny black, he picked it up for examination. Having heard the local tradition of stone coal, he took his find to Col. Jacob Weiss for confirmation. Weiss, with the assistance of friends, determined that the sample was, in fact, stone coal and offered Ginder a tract of land if he would point out the spot where he made his discovery. On this tract Ginder later erected a grist mill.[1]

This tale persisted as local folk-legend until George Korson's research into the folklore of the Pennsylvania Dutch in the lower anthracite area exploded the folk-hero role of Philip Ginder and established him as a flesh and blood human being. Instead of a poor hunter, Ginder was already a successful miller, skillful carpenter, and grinder of millstones when he made his discovery. In fact, he was on a search for suitable millstone rocks on that day in 1791 when he stopped to rest on Summit Hill. Turning over a rock which he thought suitable for his purpose, he discovered a black surface underneath and it occurred to him that this might be stone coal. He took samples of the rock to his friend Joe Neyer, a Mahoning Valley blacksmith. The blacksmith threw some of the material on his charcoal fire. After some time the stones ignited and a bright glow appeared. His find was, in truth, stone coal.[2]

Philip Ginder then took some of the samples to his neighbor, Col. Weiss, who agreed to carry them to Philadelphia for the expert opinion of some of his friends. The enthusiasm which the display of these samples generated, resulted in the organization of the Lehigh Coal Mine Company in 1792 and the purchase of a tract of ten thousand acres of land in the area disclosed by Ginder.[3]

But the organization of this company did little to advance the development of coal mining. After fruitless efforts to mine and transport the coal over the treacherous waters of the Lehigh River to apathetic and often scoffing potential buyers, Col. Weiss admitted forlornly, "We are completely discouraged."[4] The project collapsed and remained in idleness until 1818 when the property was leased to Josiah White and his associates, Erskine Hazard and George F. A. Hauto, for "a yearly rental of an ear of corn, on demand."[5]

With the vision, tenacity and inventive genius of Josiah White, the project was now assured of success. But, first much groundwork had to be laid. Obstacles in the Lehigh River must be cleared away to assure safe passage of the arks carrying coal down its water. The crude method of transporting coal by wagons from the mines over the rough mountain road was a slow and expensive job. To correct this condition Josiah White conceived and constructed the first railroad in the United States[6]—the gravity railroad, later known as the famous switchback railroad. By this innovation coal was conveyed in cars, or "waggons" as they were then called, by gravity from the mines to the river, nine miles away. Mules were used to draw the waggons back to the mines. To conserve the mules' energy and to have them available for the return trip, a waggon was built to carry them down with the loaded coal waggons. During this ride the mules also were fed to save time. Years later, Josiah White's nephew, Solomon Roberts, who rode down on the first trip, recalled with evident relish that, in addition to being the first railroad, the "gravity" also provided "the first railroad dining car! The first transportation of cattle by railroad!"[7]

Upon the organization of the Lehigh Coal and Navigation Company, a state charter, which gave the new company sole control of the Lehigh River, in addition to the coal mining rights, was granted on February 13, 1822.[8] Still, an important obstacle had to be sur-

Canal Society of New York State
The famous switchback railroad at Mauch Chunk.

mounted—the general apathy of the public to the use of this new fuel. The fireplaces and stoves in which wood was the conventional fuel were not adapted to burning stone coal. But gradually, craftsmen began to design and produce cast and wrought iron grates and stoves that were effective and economical in burning anthracite.

The Lehigh stove, cast at the Mary Ann Furnace in Bucks County, Pennsylvania, in 1820, was the first anthracite stove on the market. Production of stoves continued at this plant until 1859.[9] About 1820, Josiah White sent some anthracite to Reverend Dr. Eliphalet Nott of Schenectady, New York, with the suggestion that he try building a stove for hard coal. This remarkable man, president of Union College for sixty-two years, pulpit orator, prohibitionist and

practical inventor, was also one of the country's outstanding com-
bustion experts. Not only did he invent and patent many different
kinds of stoves, but also became the guiding member of H.
Nott and Company, the leading stove manufacturer of the day.[10]

With suitable stoves for burning anthracite available to the market,
the apathy to its use began to disappear. Industry also found anthracite
advantageous over other fuels. Soon the Lehigh Coal and Navigation
Company had no difficulty in disposing of all the coal it could send
down the rivers by arks. During 1830, the last year that anthracite
was shipped exclusively by this method, over 40,000 tons were dispatched from the Mauch Chunk area to Philadelphia. Completion of
the Lehigh and Delaware canals, together with their connecting links,
the Morris and Delaware and Raritan, was none too soon to supply
the rapidly expanding demand for anthracite. It was not long before
these canals were called the "great tidewater anthracite navigation."[11]
By the end of the first decade of operation, more than 300,000 tons
of coal per year were shipped from the Lehigh Valley mines down
these canals.

Stories of the expanding traffic and the great range of travel over
the canals then in operation were absorbing news to the general
public. Hazard reports [12] that in 1834 the *Commercial Herald* told
its readers, "We have been informed of a striking fact which exem-
plifies the great importance and benefits of the internal improvements
of our country—a few weeks since an Erie Canal boat which had
brought a load of coach lumber to Newark, took in return a cargo
of coal destined for the town of Elmira on the Tioga river near the
Pennsylvania line in the state of New York.

"It is curious to trace the route of this lot of coal on the map.
First it starts from the mines and arrives at Mauch Chunk by railroad, thence it takes the Lehigh Canal to Easton, then the Morris
Canal to Newark, then through the New York bay and up the North
River to Albany, then by the Erie Canal to Seneca Lake, then
through Seneca Lake to Salubria at its head, then by the Chemung
Canal to Elmira which, in a direct line is about a hundred miles
from the place of starting, having gone 700 miles to arrive at its
destined point."

The second decade of operation, 1844 to 1854, was the great
expansion period of coal transportation on the Lehigh and Delaware
canals. During the following year, 1855, the greatest quantity of coal
to be transported over the Lehigh Canal 1,276,000 tons was
recorded. Of this amount, 290,700 tons were transferred at Easton
to the Morris Canal, also a record for transfer to that canal, and

755,000 tons passed down the Delaware Canal, of which 156,000 tons were conveyed from New Hope to the Delaware and Raritan Canal.[13]

That same year, 1855, the Lehigh Valley Railroad was completed to Phillipsburg, New Jersey, followed a few years later by the Lehigh and Susquehanna Railroad. The competition of these railroads together with a series of disasters, including the great flood of 1862 and the financial panic of 1873, presented obstacles that the canals found impossible to surmount. The Lehigh Valley Railroad which, in 1871, acquired the Morris Canal by lease, shipped coal to Phillipsburg where it was loaded on boats for delivery along the Morris Canal and to tidewater at Jersey City. Coal shipment by the Lehigh Canal for transfer to the Morris rapidly decreased until in 1887 only 359 tons were recorded. Following the panic of 1873, coal traffic on the Lehigh Canal never exceeded 500,000 tons per year. Most of this coal, with the exception of that delivered to industries and dealers along the Lehigh, was transported over the Delaware Canal from Easton.

The decline in the coal trade over the canals in no way suggested a decrease in the volume of business produced by the Lehigh Coal and Navigation Company. The rapid recovery of industry following the depression of 1873 together with increase in business and population produced demands for anthracite greater than ever before. But these demands were supplied mainly by the railroads. The year 1911 recorded the maximum amount of coal supplied by the mines in the Lehigh Valley. That year 8,884,000 tons of coal were shipped by rail from Mauch Chunk to eastern markets, in addition to 321,00 tons shiped by canal.[14]

The impact of rail competition was not so apparent on the Delaware Canal. From 91,800 tons of coal carried in 1833, the annual volume increased to a maximum of 792,000 tons in 1866. That same year saw the maximum transfer of coal, 526,000 tons, through the outlet lock at New Hope, to the Delaware and Raritan Canal. From that time the volume of business decreased slowly until by the turn of the century about 250,000 tons of coal were transported annually over the Delaware Canal. This annual volume continued until 1915 after which not over 135,000 tons were carried per year. In 1931, the last year of operation, 65,600 tons of anthracite were carried on the Delaware Canal.

The construction of the Delaware Canal and the rapid growth of the coal trade were a great boon to the communities through which the canal passed. Suddenly, the Delaware Valley was aroused from its colonial lethargy by a new era of transportation and commerce. Most affected by this innovation was Bristol. This quiet little village at the southern end of the canal suddenly awakened to find itself a teeming river port swarming with canalboats, boatmen, mules and river and coastal boats of all sorts. The canal traffic started slowly. Within a few years the number of boats headed for Bristol became so great that, in the words of W. H. Gausler, "the canal seemed to be a solid mass of boats." Stores sprang up to provide food and other supplies for the boatmen; stables were built to house the mules. The mules of the boats continuing on to Philadelphia and New York were left behind at Bristol until the return trip. At times their number reached into the hundreds. Blacksmith shops were a necessity; and, farmers did a thriving business in supplying hay, oats, and straw for the animals. Then there were the grog shops to satisfy the thirsty boatmen. Bristol became a boom town.

The coal from some of the boats was unloaded at Bristol to be shipped by shallops, sloops and ships up and down the coast, but the majority continued on to other ports. Coal boats consigned to Philadelphia and adjacent ports were assembled in the river outside the tide lock in tows of up to twenty-one boats, three abreast, to be taken down the river by steamboats. The departure of these tows was scheduled to take advantage of the ebb tide in going down the river

Collection of Henry S. Engart
A boat load of coal on the way to Bristol.

and the flood tide upon the return trip. Boats consigned to New York were towed across the Delaware River to Bordentown where they entered the Delaware and Raritan Canal. The Lehigh Coal and Navigation Company had a fleet of three side wheel, steam boats, the *Lehigh, Herald* and *Rockland,* for towing the canalboats.

The Commonwealth built wharves along the basin and the river front for the accommodation of boats unloading and taking on cargoes. By an 1837 agreement, four of these wharves were rented to the Lehigh Coal and Navigation Company for $1280 a year.[15] After the sale of the State canals to private interests, the Coal Company controlled all of the shipping facilities at the outlet of the Delaware Canal.

The coming of the railroads and the construction of the outlet lock at New Hope were bad omens for Bristol. According to Doren Green, "The loss of the coal trade was a sad blow to Bristol. Over 300 persons left to seek employment elsewhere. The town subsided into a state of extreme lethargy. The life was completely taken out of it. The old residents walked through the quiet streets and enjoyed the balmy air of summer and sat around their firesides during the fierce blasts of the winter months and waited for something to turn up."[16] Bristol settled back to await more prosperous times which, fortunately, were not too long in coming.

To the Bristol Improvement Company, chartered in 1876, may be credited the start of the community's modern industrial growth. The function of this company was to encourage the development of local manufacturing industries by the erection of buildings which were leased to responsible applicants at attractive rates. Through this medium many industries were established in Bristol, including a worsted mill, a fringe mill, a woolen mill, a wall paper mill and a carpet mill.[17] The boisterous days of the coal trade were happily forgotten.

THE COAL BOATS

The rapidly expanding coal trade required a corresponding increase in the number of boats in service. Boat building became one of the most rapidly expanding industries of that period, which saw the erection of numerous boat yards along the Lehigh and Delaware canals. The center of boating activities was at Weissport on the Lehigh River, where the Lehigh Coal and Navigation Company constructed a large boat yard and other facilities required in the operation and maintenance of the canals. Not only were skilled workmen required at these plants but large quantities of lumber also had to be brought from the forests for use in boat construction. As the volume of boats increased, great numbers of men and animals had to be recruited for their operation.

Not much is known about the size or design of the early canal-boats. But it is reasonable to assume that, in specifying the size of his boats, Josiah White took full advantage of the lock capacity of the Delaware Canal. In its earliest reports, the Lehigh Coal and Navigation Company mentioned boat tonnages comparable to those of much later years. The annual report for 1832, in commenting on the condition of the Delaware Canal, expected that "the banks will be sufficiently consolidated the next season to admit water for boats carrying 60 to 70 tons."[18] In 1833 business on the Delaware Canal "commenced on the 25th of March, with boats carrying from 40 to 45 tons and closed on the 15th of December with a boat loaded with 60 tons of coal."[19] An invoice from the Lehigh Coal and Navigation Company to John E. Huey, dated September 25, 1862, lists twenty boat loads of coal averaging 71 tons per boat. It is interesting to note that this invoice specifies one boat load of egg coal at $3.50 per ton, one boat load of chestnut at $2.00 per ton and eighteen boat loads of chestnut at $2.50 per ton.[20] These early boats, according to W. H. Gausler, were built "in double sections with a capacity of about 60 tons." From this sketchy evidence it is logical to believe that the early boats were not much different in size and design from those of a much later date for which detailed specifications are available.

Equally vague and lacking substantiation are the number of boats reputed to have been in use when "the canal seemed to be a solid mass of boats." One source gives the number operating on the Delaware Canal as from 2700 to 3000 boats.[21] An important record contributing to our knowledge of canal operation in the early days is the *Register of Boats Clearing at Bristol on the Pennsylvania Canal— 1849*[22], and from it much information can be gleaned regarding the number of boats in service on the canal. This large volume records the names, or numbers, of all boats that daily cleared the toll house at Bristol for passage up the Delaware Canal in 1849. Also included are the cargoes carried in each boat, together with the tolls paid. The navigation season that year was unusually long, extending from March 13 to December 26 or, deducting Sundays, on which no clearances were made, consisted of 250 operating days. Throughout the life of the canal, the average season included about 212 operating days.[23]

The Register lists 8695 up-bound boats that cleared the toll house in 1849. Since this was the turn-around point in the canal, an equal number, or roughly 8700 boats must have come down the canal that year. During that season 580,934 tons of coal were carried in these 8700 boats, or an average of 66.8 tons per boat. It should be remembered that 8700 represents the number of boat loads and not the number of boats in service, since each boat made numerous round trips each season. Old boatmen say that from seven to eight days were required to make the trip from Mauch Chunk to Bristol and return. If a more conservative figure of nine is used, then during the 250 operating days of 1849, each boat made 28 round trips. It, therefore, required 310 boats to haul the 8700 boat loads of coal transported during that season. Other time consuming factors must be considered in estimating the total number of boats in service. Many boats continued on to Philadelphia or New York while others might be delayed at docks or for repairs. To compensate for these delays, and to provide cargo space for the other commodities carried on the canal, an additional 310 boats might be required, making a total of 620 boats in service during the year.

The maximum coal haulage year on the Delaware Canal was 1866, when 792,397 tons of coal were transported down the canal. If a similar analysis is applied to that year, using 212 average operating days and an average of 66.8 tons per boat, the total number of boat loads is found to be 11,900. Each boat could make 23 round trips, with the result that 520 boats would be required to haul the year's tonnage of coal. Applying the 100% factor for additional delays and other uses, a total of 1040 boats might have been in service during 1866. No doubt, by that year the average load per boat was more than 66.8 tons. Any increase beyond that figure would proportionately reduce the number of boats in service.

The first mention by the Lehigh Coal and Navigation Company of the number of boats in service is contained in its annual report for 1881.[24] The report states that 313 Company boats were on the canal, in addition to 141 free boats. That year 396,000 tons of coal were transported on the Lehigh Canal, of which 321,000 tons were transferred to the Delaware Canal. It was also reported that, "Three hundred and fifty-eight boats were engaged on the lower part of the canals in miscellaneous traffic; of these, 300 came from the Morris Canal with ore for Glendon and Durham Furnaces." The data here given is reasonably consistent with the previous estimates. In fact, it suggests that the estimates of boats necessary to compensate for delays are much too high. Until records are discovered to impart more knowledge on the subject, it is logical to believe that not more than 1000 boats were in service on the Delaware Canal at any time.[25]

THE BOATMEN'S STRIKE

The year 1843 started poorly for the boatmen on the Lehigh and Delaware canals. The damage to the waterways caused by the great flood of 1841 had been repaired; and, the men were expecting a prosperous year. But, the lateness of the season delayed navigation for about thirty days. When the boats started to move, a series of breaks in the banks of the Delaware Canal caused further delays of about sixty days.

In the meantime, large numbers of loaded boats were accumulating in the basin above the guard lock at Easton. The jobless boatmen, idling away the days "without wages, gathered into an angry mob to protest; and when the 'Delaware Branch' eventually was pronounced ready to resume, the men declared a 'turnout'—a strike. They claimed . . . they had been week after week without pay, and before returning to their jobs demanded assurance of regular work at larger wages."[26] W. H. Gausler remembers, "that a boat was sunk at the weigh lock where the Lehigh Canal enters the Delaware Canal, preventing the passing of boats . . . The militia was called out several times to quell a riot and prevent depredation. The Lehigh Dam at Easton was packed solid with boats. I remember when Asa Packer and officials of the Lehigh Coal and Navigation Company came down to Easton to break the strike they came near being thrown overboard."[27]

In its report for 1843, the Coal Company recorded that the boatmen, "regardless alike of their written engagements, and of the serious injury inflicted by them upon a large class of unoffending individuals and upon the commonwealth, entered into a combination forcibly to prevent the transportation of coal, except upon conditions dictated by themselves."[28]

When the miners at Mauch Chunk joined the strike, the news was a hard blow to Josiah White, then in the twilight of his career. He hurried quickly to "his valley." This gentle, but demanding, Quaker had always treated his men with paternalistic consideration; their pay was the highest in the industry, schools were provided for their children and a hospital for their sick; but their first loyalty must be the welfare of the Company. The answer to the strikers was a resounding negative.

In August, the men returned to work; but "the boatmen were, beyond question, in a worse condition at the close of the season, than they would have been, had they gone on in the honest discharge of contracts deliberately and voluntarily entered into."[29] It is doubtful if anyone realized at the time that these were the first rumblings of a new order in labor relations. Before that time arrived, however, the industry had to undergo the ordeal of the Molly McGuires and a series of strikes culminating in the great anthracite strike of 1901.

WHEN THE LEHIGH COAL AND NAVIGATION COMPANY LOST CONTROL OF ITS CANALS AND COAL MINES

During the wave of prosperity following the Civil War, most of the business expansion was conducted on borrowed money. To obtain money to repair the heavy damage to the Lehigh and Delaware Canals caused by the flood of 1861 and to extend its Lehigh and Susquehanna Railroad to Phillipsburg, the Lehigh Coal and Navigation Company assumed heavy floating debts which it expected to protect through the constantly increasing demand for anthracite. Upon completing its extension in 1868, the railroad was leased to the Central Railroad of New Jersey to secure continuous rail transportation to the east coast.

The aftermath of this wave of speculation that produced the inevitable spiral of inflation was the financial panic of September 1873, followed by a flood of business failures. Later that year, the Coal Company reported that "when the panic checked negotiations in the middle of September, our floating debt was at its maximum and great difficulty was experienced in meeting maturing obligations."[30] To escape bankruptcy, the Company negotiated a lease, effective December 31, 1873, of its two canals and all of its coal properties with the Central Railroad of New Jersey. The latter company, however, was not spared the effects of the depression and by late 1876 was forced into receivership. The receiver refused to continue operation of the canals and, through an option in the lease agreement, the Coal Company, "resumed possession of both canals and mines in the early January of this year (1878)."[31] Thus, from January 1874, through December 1877, a span of four years, the Lehigh Coal and Navigation Company lost control of all of its properties.

HOW COAL DRIBBLED AWAY

One of the minor irritations that plagued the Coal Company during most of its existence was the disappearance of coal while boats were enroute from the mines to their destinations. In general, the quantities involved were not large and the practice was accepted by the company as a business hazard. In fact, as Ted Sherman said, "When you got weighed at Mauch Chunk, there was always allowed so much—what lock keepers took, what boatmen took and what disappeared in other ways."

Some of this coal might be legitimately claimed by the boat captain as a reward for keeping his boat shipshape. The shovellers who unloaded the boats were not too particular about removing all the coal from the hold; broken, or loose lining planks allowed coal to sift into the bilge and the openings through which the bilge pumps passed permitted more coal to accumulate in this section. During the return trip the boatmen collected this coal in sacks or other containers and, for their efforts, might be rewarded with a ton or more of coal. This accumulated coal usually was referred to as "sweepings."

Of course, there were other ways, not so legitimate, by which some boatmen acquired coal for their own disposition. One or more lining planks might be removed to allow more coal to enter the bilge. A little money distributed to friendly shovellers made them careless in cleaning out the hold. Or, as one boatman recalls, during prohibition, an occasional bottle of moonshine accomplished the same result. One method the Coal Company particularly frowned upon was shovelling coal directly from a loaded boat. Joseph Lum remembers that sometime during his years on the canal (1883-1895), the hatch covers were sealed, similar to the doors on freight cars. But the results hardly justified the effort; and, this procedure was abandoned.

A new canal superintendent, John Ruddle, appointed about 1890, decided to do something about the more flagrant abuses. The Pinkerton's National Detective Agency was employed to conduct an investigation, which extended from October 19, 1891, until November 20, 1891. Following are extracts from the daily reports of operative G.E.S.[32]

Monday, Oct. 19th, 1891.   Philadelphia

"I was instructed to proceed to New Hope, then tramp the canal and try and locate the persons stealing the coal.

"In accordance with these instructions, I left the Agency at 3-25 P.M., took car to the 9th and Green Sts. depot of the P.&.R.R.R. Co., and after purchasing ticket, I boarded the 4-20 P.M. train for New Hope, arriving there at 8 P.M. I took a walk, then went to the Logan House, secured a room and at 9-30 P.M. retired."

*   *   *   *   *

Tuesday, Oct. 20th, 1891.   In New Hope

"In continuation of operation, I left the Logan House at 7-30 A.M. and went out on the canal, walked down to the New Hope locks, where I found boats 2101 and 2084 going through. I asked the Captain of No. 2084 if he would give me passage up to Point

Pleasant. 'Yes, jump on,' was his reply. I boarded the boat, and entered into conversation with him. He stated, in answer to my inquiries, that he took the boats as far as Bristol, then returned with the light ones to Mauch Chunk; that the coal was weighed and the boat gauged when she left Mauch Chunk; . . . that there was considerable difference since the new Supt. was in charge; that none of the boatmen had any love for him. He showed me several small houses along side of the canal, and said boatmen resided in them. He also explained how they got their coal, and said that last fall he had had 6 tons of coal in his house, but he did not have as much this fall; he would, however, get some on the next trip down, viz.— if he loaded with chestnut coal.

"No. 2102 was light and was lying at Bridgeton, with a small pile of coal (about a ton) on the bank, along side of her. It looked as if it had just been put ashore. No one being on board, the Captain on No. 2084 did not know who was running it. Outside of this pile of coal I saw but one other. It was located about a mile below Point Pleasant, and I was informed it was the property of a boatman, who lived about a mile distant, over the hill. . . . At 5 P.M. we tied up at Bridgeton. I walked about for half an hour, but did not see anything of interest to report. I then crossed the bridge, went to the Gibson House, Milford, N.J., and registered."

* * * * *

Wednesday, October 21, 1891. On the Canal, between Bridgeton and Uhlertown, Pa.

"In continuance of Operation, I was up and abroad at a very early hour this morning after breakfasting, and went over to Bridgeton. Just as I got there, which was about 7 o'clock, I saw the captain of one of the Uhler boats, the 'Charles F. Howell' by name, passing out of the hold some pig-iron to his man or driver, who was putting it on a wheelbarrow. The boat was then lying abreast of Mike McIntee's stores. As near as I could judge by sight, there was about 150 pounds of pig-iron handed out in this way. . . .

"The driver then came, whipped up his team and started up the canal. I walked up that way for about a mile, then came back. . . .

"I had not gone more than a mile or so when I met the Captain of boat No. 2084 coming up. He said he had been down to Frenchtown on business, and was now going to his boat to make a start for Mauch Chunk. He told me I should ask for him any time I happened down this way, and to ask for Bill Rayner—saying that everybody knew him. I kept on my way down canal after leaving Rayner, and saw a couple of small piles of coal (perhaps half a ton in each pile) that had been put out since I had been up here before, last night. I stopped at a house close by, but could not find out who left the coal there or to whom it belonged. No one knew, not even the lock-tender.

"I remained about Uhlertown until about 9:30 P.M., when I took a walk about a mile up canal, where, as captain Rayner had told me, a good many of the boats tie up at night, that is to say the down boats, and where a good deal of coal has been taken off the boats. I waited there until 10:30 P.M., when, as none of the boats had come down, I went back to Uhlertown."

*   *   *   *   *

Friday, October 23, 1891.   Point Pleasant and New Hope.

"Captain of 2131 lives near Point Pleasant and did not hesitate to tell me that it costs him nothing for his coal; he added, however, that he never takes any from a loaded boat, but can always manage to get enough left behind by the shovellers to be of service to him when he gets home light. He went on to say that some of the lining-boards were loose, so that considerable coal always got under them; the shovellers would not take the time necessary to get out this coal, and in consequence he could always be sure of finding it there.

"He also said he did not think there is a boatman on the canal but gets his winter coal without paying for it. He added, that there is not so much of that sort of work going on now as before, since Ruddle, the new Supt. is a very watchful and strict man."

*   *   *   *   *

Saturday, October 24, 1891.   New Hope to Yardley

"A Uhler boat, the Morgan, capt. Taylor, had been on the canal for 20 years. He said that in the early days a captain had a fair chance of selling enough tons of coal to the farmers and others to pay his own board-bill; but that as things are at present, these people do not any longer care to risk buying coal from the captains of the boats."

*   *   *   *   *

Tuesday, October 27, 1891.   At Bristol.

"I left the hotel at 6:30 A.M. and went down among the boats at the Basin. . . . However, there were not many of the captains around, and I went to the Hotel presently and got my breakfast; then up canal to Leedom's coal-wharf. But there was nothing of any account to be got there in the way of information, and I soon strolled down to the lower locks, where . . . several empty boats were on their way up canal. The wind was blowing so fresh at this time, that they determined to wait there until it moderated somewhat. I got in with these captains, but could not learn anything as they seem to be very careful as to what they say and to whom they say it. They appear to think that every stranger who comes along is a spy in the employ of Ruddle; indeed, I have heard them say as much as this; and they are a bad lot too, and would not hesitate long about throwing a man into the canal . . . I took another round among the captains after supper and as all of them had been drinking pretty hard meantime, there was some one knocked down every twenty minutes or so."

*   *   *   *   *

Wednesday, November 4, 1891.   In Milford, N.J.

"I left the Hotel at 7:30 this morning and crossed over to Bridgeton, Pa., where I made inquiries of Constable Charles Shaw for the Justice of the Peace. He told me where I could find Mr. John Nice Jr., and I went to the latter's store, where I was told Mr. Nice was out of town. Then back to Shaw's blacksmith shop. I got Charles Shaw to go with me [to see Michael McIntee] . . .

"While we three were together, 2137 came along, and also the 'Volunteer.' They came up canal and stopped at the bank, just below McIntee's store. I saw the men of the 'Volunteer' bring a wagon alongside, put into it about three-fourths of a ton of stove coal and haul it away to the captain's house, in Bridgeton. When this was done, the captain of 2137 came along with a double team and commenced to load up the wagon with coal from his boat; he did not stop loading until he had taken from his boat about two tons, or about as much as the wagon would hold. This wagon load of coal he hauled to a frame house about one-half a mile up the road from Bridgeton. Shaw saw this, and remarked that it was 'nothing new,' adding that 'the captains all say this is the sweepings of their boats.' At this time, seeing another one-horse wagon standing behind McIntee's store, I asked McIntee if that was his coal (this wagon was loaded); he answered that it was not, but belonged to a . . . captain of one of the liners, living down the hill—who had taken this coal out of his boat this morning.

"McIntee told me he had been often asked to buy some coal, but had always refused to do so because he thought it 'very queer' that so much coal could be gotten together by cleaning up a boat. He had, he said, seen as much as two tons put out at one time."

*   *   *   *   *

During this investigation evidence was obtained that merchandise was stolen from the boats and disposed of to merchants in Allentown. On the basis of this evidence a number of subpoenas were issued.

*   *   *   *   *

Friday, November 20, 1891.   In Philadelphia
"In accordance with instructions, I left the Agency at 9:30 A.M. to appear before the Grand Jury . . . ."

*   *   *   *   *

As the twentieth century approached, the Lehigh Coal and Navigation Company had more pressing problems than the small amount of coal disappearing through unauthorized channels. Over several years, a series of floods periodically had disrupted navigation. The time lost by these interruptions, in addition to the normal winter idleness, was causing more and more boatmen to look for employment elsewhere. The Coal Company found it difficult to obtain men to operate the boats. In its 1907 annual report the Company said, "Operation of the canals is very seriously handicapped by lack of competent labor to handle the boats. Due to loss of work in former years by floods and high wages elsewhere, many employees have left, and it is found about impossible to secure enough men to operate equipment. This condition can only be overcome by increase in wages."[33]

After 1900, the annual shipments of coal over the Company's canals were never more than 3 percent of that shipped by railroads from the Company's mines. Thus the coal appropriated by the boatmen was too insignificant to further irritate them by stealthy policing. As long as this loss didn't get out of hand, I. M. Church, then superintendent of canals, was inclined to look the other way. As Joe Reed said, "The super was a wonderful guy. He used to say, 'you make a little extra money, it gives you more spending money.'" It is this period, following 1900, that is remembered by the boatmen living in the Delaware and Lehigh valleys. Any one of them has stories of how coal disappeared through unauthorized channels.

During a call at the canal office at Lock No. 19, I absorbed some canal stories from Russ Paetzell and W. A. Minder. The subject of coal was included. Bill Minder recalled the weigh lock at Mauch Chunk where loaded boats were weighed before starting down the canal. "A mark was put on the boat at the water line," he said, "to indicate the loaded depth. On the way down the boatmen would take off a little coal here and there. Before they got to New Hope where the collector put this gauge on, they would pump water in the boat to get it down to its natural depth. Then when they got down where they were safe, they would pump the water out."

"You remember old Andrew Goodyear," Russ said, "He used to take coal off and pump water in. He'd sell the coal to my father." That reminded Bill Minder of a "fellow down the canal—ran a big farm. You give him a couple of buckets of coal and he would give you a chicken, or milk or anything you wanted." "Yes," said Russ, "If you got a few buckets from each boatman, you soon had enough coal to last all winter."

Most boatmen had stories about coal. "In the hills above Lodi," Charles Solomon recalled, "nearly everybody boated. They never bought coal. The coal that accumulated below the lining planks, they shoveled out and put in bags to haul home. The Company knew about it, but as long as you didn't abuse it, they never said anything."

Coal was also a convenient means for repaying favors. "Old Ike Wood, he was at the level ahead of New Hope—Lumberville," Joe Reed said. "When I came down loaded, he would come out with four or five buckets and take coal off. I never said nothing. So, if I came down after hours and he wasn't around, I'd run ahead and open the lock and run the boat through and then leave the lock in the same condition it was. He showed me where he kept the key. The lock tender would put a pad lock on the gates at night."

"One time I unloaded at C. K. Williams," Joe Reed recalled. "I had cement bags to put the extra coal in. So we bagged this coal up— might have been a ton—to unload here at Freemansburg to keep for the winter. We put the bags at the hinges. When we came up past Chain Dam, we let the mules go alone up to the lock. My driver said, 'I believe I. M. Church is up at the lock now.' He said, 'Quick get a canvas and cover the bags up.' Naw, I said, don't worry about it. We went in the lock, and there was Church. He said, 'How you doing Joe? Is potatoes pretty cheap now?' Yeah, I said. And he walked away. That's all he said. He knew what they were."

"The Company wouldn't say anything about the loss of coal," Joe said. "On our boat we had a hatch at the bow. At the chutes, if the operator liked you, he'd shoot the coal in pretty fast so that some of it would fill up the hatch. On unloading, some of the fellows would take the coal out of this hatch and some wouldn't. That left more coal for me."

"Where did you sell most of your coal," I asked Joe.

"Oh, down along the Delaware, at Black Horse Tavern and the hotels. At Upper Black Eddy, the fellow that ran the Hollyhand Hotel had a number of girls there. One time I came up from Bristol. I had about two tons on. We went in for a beer. He said, 'Hey, Joe, you got any coal on?' Yeah, but I'm too tired to carry it off. 'The hookers will carry it off,' he said. These girls got buckets and had the coal off in no time. Everybody did that, everybody. They sold coal and had a lot left for the winter. I never did anything sneaky. The Company knew all about it."

Some people used ingenious methods to obtain coal. Mrs. Mann remembers a family who lived along the Morris Canal. Their fence paralleled the canal. They put a row of bottles on the fence, hoping the boatmen would throw coal at them. Here was something to break the monotony of a boatman's life, as well as challenge to his throwing skill. By the end of the boating season, quite a quantity of coal had accumulated.

"We used to trade a lot along the canal," Mrs. Mann said. "People who had vegetables and things. We'd give them coal and they'd give us cabbages, tomatoes and things like that. Then there were lock tenders whose wives made good bread. We'd give them coal for bread."

OTHER COMMODITIES CARRIED ON THE CANAL

Were it not for the tremendous quantities of coal carried over the Lehigh and Delaware canals, the volume of other commodities would appear quite impressive. From the very beginning of canal transportation advantage was taken of these waterways to supply the necessities of life to the then isolated communities in the Delaware and Lehigh valleys. But this traffic rarely amounted to more than twenty percent of the total annual volume. Complete records are preserved in the annual reports of the Lehigh Coal and Navigation Company of all commodities transported over the Lehigh Canal, most of which were transferred to the Morris and Delaware canals.

Logs, lumber and other wood products, including cord wood, were the principal commodities shipped in the early years, followed closely by grain, flour, lime and limestone. The greatest volume of lumber was shipped in 1859, when 73,000 tons were transported over the Lehigh Canal. As soon as the iron industries became established in the Lehigh and Delaware valleys, iron and iron ore became the leading commodities. By 1847 their volume reached 77,000 tons,

Courtesy, Palmerton Camera Club
Seitz beer boat, typical of cabin type cargo boats.

with a maximum of 184,000 tons in 1857. After that time, the volume of iron and iron ore gradually decreased. Whiskey appeared in the earliest shipping records, reaching its greatest volume in 1853 when 1887 tons were shipped, equivalent to 15,100 standard barrels. Most of the whiskey was in descending traffic, from distilleries in the grain growing sections of the state.

The greatest traffic on the Lehigh Canal occurred in 1855 when 1,544,000 tons, including coal, were recorded. This tonnage consisted of both descending and ascending traffic.[34] (See Table IV). The boatmen called ascending traffic back loads. The back loads seldom exceeded fifteen percent of descending traffic.

The first year for which the Coal Company reported traffic on the Delaware Canal was 1867, when a total of 901,000 tons were transported. (See Table V). Of this quantity, 764,000 tons were coal. At that time and for a number of years to follow, one of the largest back loads was manure and guano. Back loads on the Delaware Canal were rarely in excess of five percent of the descending traffic.

During the time that the Commonwealth owned and operated the Delaware Canal, tolls were collected at Easton, New Hope and Bristol. A tabulation of toll charges is given in Table VI.

THE LAST EFFORT TO SAVE THE CANAL COAL TRADE

In spite of the devastating floods of 1901 -2 -3, during which time traffic on the canals was practically suspended, together with the heavy expense of making repairs and the difficulty of obtaining competent labor to handle the boats, the Coal Company was in no mood to abandon its waterways. Almost pridefully, as if influenced by the tenacious spirit of Josiah White, the Company announced in 1907: "Our canals are among the very few that are left in active business. The D & H canal has been abandoned, the Morris Canal abandoned by the Lehigh Valley RR, the Pennsylvania Canal abandoned, business on the Schuylkill Canal has been almost extinguished, the Monongahela navigation has been sold to the government, and the James River Canal has been abandoned, as well as the C & O."[35]

The following year the Company reported, "A study of the canal situation, both as to its business and physical features, was carried on during the year, the results of which were so satisfactory that it has been decided to increase the equipment by the addition of 50 new boats during the coming year: this number to be again increased during 1909 if the additional business secured in 1908 seems to warrant it."[36] That year 165 boats were reported available for service. In 1909, 35 boats were under construction, and 11 more in 1911. In spite of this flurry of boat building, old boats were wearing out and being withdrawn from service, so that in 1913 the Company reported only 176 boats available for service.

These courageous efforts by the Coal Company to save its canal traffic showed evidence of success. From a low of 75,000 tons in 1904, the year following the floods, the annual coal business increased to 203,000 tons in 1908 and 321,000 tons in 1911. But the tide of modern transportation was too far advanced to be challenged by ancient canalboats and mule teams. From that time the canal business gradually declined. By 1929 the annual traffic had decreased to 108,000 tons. The final year of canal operation, 65,000 tons of coal were transported.

In closing his diary on December 31, 1917, the canal superintendent, I. M. Church, lamented, "This was one hell of a year— labor scarce, high water, no boatmen, food high, cost sheet going wrong way and everybody with chips on their shoulders. Nothing but fight, fight. Hell has no terror—can't be anything worse than trying to run a damn old ditch like this."[37]

Chapter 8
Other Canals In The Delaware Valley

LOST CHILD

About this time three years ago my son Lawrence Walsh, who was hired as a driver to the boatmen of a Mauch Chunk scow, left his employ at the lock of Tho. Hope Esq. on the Lehigh Canal and has not since been heard of. If found please notify his parents.

Easton Sentinel, Easton, Pa., June 23, 1837

LEHIGH CANAL

When Josiah White and his associates, Erskine Hazard and George Hauto, decided to exploit the anthracite coal fields at Summit Hill, near Mauch Chunk, Pennsylvania, they were confronted with the serious problems of transportation. Philadelphia, the logical market, could be reached by natural waterways; but, the treacherous Lehigh River posed a serious challenge. Undaunted, however, by this difficulty, White and his partners petitioned the State Legislature for permission to make the Lehigh River navigable.[1] A bill was passed March 20, 1818, authorizing development of the river for navigation from Stoddartsville to Easton.

This development was undertaken in three stages; the first from Mauch Chunk to Easton, originally for descending navigation only, accomplished by means of artificial freshets resulting from a series of "V" shaped dams in the center of which were located the so-called "Bear Trap Locks"; the second from Mauch Chunk to White Haven; and the third from White Haven to Stoddartsville. Work on the first section progressed rapidly. By 1823 ark loads of coal were regularly being dispatched to Philadelphia via the Lehigh and Delaware rivers. This method of transportation was continued until 1832 by which time shipments to Philadelphia exceeded 40,000 tons of coal per year.

The arks used on the Lehigh River were built of dressed logs, held together by iron straps. They were from 16 ft. to 18 ft. wide and from 20 ft. to 25 ft. long, and were equipped with large box arrangements for holding coal and other cargo. At first single arks were sent down the river; but, as the rivermen became more adept, two or more arks were hinged together until a total length up to 180 ft. was attained. Since these clumsy devices could not be navigated upstream, the arks were disassembled at their destination and sold for lumber.

In the spring of 1827 work was started on providing two way navigation between Mauch Chunk and Easton by means of canals and slack water navigation in the river. To supervise this work, Canvass White, of Erie Canal fame, was obtained as chief engineer. On June 2, 1829, this section was opened for navigation. In the 46.2 miles from Mauch Chunk to Easton the river drops 353 feet, which required the installation of 48 locks, none of which had a lift of over 9 feet. The locks were 22 ft. wide by 100 ft. long, except the four upper ones near Mauch Chunk, which were 30 ft. wide by 130 ft. long. The canal prism was 45 ft. wide at the bottom and 60 ft. wide at the top, with a depth of 5 ft., later increased to 6 ft.

One of the first boats to navigate the new canal was the packet *Swan,* which had been brought up the river from Philadelphia to carry passengers to and from Mauch Chunk. When the second section of the canal was completed, passenger service was extended to White Haven.

Pennsylvania Canal Society
Ticket for passage on packet "Swan".

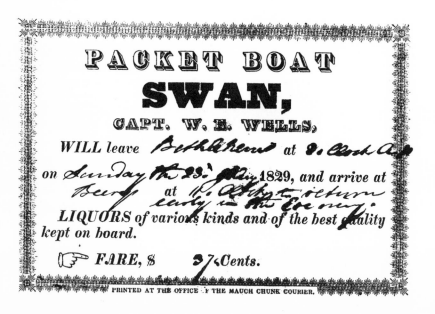

With two-way navigation established on the first section, Josiah White was ready to undertake development of the second section from Mauch Chunk to White Haven, a distance of 26 miles. But here a formidable difficulty arose. In this distance the river dropped 600 feet. To install conventional locks of not over 10 ft. lift, which was considered the maximum at that time, would have been impractical due to the time consumed in navigating this distance. Josiah White was convinced that the problem could be solved through the installation of high dams and locks of unprecedented lift. But who would supervise the undertaking?

There was one engineer he knew could have guided this project to a successful conclusion. But that man, Canvass White, had died the year before at the age of forty-four. Finally, Edwin A. Douglass, a young man with faith in White's ideas, not only supervised construction of the second section but also remained with the company the rest of his active life.[2]

The project, which consisted of a series of high dams, slack water navigation and a few short canals, was started in 1835 and completed in 1838. Twenty-nine locks, 20 ft. wide by 100 ft. long,

Collection of Harry L. Rinker
Remains of one of the huge lift locks on the upper section of the Lehigh Canal. This section was abandoned over a hundred years ago.

were installed. These locks were the highest built up to that time, one near White Haven having a lift of 30 ft. The canal prism was 40 ft. wide at the bottom and 60 ft. wide at the top, with a depth of 5 ft.

The great flood of June 6, 1862, completely destroyed the canal above Mauch Chunk, as well as doing great damage to that portion extending to Easton. The second section from Mauch Chunk to White Haven was never rebuilt.

In the meantime the third section of about 12 miles, between White Haven and Stoddartsville, was opened to down-stream navigation by clearing out the channel and installing two Bear Trap locks in the vicinity of Stoddartsville. About the only traffic of any consequence on this section was the transportation of logs to White Haven and Mauch Chunk.

MORRIS CANAL

When the fish were not biting for George P. M'Culloch at Lake Hopatcong, his usual fishing spot, he often did a bit of day dreaming on his favorite subject, a canal across northern New Jersey—Why not use the lake as a feeder for a canal extending eastward to Newark and New York Bay and westward to Phillipsburg and the Delaware River? That was in 1820. The idea proved a good one; but, it was not until December 29, 1824, that the New Jersey legislature chartered the Morris Canal and Banking Co.[3] On October 15, 1825, construction of the canal began with ground breaking ceremonies at the summit.

The canal had potential as a successful venture; it connected with the rich anthracite coal area up the Lehigh River; it traversed a rich farming area requiring fertilizer and transportation for the farm products; and the numerous iron furnaces in the area would soon require anthracite to replace charcoal made from the wood of the rapidly depleting forests. These factors were compelling incentives; but, serious obstacles were encountered. The mountainous terrain over which the canal was projected presented many engineering problems and, in later years, association with its banking interests proved a white elephant.

In the spring of 1832 the canal was opened for navigation from Phillipsburg to Newark. Five years later the Morris Canal was extended to Jersey City. The air line distance from Phillipsburg to Jersey City is 60 miles but the course laid out for the canal involved a distance of 106.7 miles. From Phillipsburg to Lake Hopatcong the canal climbed 758 feet and from that point to tidewater at Jersey

City it made a descent of 913 feet. To overcome these great changes in elevation a combination of locks and inclined planes was used; there being 7 locks and 11 planes between the Delaware River and Lake Hopatcong and 12 planes and 16 locks between Lake Hopatcong and tidewater at Jersey City. Plane No. 9 west, near Lopatcong, with a lift of 100 feet, was the highest on the canal.

This combination of locks and planes made the Morris Canal unique in canal construction of that era. The planes were designed by Prof. James Renwick of Columbia University who was retained as consultant to the Morris Canal and Banking Company. In principle the planes consisted of inclined railways for transporting the boats, supported on cradles, over elevations much higher than practical for locks. Power for hauling the cradle up the inclined plane was supplied by a water turbine and drum which activated the pulling chain, later replaced by a steel cable. The turbine was housed in a building near the summit of the plane, with a flume connected with the higher canal level to supply water to the turbine. After the water passed through the turbine, it was discharged into a tailrace to supply water to the lower canal level.

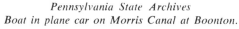

Pennsylvania State Archives
Boat in plane car on Morris Canal at Boonton.

The original locks measured 9 ft. x 75 ft. with the canal prism being 32 ft. x 20 ft. x 4 ft. As was true with most canals of that era, the original dimensions were too small to accommodate the boats bringing coal from the Lehigh Canal, with consequent delays due to transferring the coal at Phillipsburg. An expansion program begun in 1844 resulted in a final prism of 40 ft. x 25 ft. x 5 ft. and locks 11 ft. wide by 95 ft. long, with the capacity of the planes increased correspondingly.

"Flickers", or "stiffs", with a capacity of about 20 tons, were the first boats used on the canal. When the enlargement program was completed in 1851, the "hinge-boats" of the Lehigh Canal, with a capacity of about 100 tons, could be used on the Morris Canal; in fact the hinge-boats were designed primarily for use on the inclined planes. On the Morris they were frequently called "squeezers" or "lemon squeezers". Packets were used for a short time on the Morris, principally for carrying passengers between Newark and Paterson.

In 1871, the canal was leased by the Lehigh Valley Railroad; and, its decline began. In 1922 the canal was transferred to the State of New Jersey. On March 12, 1924, an act of the Legislature provided for draining the canal, thus ending canalling in northern New Jersey.

DELAWARE AND RARITAN CANAL

When improved transportation facilities across the "waist" of New Jersey was under consideration, there developed heated competition between advocates of a canal and advocates of a railroad. To settle the argument the Legislature on February 4, 1830, granted simultaneous charters to the Camden and Amboy Rail Road and Transportation Company and to the Delaware and Raritan Canal and Banking Company.[3] To further cement (or confuse) the under-takings the Legislature on February 15, 1831, adopted the "Marriage Act" by which the "Joint Companies" was organized under which each company retained its own organization but all revenues and expenditures were combined.

The canal company appointed Canvass White as chief engineer. Construction began in November 1830. By May 1834 through navigation was established. The canal extends from Bordentown on Delaware Bay, through Trenton, which was the summit, to New Brunswick at tide water on the Raritan river, a distance of 43 miles. Water for the canal was supplied by a feeder extending from above Lumberville dam, along the east side of the Delaware River to Trenton, a distance of 22 miles.

New Jersey State Archives
Canal basin and lock at Bordentown, entrance to Delaware and Raritan Canal.

The relatively flat country through which the canal ran required a minimum of locks. From Bordentown to Trenton, a distance of approximately 6 miles, there was a rise in elevation of about 57 feet, necessitating the installation of 7 locks—From Trenton to New Brunswick, a distance of 37 miles, a corresponding drop also required the installation of 7 locks.

Recognizing the potential importance of this canal as a coastwise connection between New York and Delaware bays, the canal was made larger than most canals of that period, with a prism of 75 ft. x 60 ft. x 8 ft. and locks 22 ft. wide by 110 ft. long. The feeder prism was 60 ft. x 50 ft. x 6 ft., with one lock of 10 ft. drop at Lambertville.

The size of the canal channel permitted the passage of sloops under tow; and, by 1850 propeller driven vessels made their appearance. Operation of the latter created a wash which deteriorated the canal banks. To overcome this problem the banks were "rip-rapped" to a depth of about 3½ ft. below the water line. During this improvement the locks were lengthened to 220 ft., the width remaining 24 ft. After the introduction of propeller driven boats, the use of mules gradually declined until it was a common sight to see strings of canalboats being towed by steam tugs. In spite of the number of sloops and other coastal vessels seen on the canal, including the passage of gun boats during the Civil War, the bulk of the tonnage was coal in boats from the Pennsylvania canals.

With a railroad paralleling the canal, there was little need for packets, although several were in service for a time. Their passengers usually took the ride to enjoy the scenery and the novelty of a canal ride and passage through its locks.

In June 1871 the Pennsylvania Railroad leased the properties of the Joint Companies for 999 years. Later, in 1876, the Reading Railroad established its own line across New Jersey. As this was a major coal carrying line, the business of the canal dropped rapidly. The canal was returned to state control in 1934 after which it was no longer important for the transportation of goods.

DELAWARE AND HUDSON CANAL

Maurice and William Wurts explored and developed the anthracite coal area near Carbondale, Pennsylvania. In 1822 they rafted the first coal to Philadelphia but found the market already being supplied from the Lehigh area. So they turned their attention to New York City.

In 1823 Benjamin Wright, of Erie Canal fame, made a survey from the Hudson River to the vicinity of the mines at Carbondale. This survey was the basis for organizing the Delaware and Hudson Canal Company[4] in March 1825. Mayor Phillip Hone of New York City was elected the first president. On July 13, 1825, a ceremony inaugurating the start of the canal was held at Summitville, about midway between Ellenville and Wurtsboro.

The canal was considered functional April 1, 1828, although very little traffic occurred that year. The canal extended from Eddyville on the Rondout at tidewater (near Kingston), through the Rondout and Neversink valleys to Port Jervis. From there the canal paralleled the Delaware River to the Lackawaxen River which it followed to Honesdale, the western terminus of the canal. The canal covered a distance of 108 miles, of which 25 miles were in Pennsylvania.

The original canal prism was 32 ft. by 20 ft. by 4 ft. deep. The locks, of which there were 108, with an average lift of 10 ft., were originally 9½ ft. wide by 75 ft. long to accommodate boats of 20 tons capacity. These small boats were called "flickers". By 1842 enlargement of the canal began and continued in various stages until a depth of 6 ft. was attained, and locks increased to 15 ft. wide by

90 ft. long, permitting the passage of boats of 130 tons capacity. Packet boats appeared on the canal soon after it was opened; but, by 1850 this traffic had disappeared.

A pioneer development occurred on the canal when John A. Roebling constructed steel cable suspended aqueducts across the Lackawaxen and Delaware rivers. These were completed in 1848. The Delaware aqueduct, somewhat modified, is still in use as a highway toll bridge.

Eight hundred D & H boats were operating on the canal in 1890; but, by 1898 only 387 were still in use. On November 5, 1898, Boat No. 1107 pulled out of Honesdale with the last load of coal. Various sections of the canal continued in use for several years thereafter.

TRENTON DELAWARE FALLS COMPANY

A short, artificial waterway that should be included in this category of Delaware Valley canals is the Trenton Delaware Falls Company,[5] authorized by act of the New Jersey legislature, February 16, 1831, with authority to build a waterway from above Scudder's Falls to Trenton, a distance of 7 miles. The fall of 18½ ft. in the waterway provided an estimated capacity of 530 H.P. of hydraulic power to certain industries in Trenton.

For many years the stock of the Trenton Delaware Falls Company was owned by Cooper, Hewitt & Co.; and, the power was used by their plants. After Cooper, Hewitt disposed of their plants, about 1908, the power company was sold to other parties and gradually was abandoned. The portion through the city of Trenton was filled in; and, it is doubtful if any evidence of the canal now exists.

Courtesy, Grant G. Emery
"Little Freddy" at Delaware River aqueduct.

Collection of James Lee
Bow of canalboat showing towing posts, nighthawker, bilge pump and, on the lock wall, a dog-house.

Collection of Henry S. Engart
An empty boat leaving Guard Lock No. 24 at Easton.

Chapter 9
Life and Times Along The Canal

Accident—We learn that on Wednesday last, as the boat Commerce, belonging to the Union Line Transportation Company, was about passing under the Yardleyville bridge, the wind and strong current in the Delaware drew her against the pier, which she struck with such force as materially to damage her. She was laden with wheat and buckwheat flour, whiskey, nails, wire &c. . . .

The Whig, Easton, Pa., March 4, 1840

LIFE AND TIMES ALONG THE CANAL

Old boatmen living in the Delaware and Lehigh valleys have their nostalgic memories of life on the canals. With a little encouragement, they may be induced to recount their recollections of the good old days when a team of mules pulled their coal laden boats at a speed of two miles an hour down the waterways to the metropolitan markets. Yet, these memories do not adequately portray the primitive scenes and experiences encountered by the boatmen of the mid and latter nineteenth century—that era when the canals were teeming with boat traffic. With one exception, the recollections of the boatmen interviewed extended back only to the beginning of the twentieth century. By that time, the tonnage carried on the Delaware Canal had dwindled to less than twenty percent of its peak years; and, the number of boats in service had correspondingly declined.

Following the turn of the century, the roar of steam trains, which had long since become a familiar sound to residents of the valleys, increased in even greater volume; the clang of trolley cars crescendoed and then decreased to a murmur; and, increasingly, the sounds of automobiles and even the whir of airplanes were proclaiming a new and faster era; all of which sounded the death knell of mule drawn canalboats.

At the time the Delaware Canal was started, the countryside through which it was dug had not changed much from colonial times. The existing villages were scattered and sparsely settled; in fact, construction of the canal began at tidewater in a little community of less than a thousand inhabitants, progressed along the river through a heavily wooded region with but few inhabitants, and terminated at the junction of the Delaware and Lehigh rivers opposite a village of some four thousand people. The canal trade was a boon to the previously settled communities, while others sprang up during the

construction and subsequent operation of this waterway. Of the
latter, only a few have survived the abandonment of the canal traffic.
Such place names as Uhlersville, Limeport, Lumberton, Hard Times,
Monroe, Lehnenburg, Coffeetown and Stuckertown now remain only
in the memories of the older inhabitants.

Even when the canal was operating at full capacity, the countryside presented much of its primitive, colonial appearance. For the
small boy of eight or ten years, who guided his mules down the
towpath, the days could be pleasant and friendly. But when night
closed over the thickly tree lined banks of the canal, he, no doubt,
longed for the comfort and warmth of his boat's cabin. As he plodded
along, sometimes in rain or sleet, through the shadowy light of his
boat's night-hawker, his lonely monotony broken only by the flicker
of a candle in some remote dwelling, the splash of a shad in the
river or the brief excitement of passing an upbound boat, it is no
wonder that he snuggled against the side of his mule for warmth and
companionship. It is this memory that lingers in the minds of old
boatmen as nostalgic affection for these friendly animals.

Regrettably, no historic novelists of the caliber of Walter D.
Edmonds and Samuel Hopkins Adams have appeared to popularize

Collection of Ted Sherman
Two drivers and their mules. Ted Sherman (left) and Frank Walls.

the folklore of the Pennsylvania canals. Aside from an excellent chapter in *Pennsylvania Songs and Legends,* edited by George Korson, and occasional articles in historical magazines and the publications of historical societies, most of this folklore is unpublished or is forgotten. A recent novel by Thomas Fall[1] gives a somewhat sketchy picture of early life on the Delaware and Hudson Canal.

The boatmen who plied the waters of the Lehigh and Delaware canals were equally at home on the Morris and Delaware and Raritan canals. It is, therefore, not surprising that their recollections and personal experiences may involve all of these canals.

One of the early recollections of life on the Lehigh and Delaware canals was recorded by W. H. Gausler.[2] "I commenced to drive a horse," he said, "on the towpath of the Lehigh Canal in 1840 for board and clóthing, and by 1856, when the Lehigh Valley Railroad was built, I was proprietor and owner of a line of twelve transportation boats plying between Philadelphia and Wilkes-Barre." [From White Haven to Wilkes-Barre transportation was via the Lehigh and Susquehanna Railroad.]

"I was first employed as driver by John Backman of Freemansburg, Pennsylvania. Mr. Backman was the owner of two canal boats, or scows, built in double sections, with a capacity of about sixty tons, used to freight coal from Mauch Chunk to Bristol and Philadelphia via the Lehigh and Delaware canals. I drove the horse of the boat "Bear" that brought the first load of iron ore from South Easton to Catasauqua, Pa. for the Crane Iron Furnace Company in September, 1840.

"About 1850 the Hockendauqua Iron Furnace was built at Schwartz's Dam above Catasauqua. I freighted pig iron from Catasauqua and Hockendauqua to Philadelphia for $1.46½ per ton up to December 1852.

"Our expenses for one boat for one trip from Mauch Chunk to Philadelphia and return were $3.00 for provisions and horse feed. Bacon (or fletch) cost 4¢ per pound; shoulder 4¢; ham 6½¢; butter 12¢; coffee 12½¢; brown sugar 4¢; potatoes from 2 to 3 shillings per basket; oats from 2 to 3 shillings per bushel; hay and stabling over night, 1 shilling; and other provisions and feed in proportion.

"Up to 1843 the boats ran Sundays, the canal being the only means of bringing freight to Philadelphia . . . Nearly all boatmen kept going day and night, boats being so numerous that the canal seemed to be a solid mass of boats. The salary of a boat captain was from $14 to $20 per month; bowsman from $8 to $14 per month, and drivers $5 per month. The boatmen often encountered dangers from high winds at Easton dam at the weigh-lock, the Chain dam and Lehigh Gap."

Mrs. Martha Best remembers what the winds were like along the canal. "I had an experience one time at Lehigh gap," she said, "when it was windy. He [her husband] was driving. I said I would steer. When we came out of the lock, the wind caught and turned the boat right around. I crawled on my hands and knees up to the hinge to loosen the line. Then I crawled back and put the line on the stern. So he took me backwards up the bank till we got up above the Lehigh Railroad bridge. Then I crawled again—it was dark, five o'clock in the morning, and it was bitter cold. So I crawled and took the line up again and fastened it to the bow and he turned me around. Then we were all right again to go."

Joseph A. Lum, who in 1883 at the age of seven, started driving mules on the Morris Canal for a boat captained by his father, has only hazy recollections of that period. "I was very young when we were on the Morris Canal and do not recall much about it. One thing I do remember. From Newark to Jersey City the canal ran through the meadows and the mosquitoes nearly ate us up. One man asked if I knew why they bit me. I said, 'no I don't know.' He said, 'You're from Pennsylvania and they don't like any one from Pennsylvania.' "

"One thing," Lum said, "you were never bothered with insomnia. You arose about 3:30 A.M. and you wouldn't retire until 11:00 P.M. I recall one time on the Raritan, in the early morning I fell asleep and walked off the towpath in the canal. After I did this twice my dad said if I couldn't keep awake driving, I had better get on the boat and steer. I never could figure it out—if I couldn't stay awake on the towpath, how was I going to keep awake on the boat. I must have, for I know I didn't fall overboard."

A TYPICAL DAY ON THE CANAL

The working day was long and hard on the Delaware Canal— from 4 A.M. until 10 P.M. On some other canals, notably the Erie Canal in New York State, where traffic continued throughout the 24 hours, the work might seem harder; but there, the boats were large enough to carry an extra team and driver. A change was made every 6 hours. On the Delaware there was but one team and one driver for the long 18 hour day.

The boatman's day, however, began well before 4 A.M. His mules had to be cleaned, harnessed and on the towpath ready to moved by that time. Most of the stables on the Delaware Canal were located along the berm bank, with a bridge in the vicinity over which the mules crossed.

Grant Emery, whose father and two grandfathers were boatmen before him, lived as a boy near Uhlertown. It was in this vicinity that many of the boatmen of that period lived. "I was about 10 or 11 when I went along with my father as a regular hand," he said. "I was the mule driver." Before that he frequently went along just for the ride. "I used to go with my granddad Gray. He boated coal to the Union Paper Mill. Big Mag ran the store at the River House— Mag Featherston. She knew all the boatmen. I would go up to the store and buy penny candy."

If their boat passed a lock before tying up for the night, they might start early enough in the morning to be at the next lock by opening time. "When the alarm went off, possibly 2:30 or 3 o'clock, all depending on where we were located, dad would drop out of his bunk—the captain always slept in the top bunk, the driver in the lower one—and light the lantern to go to the stable. I would put the feed baskets over my shoulder and carry the curry comb and brush. When we arrived at the stable, dad would hang the lantern on a spike; there was always some place to hang it on. I would set the baskets. We'd only give the mules a light feed while we were brushing them down and cleaning them off and putting the harness on—probably a couple quarts of oats and a half measure of corn, usually cracked. By the time the harness was on, the grain was all eaten up. We'd lead the mules out of the stable, snap on the middle traces, putting them together as the mules were hooked up for the towpath."

Not all boatmen fed their mules before starting in the morning. When they were put in the stable at night, they were given a good supply of hay. "We gave them what we called a cut feed meal and long hay," Joe Lum recalled. "They got four meals a day. We started out first and the mules didn't get anything to eat until we had gone about an hour—about 5 o'clock. Then we hung the feed baskets on."

Upon going to the stable in the morning, Joe Reed brushed and harnessed his mules but delayed feeding them. "They weren't fed before we started out," he said. "When they needed it, we would hang the baskets on the mules. We would figure to stop for the night at a lock where there was a stable, where the mules were given hay. If we didn't make it, we would just let them stand along the towpath, where they wouldn't get in any trouble or get hurt."

Most boatmen were particular about thoroughly brushing their mules in the morning. This may have been due to the fact that most mules, after their harness was removed, liked to roll. "My husband would never bring his mules out in the morning unless they were well brushed," Martha Best said. "At night, after he took the harness off, he would let them roll in the sand."

After Grant Emery and his mules arrived on the towpath he was ready to hook on the towline and begin the day's journey. "Dad would throw off the mooring lines and throw out the towline. There was a knack to throwing the line from the boat across the canal to the towpath. You'd make about 18 inch curles of enough line to reach across the canal. Then you'd take half in each hand, swing it over your head like a cowboy would a lariat, then give a heave. A good boatman would make it every time. I would hook the towline on the club stretcher and we would be on our way.

"If the next lock was not too far away, we would wait to start breakfast until we were going through the lock. In the meantime, dad would get the coffee pot on, get fresh water from the barrel in the pot, run back and straighten the boat out—she would run herself for a length or two before you would have to run to the tiller again. As a rule we had bacon and eggs or ham and eggs, with bread and butter. After dad ate, he would get off, usually at the next lock,

Courtesy, William A. Barnhill
Taking on fuel enroute.

and drive while I had my breakfast. Sunday morning the usual was mackerel, home fried potatoes and rye bread—about as regular as Sunday morning came along. We didn't have to hurry and both could sit down to eat.

"Then we'd go along till, maybe, ten or eleven o'clock,when we started to think about dinner. It was most always cured meat. Seldom did we have time to do fresh meat. Probably a piece of ham, or a piece of bacon or salt pork. A lot of boatmen used plain salt pork. We had all the cured meat that we raised at home. We'd take out of the smoke-house bacon, shoulder, ham, whatever. We didn't know about cereals in those days. If we used milk it was condensed milk. We'd put the pot on, peel a few potatoes, cut a head of cabbage in four pieces and, if a pan of beans had been soaking, we would put them in. We might just make a stew; some potatoes and some carrots we brought from home or got at the store, or the lock keeper might have a little garden. He might have some string beans setting there on the bench he'd sell you for a dime. Or, we might buy a dozen ears of corn from him.

"Then we'd switch around, we never stopped. Whoever cooked dinner would eat and then get on the towpath. A lot of times dad would say, 'I think the mules will be all right alone; I don't think we are going to meet any boats,' and we would let them go alone. Then we could both eat. Our mules would never bushwack—they'd always stay away from the bushes. Some mules, if you didn't walk along side of them would always be biting at the bushes, with the towline flopping in the water. That didn't go good.

"If we ate alone, whoever ate last would clean up and wash the dishes. We had a dishpan with a long bail, to dip water out of the canal, that we put on the stove. When hot, we would take it back on the cabin slide and wash the dishes while steering. Always doing two or three things at the same time.

"Probably about five or six o'clock we would think about supper, all depending where we were. My mother would have a lot of baked goods ready when we passed by. We were very fond of her white crumb cake. Dad would say, 'What will we have for supper, Grant?' Well, let's settle for coffeebruckle. That would be coffee and crumb cake. If we didn't have special food from home, our supper would probably be warmed up leftovers from dinner."

As ten o'clock approached the captain began to think about tying up for the night. While there were mule stables at most locks, others were located at intermediate points such the *Cake and*

Beer House and the *Milk House*. Most captains preferred to stop where a stable was available to provide shelter for his mules and hay for fodder during the night. He disliked reaching a lock just at closing time. That meant delay in getting started in the morning, especially if several boats were tied up ahead of his. Should he clear a lock an hour or so before closing time he might tie up as soon as he passed through the lock. Then he would start early enough the following morning to arrive at the next lock by four A.M., the time at which it opened. As his experience accumulated, a captain gauged his starting and stopping time to make the maximum use of the hours available for navigation. That was about the routine most boatmen followed.

A boatman's wife, who was not part of the regular crew, often made several trips during the summer. This was a boon to the boatmen as they were relieved of the cooking chore. Since Joe Lum's father had only one arm, most the cooking as well as many other jobs fell to his lot. "My mother went along four or five times a season," Joe said. "She did the cooking and steered the boat so that I could eat in peace. Sometimes my sisters would go along; and, they would be

Collection of James Lee
A captain and his family guides a coal loaded boat down the Delaware Canal.

the cooks. One or more of the boys around our home at Glendon sometimes went along just for the ride. They would drive the mules and steer the boat. Of course, they didn't know anything about cooking, so I would have to do that."

Mrs. Best, who regularly boated with her husband, often had her family aboard. "I had seven children on the boat," she said. "They slept on the two bunks, on a straw tick I put on the floor, and on deck. We managed. They never slept in the stable." Afternoons when the children were in the towpath. Mrs. Best would "make sandwiches and roll them in paper and throw them out on the towpath for the kids. They would sit on the mules and eat them."

Preparing meals was merely an incidental in the daily activities of a boatman and his driver. Contributing most to his day's work was the long haul from Mauch Chunk to Bristol, and often to Philadelphia or New York. Before the destruction of the upper section of the Lehigh Canal between Mauch Chunk and White Haven, by the great flood of 1862, many boats went up to the latter port to take on coal from the upper coal fields. This added 26 miles to the total distance as well as passage through the 29 huge locks on that section some of which were 30 feet high. Available records contribute little to the life of the boatmen on that portion of the canal during its period of operation.

The cargo of most descending boats was coal, loaded in the vicinity of Mauch Chunk. Then began the 106 mile journey to Bristol, including passage through 71 locks enroute. If the boatman maintained a regular schedule throughout the boating season, his driver and mules walked the incredible distance of about 3000 miles during that period.

The recollections of old boatmen vary considerably regarding the time necessary to pass through a lock. Most of their recollections vary from ten minutes to half an hour. Within the period of their experience, traffic on the canal was much less congested than during the nineteenth century, and they probably gave little thought to the passage of time. Richard DeWalt, who operated Lock 38 on the Lehigh Canal, recollects the time to be about ten minutes while Ted Sherman, who was lock keeper for a time at Allentown, gives it as five to ten minutes.

Arlington Greenzweig was one boatman who had definite recollections about the time required to go through a lock. "We had a good team," he said. "When we got to the nigger head to snub the boat, they would slack off and we would unhook the line. Then you would run down along the lock and run it underneath the lock bridge and pull the line through so it wouldn't get snagged. I would then pull two wickets on the lower gates; that would help the lock tender pull the drop gate up. As soon as the gate was up you would pull all the other wickets on the lower gates. Those mules, as soon as I unhooked the line, would go down and stop and wait for me to bring down the line. I would open one of the lower gates. That would save the lock tender time. It didn't take long to go through a lock, maybe three or four minutes. Because we helped, you see. If you didn't help, the lock tender would have to open one gate then go across the lock bridge and open the other."

Following inspection of the completed lower section of the Lehigh Canal, it was reported to the Canal Commissioners that, "Notwithstanding the size of the locks (25 feet by 100), everything being new, and the lock keepers inexperienced, the average time of passing the locks was about five minutes."[3] During a later inspection of Lock No. 29 near White Haven, which was 100 feet by 20 feet, with a lift of 23 feet, the inspectors reported to the Canal Commissioners, "the time occupied in passing this lock, both filling and emptying, being two and a-half minutes."[4]

Further evidence suggests that not much over five minutes could have been consumed in passing boats through the locks during the years of heavy traffic. In a letter, dated August 2, 1849, to the Canal Commissioners, Erskine Hazard complained, "They only pass at the weigh lock here [Easton] from 65 to 70 loaded boats in a day. They say they cannot pass more on to the next lock below. If they do not pass more than that number per day, I do not know when they are to get them all away from here. I suppose there are over 100 boats here at the present and from 60 to 70 arrive per day."[5] A corresponding number of light boats must have passed up the canal; thus 140 boats passed a given lock each 18 hours. At an average of eight boats per hour, each boat could consume only 7.5 minutes in passing through the lock. And 1849 was considerably below the peak period for the canal.

From a group of 116 regulations established by the Canal Commissioners[6] in 1833 for the operation of the Pennsylvania Canal, only a few simple rules of the road were in effect on the Delaware Canal during its later years. Among these, the passing rule was standard procedure. When boats were passing in opposite directions, the light boat, or the one on the towpath side, had right of way. The loaded boat steered to the berm side, its mules stopped on the land side of the towpath, allowing the towline to sink to the bottom of the canal. The approaching mules and boat passed over the towline, after which the loaded boat proceeded on its way. To guard against fouling the towline being passed over, the Act of 19 March, 1830, Sec. 3 was passed. "Every boat to have a guard plate or iron attached to her keel, and extending under the rudder in such manner as to cover the opening between the stern-post and rudder, to prevent the line of any other boat from entering the said opening, or be liable to a penalty of twenty dollars, and all damages occasioned by the want thereof."

Overtaking and passing a boat going in the same direction was quite another matter. An old regulation of 1826 specified that "slow boats shall turn out and give the towpath side to boats going faster, the same way, and, if necessary, stop till they pass" or be liable to a penalty of twenty dollars. But this regulation was as frequently breached as it was obeyed. It might depend upon the mood of the lead captain that particular day or his reputation as a fighter. His reluctance to allow the other boat to pass might precipitate a fight later on when the two captains met at a lock or in a pub. If a lock was being approached, the lead boat might hold its position until it passed the lock and thus gain time on the other boat beyond the lock. In general, however, the lead captain would steer to the berm side, drop his line and allow the other boat to pass. "If a man had

Collection of James Lee
Two boats passing.

a better team than me," Joe Reed said, "I would just let him pass. Maybe he would tie up early, then I would pass him. I never was cruel to my animals just to hold my position." Mrs. Mann recalled that, "If a man was beating us and wanted to get past, we would drop our line and let him go. Often we didn't like it but we would let him pass."

In the days of heavy traffic there were "locking distance" markers at each approach to a lock. The first boat within the locking distance was supposed to have right-of-way through the lock. But which boat went first depended mainly on the judgment of the lock tender. "If he had the lock set for the boat coming up," Grant Emery said, "he probably wouldn't close the gates and fill the lock to let the boat above through the lock, regardless of locking distance. Of course, there were quite a few fights over locking distance." Here the lock tender might find himself in the midst of the brawl. One way to cool off the contestants was to throw them in the water. "I remember one day," Flora Henry said, "my dad grabbed both the driver and captain and threw them in the canal. My dog, Buster, got one of the captains by the seat of the pants and really tore his pants off. He got his wife to steer while he went in the cabin to get on another pair of pants — just by acting fresh."

The "pull-out side" rule applied to all of the locks on the Lehigh Canal and the double locks on the Delaware Canal. Of two boats entering a lock, the one that snubbed on the berm side had right-of-way upon leaving the lock. "If we were approaching a lock," Grant Emery said, "and the boat following me had more mule power and wanted to pass, I might snub on the towpath side of the lock and give him the pull-out side. If I didn't want him to pass me on that level, I would take the berm, or pull-out side, and he couldn't go out ahead of me. Quite a few fights occurred over this rule. I saw what happened on one occasion. The captain on the towpath side tried to pull out first. The other captain came up with a good sharp axe and went boom on his towline. Then there was a free-for-all around there. The two drivers also got into it; and, there was a real brawl. But there weren't too many of these. I guess sometime ago there was more of it when a tougher gang ran on the canals than in later years. Most of the people I knew were nice family people. They had homes and little pieces of ground down in the Bucks County area. There were the Menninghoffs, the Millers, the Breiners, Smiths, Wells, Grays and, of course, the Emerys."

I asked Grant if there was a passing rule at the aqueducts. On the Delaware Canal an aqueduct trunk was only 20 feet wide, which did not allow two boats to pass through at the same time. "In general, the light boat would hold up. To stop the loaded boat, the captain would have to put a line out and snub. I never recall any fights over this."

The captain of a boat approaching a lock gave a blast on his horn to let the lock tender know he wanted to enter. During daylight hours the tender at most locks could observe the approach of boats and would call that the gates were open, or that the captain should hold up; but after dark the horn was a necessity. These instruments were of various kinds, including tin horns, both straight and curved, bugles and conch shells. The latter was probably the most popular with the boatmen. With it an expert captain could produce a tremendous blast. A family named Keener was celebrated for the dulcet tones they produced on the bugle. "When that instrument echoed through the river valley," one old boatman said, "people along the shore would say 'Keener's coming.' "

After dark the lock keeper would signal by waving a lantern that the gates were open. In the wicket house at the head of double locks, a small window equipped with a ruby glass faced upstream. A lamp placed at the window produced a red glow which warned the boatman that the gate was closed. Removing the lamp was the signal that the gate was open.

By the turn of the century, ferrying boats from Easton to the Morris Canal had practically ceased. The railroads had long since drained off coal shipments which had previously transferred to the Morris Canal from Easton and what traffic remained was mainly iron ore from New Jersey for the iron furnaces along the Lehigh and Delaware canals. This traffic continued until those furnaces were abandoned. Joseph Lum, who boated on the Morris Canal until 1887, said he had seen a few boats ferried across but had never made the crossing himself. The 1903 flood destroyed the Easton outlet lock, ending transportation between Pennsylvania canals and the Morris Canal.

The erection and operation of a hydroelectric plant, about 1902, adjacent to Ground Hog lock, produced conditions in the six mile level from there to Easton, not encountered in other portions of the canal. The volume of water taken from the canal to operate the plant caused a swift current in that level which frequently created problems for the boatmen. A loaded boat sometimes acquired a speed greater than that of the mules so that they had to be prodded to keep the towline taut. Snubbing posts were installed along the towpath above the lock, to which lines could be attached to reduce the speed of the boat as it approached the lock.

This strong current presented hazards to boatmen delivering coal to the papermill just above Ground Hog lock. "Pete Notzer and I used to take a lot of coal to the papermill," Ted Sherman recalled. "Pete would never stay on the boat to snub. I'd always have to take care of that. You'd have to start snubbing way up the canal." A feeder around Ground Hog lock, between the lock and the present road, which existed until after the papermill was destroyed by fire, also added to the problem of landing boats at the papermill.

Even with light, or partly loaded boats, the captains found navigation difficult through this six mile stretch of canal. Joe Reed remembered one night when he arrived at Ground Hog lock at about 10 o'clock. "The guy at the power house was sitting out front. 'Hello, Joe, going to tie up here tonight'? I said if you shut down a little bit with the water, I'm going on up to South Easton. He did, he gave me a good break. Sometimes when they drew that water fast, it was hard going."

That reminded Ted Sherman that turnbuckles were often used on a light hinge boat to aid in towing and steering. "The bow and stern were built higher than the rest of the boat, which added weight to the ends. If your boat was empty, you might draw two or three more inches at the bow and stern than you did in the middle. You might say, there was a hump there. We would attach turnbuckles to the cleats on each half at the hinge and draw them up to give an even keel. That made towing and steering a lot easier."

The strong current in the six mile level, nearly produced a tragedy one time at the overflow just north of Raubsville to which Clinton Kreitz was a witness. The mules of a loaded boat decided to stop for a drink when they arrived at the overflow. As frequently happened, the driver was riding on the boat at the time. "There was considerable current due to the power house," Kreitz said, "and the boat kept going. The men kept hollering but couldn't get the mules going, and before they could get the line unhooked the boat pulled the mules into the canal. They could swim, of course, but they were pretty well mixed up with the harness. They had a Newfoundland dog on that boat. You ought to picture that. The dog made a leap overboard and got the lead mule by the bridle and took them to the shore."

As the boats proceeded down the canal, some delivered coal to the Durham furnaces while others might have consignments for coal yards between Durham and New Hope. Coal boats for New York crossed the Delaware River by cable ferry from New Hope to the feeder of the Delaware and Raritan Canal.

A popular stopping place for boats with cargoes for Bristol and beyond was the *Cake And Beer House,*[7] located about one and a half miles north of Centre Bridge, opposite Hendrick Island. A bridge, formerly spanning the canal at that point, has been replaced by a culvert and fill. This marks the northern limit of the mule drawn pleasure boats from New Hope. "We stopped there quite often on the way down," Grant Emery said. "We tied up on the berm bank and took our mules over the bridge to the stable owned by the old fellow at the house. He didn't serve beer in my time, but prior to that time it picked up its name from earlier boatmen. We would leave early enough in the morning to get to New Hope by 4 o'clock when the locks would be open. In that way we would get into Bristol that day in time to catch the tow, if we were going on to Philadelphia."

During his years on the canal Joseph Lum made the crossing at New Hope many times. "We would leave Coalport, above Mauch Chunk, at noon on Friday," he said, "and arrive at New York the following Thursday afternoon—almost a week. It would be about a day shorter coming back. A loaded boat, as a rule, could go two miles an hour and a light boat four miles an hour. We were paid on a tonnage rate of 70¢ per ton to New York, and we hauled 100 tons, about $70 for almost two weeks' work. We averaged about twelve trips a year. The Coal Company deducted 10% of your pay which would be held until about January, when you would be paid what was due you. This, they called back pay. That came in very handy for the boatmen to live on during the winter.

"While we crossed the river at the outlet lock, the driver had to take the mules back to the New Hope-Lambertville bridge. That was quit a distance, about a mile, I guess, and the same distance on the other side, down to where we crossed by cable. The driver usually rode one of the mules during that trip. If we were going to New York, we left our mules when we got to New Brunswick. They had stables there where they took care of your mules until you got back. I think the rate at that time was a dollar a head; and, they fed and cleaned them. That would be three or, at the most, four days; one day going from New Brunswick to New York, one day coming back and one day to unload, if there was no delay.

"During our trips through the Delaware and Raritan Canal," Lum said, "we saw boats of all kinds—canalboats, power driven barges and big ships that had to be towed, either by tugs or mules." Prior to that time, the banks of the canal had been rip-rapped to prevent damage by the wash of power driven boats. "The locks were real big," Lum said. "You could put four Lehigh boats in one lock. Two barges

Courtesy, Robert J. McClellan
*Crossing the Delaware River by cable ferry from the Delaware Canal to the
feeder of the Delaware and Raritan Canal.*

would go through at one time, one would tow the other. The locks
had miter gates that were opened and closed by steam engines. They
were so big I don't believe a man could push them." At New Brunswick, the boats were collected in tows and drawn by tugboats through
the Raritan River and New York Bay.

After Joe Lum's boat arrived at its destination in New York, it
was unloaded by two men supplied by the purchaser of the coal.
The coal was shoveled into a large bucket, lowered and raised by
a derrick on the wharf. The captain was required to "hold guide,"
the line that swung the bucket from the wharf to the boat and
guided it into the hold. "It was right on the bill of lading—Captain
to hold guide," Lum said. "I remember one time it wasn't on there
and the captain refused to hold guide. But that didn't happen often.
Unloading took about eight or nine hours. A hundred tons was a lot
to handle by hand. It was a lot different at the chutes at Mauch
Chunk. Our boat could be loaded in about half an hour."

"Once we had a consignment of coal for delivery all the way
up the river to Hudson, New York," Joe remembers. "You should

Pennsylvania State Archives
A miscellaneous tow of boats on the Hudson River near West Point being
towed by a steam tug, out of sight at the left.

have seen that tow we were in. There were boats of all sizes and descriptions. The tow was pulled by a sidewheel, steam boat."

Continuing on their way down the canal from New Hope, some of the boats might deliver coal to Yardley or Morrisville, while the remainder would proceed to Bristol or to Delaware River ports.

Another place where boatmen frequently stopped was the *Milk House,* located about a mile north of Lock No. 7 at the foot of the 9 mile level. The farmer who lived there dispensed excellent fresh milk as well as other farm produce to the boatmen and the name, *Milk House,* became well known on the canal. During hot summer weather many boatmen stopped there for the night and made an early morning start to get through the 11 mile level to Bristol before the day became too hot.

Before reaching the last three locks on the canal two unusual road bridges were encountered, one on each side of Grundy mill. These swing, or bump bridges, as the boatmen called them, were located above Lock No. 3 in the 2 mile level. An old boatman explained that, "there was a high control section with iron rods extending up from the ends of the bridge to carry the weight. A heavy, spring supported plank about 8 feet long, was attached to each side of the bridge. An approaching boat bumped into the plank, causing the bridge to swing open. After the boat passed, the bridge would swing back into place."

Just above Lock No. 1 the canal made a sharp, right angle turn to the left. Ted Sherman recalled that, "at the turn there was a big snubbing post. When you got there, the driver would stop the team

Courtesy, Naomi Tomlinson
One of two bump bridges on the Delaware Canal at Bristol.

Smithsonian Institution
A collection of canalboats waiting outside the tide lock at Bristol to be towed down the Delaware River by the steam tug in the background.

and would take up the slack in the towline until the boat was even with the post. Then he would gradually snub the boat and that would pull it around. The curve was that sharp, it was impossible to steer around. That snubbing didn't stop the boat at all—it just turned it, and it would continue on into Lock No. 1."

Some other boatmen used other means for getting around this sharp curve. Arlington Greenzweig was one of these. "We shortened our towline," he said. "We adjusted the line to pull us around. You'd put your line on the bow cleat and the mules would pull it around. Below the lock we didn't use mules. If there was the least bit of current, the boat would float down or the men would use the towline to pull it."

Since the mules were no longer needed after passing the snubbing post, or lock, they were taken to local stables to await return of the light boats. "We always stabled at No. 2 Lock—with Larry Mutz," Grant Emery said. "He would pick up our mules when we were snubbing around for No. 1 Lock, and bring them back to us when we came up. He would have the mules cleaned nicely and the harness and brass in good shape." Most captains had their favorite stable keepers. Arlington Greenzweig recalled a big, long barn above the lock. "You would put your mules in there where there was good food for them; and, he would take care of them until you returned. When we came back, we took our mules down and connected on as we came in from the river. There was a bridge at Lock 1 that we crossed to a towpath along the west side of the basin down to the tide lock."

The basin was a convenient place for the boats to tie-up to await the arrival of the up-river tow. Since anchors were not a part of a boats's regular equipment, a number of them were always available at the toll house adjacent to the tide lock for the use of boat captains who might need them on the down river trip. Boats with cargoes consigned along the Jersey shore or to ports not accessible to the entire tow would drop off and anchor in the river to await the return of the tug. Upon its return the tug would tow the individual boats to their destination.

When the time approached for the up-bound tow, the toll keeper would direct the boats in the basin to clear through the tide lock and assemble in the river above the basin entrance to permit free access for the returning boats to the basin. Here, there seems to be a difference in the recollections of boat captains. Some maintained that the loaded boats remained in the basin until the light boats returned and were safely in the basin. At high tide, which was the time the up-bound tow arrived at Bristol, the river level was usually the same as that in the basin, permitting free passage without locking through.

After the tug captain released his up-bound tow, to be poled or pulled by hand through the slip and tide lock into a basin (there were usually loiterers along the slip to lend a helping hand to lines thrown from the boats), he would check with the other captains as to their destinations. "I remember Big Jim; never did know his last name," Grant Emery said. "He was captain of the tug, *Wm. S. Cramp*. That was a big propeller driven boat, carrying an engineer, fireman and cook. As a kid I often went down the river with my dad. Sometimes I would go hand over hand along the big towing hawser to the tug. How Big Jim would bawl me out if he caught me doing it. But once aboard, he never said much. I know I never left without a good meal. That cook served excellent food; and, it's a funny thing. His name was Hungry.

"Big Jim, who knew about everybody on the canal, would come along with a little notebook to find out where the boats were going. Perhaps a number were consigned to the Glass House. That was the office of the Lehigh Coal and Navigation Company at Philadelphia, with W. R. Bernard in charge. A lot of coal was delivered there. Other boats were going to League Island or Cramp Ship Yard. Some would be going to the Schuylkill or Camden, Cooper Creek or maybe, Gloucester City. Four of five might be going to a certain ship where they would be unloaded. Sometimes we took a load of lump coal up to the iron foundry at Florence, New Jersey. Big Jim would have to run us up there, first. He didn't like that much as it was kinda out of his way. Of course, when we were unloaded, we had to wait until he came up to get us."

THE CANAL MULE

The mule is an asexual animal which for generations, in fact, for centuries, has been of inestimable service in lightening the burdens of man. It is long-lived, almost immune from disease, sure-footed and has great powers of endurance. In spite of its docile demeanor, the mule can, upon provocation, lash out its hind legs with devastating results and display other "mulish" characteristics. As the chief motive power on the canals of America, the mule established an enduring reputation. Horses were used to some extent on the canals, mainly because they walked faster, but they could not otherwise match the endurance of the mule. On the Delaware Canal the mule was the main source of motive power.

Boat operators were required to supply their own mules and harness which were purchased chiefly from the Coal Company at its stables and equipment stores located at Weissport. Not only were prices lower there than elsewhere; but, the Company also offered liberal terms of payment, deducted from the men's pay.

Periodically the Coal Company received a herd of young mules from Kentucky or Missouri. "The Kentucky mules were better, or fancier, looking," Grant Emery said, "but they didn't seem to do as well, didn't seem to hold up as well. I know my people were always Missouri mule men. The first time I went up to buy a mule I was rather young, but dad said it would be good experience and if I didn't get what I wanted it would be my own fault. I looked the herd over for one with good legs, strong shoulders and broad hips. When I saw the one I liked the man brought him over to the bench where you would try to make up to him a little.

"These were all young mules that had never been broken, no shoes on him, or anything. All he previously had on was a halter. Some of them were pretty wild, some pretty good. After the mule was broken to the harness, the next thing was to have him shod. Then they would take a branding iron and put a number on one front hoof, burn it in pretty hard, up about two to three inches above the shoe. That number would be recorded as your property. Each trip when you came back and drew your pay a certain amount would be taken out to go towards the mule.

"Most boatmen liked to have good harness, then there were others who were careless and shiftless, like some people with automobiles. Our bridles had a brass rosette and a brass band across the headstall, a brass ornament below each ear and buttons on the backstrap. The bridle had a bit and short reins. The reins were never used; they were just part of the bridle. The rein was just an endless strap from one side of the bit up over the mane to the other side of the bit. When we fed the mules, before the basket was put on, we unstrapped one side of the bit, took it out and let it hang down while the mule was eating.

"The collar had wooden hames strapped to each side that the traces were attached to. Then there was the leather "housel" with two holes in it for the ends of the hames to pass through, that covered the top of the collar to keep rain off the mule's shoulders. Some men used canvas but we always used leather. The mules' shoulders were always a vital part that couldn't be neglected.

"Most mules carried bells. We tried to get bells that would make a musical tone. We usually used four bells, two on each mule. From the bottom of the collar a strap about 1½ inches wide went between the front legs to the bellyband. The bells were attached to this strap, below the collar.

"When two mules were used in a team, they were called the lead mule and the shafter. The lead mule's traces were hooked to a wooden spreader with hooks at each end. The back of each hook consisted of a ring that the middle traces, coming up from the shaft mule, snapped into. Then there was a carrying strap on the shaft mule that hung from his hame ring. The middle trace ran through this so that when the lead mule stopped, the middle trace would not drop down. At the back of the shafter mule was the club stretcher with odd shaped hooks at each end. The middle traces as well as the shafter mule's traces snapped into these hooks. I always called them the crooked hooks. The traces would never come out if the mules ran away. The middle of the club stretcher had a hook to which the towline was attached." If more than two mules were used in a team, the additional animals, each with its own middle traces and spreader, were inserted between the lead and shafter mules.

Collection of James Lee
Canal mules and their harness.

Another type of hook-up, called a pulley hitch, was sometimes used on the Delaware Canal. In place of the middle traces, a line extended back from the mid point of the lead mule's spreader, through a pulley and up to the shafter mule's club stretcher. The towline was attached to the pulley. A problem of this hitch which many boatmen disliked was the fact that if the shafter mule tended to lag, a disproportionate amount of load was placed on the lead mule. To correct this situation, a strap from the shafter mule's bit was attached to the harness of the lead mule. It was this pulling on the mule's mouth that the considerate boatmen objected to.

Other items of the mule's equipment were a fly net for use in the summer, a waterproof blanket to cover his back and shoulders in stormy weather and a straw hat. In the broad brim of the latter were two holes through which the mule's ears passed. A band tied under the chin held the hat in place. Whether these hats served any useful purpose may be questioned, but they did lend a picturesque appearance to the mules as they trod along the towpath. To use a Pennsylvania Dutch expression, they, together with the bells, were probably "yust for nice."

Most boatmen were considerate of their animals. But a few were as careless and as thoughtless of their mules as they were of their equipment. Inspectors periodically patrolled the towpath to check the condition of the mules. "You didn't dare to be mean to your animals on the Delaware," Joe Reed said. "Boy, they'd arrest you right away. They had a woman down there, she'd make you stop the mules and lift the collar; and, if there was a sore on his shoulder, you had to take that mule out, you couldn't use him. They'd slap a fine on you. She was all through the Delaware. You never knew when you'd run into her." Grant Emery recalled that this SPCA representative was Eva Huston.

After a long day of work on the canal, most mules, as soon as their harness was removed, liked to lie down and roll. They would twist their necks and flex their legs and this exercise seemed to revive them. "Sometimes I would clear the lock at the head of the 11 mile level about 10 at night," Joe Reed recalls. "I wanted to get down near Bristol before tying up. So I'd take the harness off, let the mules roll and give them a good meal—they were ready to go the extra 11 miles. A mule is a tough animal. I never used horses. Some of them did, but horses didn't last." Occasionally a boatman was unfortunate in getting what was commonly called a "roller." This type of animal would roll at the slightest opportunity, even in harness, and that made a pretty mess of things. The only choice was to get rid of the beast.

The inherent intelligence, or instinct, of mules was always a source of interest and amazement to boatmen. The faculty of well trained mules to plod, unattended, along the towpath for hours was often taken advantage of by the drivers. They could board the boat for a little rest or for a leisurely meal with the captain. Near the end of canal operations, this faculty of mules to go unattended was of inestimable value to boat captains who found it impossible to hire drivers.

Alvin Harlow observed this dilemma during a trip up the Delaware near the end of the canal era. "'We pass a boat going southward with only one man aboard, and he necessarily at the tiller. The two gray mules are taking their own sweet time, perfectly well aware that the captain's occasional threatening yells do about as much harm to them as the small lumps of coal which he throws now and then and which miss their targets more often than they hit.

" 'I see Whitman's lost his crew,' remarks the captain. 'Mighty hard to keep men nowadays, workin' these long hours, even if they git more money.' "[8]

Joe Reed used a different method of prodding his unattended mules. Even though Joe put muzzles on his mules, they would sometimes nearly stop to try and nibble grass. "I had a BB gun that I would shoot at their rump. It would sting a little and they would start up with a jump. One time on the 7 mile level I tried this. There was a little extra slack in the line. When they tore into it, the line broke. I didn't catch them until I chased them down to the New Hope lock."

Sometimes the captain of a one-man outfit would become discouraged with his lot and just take off leaving his mules and boat along the towpath. Mark Wismer, who was bank boss between Freemansburg and Ground Hog lock, would occasionally find an abandoned boat and team. He would pilot the boat upstream to the next bank boss who, in turn, would pilot it to the succeeding one, and so on until the boat was delivered to the Company's headquarters at Weissport.

Mrs. Mann thought a mule was more intelligent than a horse. "When we were using a mixed team we would never let the horse lead. The horse would walk off in the water and a mule wouldn't. Places where it was hard to pull, like some of the curves, the horse would keep right on going off the towpath but a mule would pull the other way and keep on the path, at least that's the way we found them. And a mule hardly ever stepped on your foot, but a horse would. We never could figure out why."

Mules had their own ideas about drinking. Joe Lum said his mules usually stopped for a drink while crossing an overflow. "If I wouldn't give my mules a drink at a certain place where they wanted water," Joe Reed said, "and you went past there — you might have gone half a mile — they'd walk out in the canal and drink." The mules used to pull the pleasure boats out of New Hope never eat or drink on the towpath, Pete Pascuzzo says. But when their harness is removed after they return to the stable, they have a good roll and are then ready for water and food.

Joe Reed said that his mules, similar to most other mules, liked to eat tobacco. "I chewed a little and if I left the pack sticking out of my back pocket, when I went by a mule he would pull it out of my pocket. I often gave them some. It was good for them."

The intelligence of mules was always a source of interest to Josiah White. Upon completion of the gravity railroad at Mauch Chunk, "waggons" were constructed to carry the mules down with the loaded train so they would be available at the end of the run to pull the empty cars back to the mine. White thought an episode in connection with these waggons of sufficient interest to be recorded in the annual report of the Lehigh Coal and Navigation Company. "So strong was their attachment to riding down, that in one instance, when they were sent up with the coal waggons, without their mule waggons, the hands could not drive them down, and were under the necessity of drawing up their waggons for the animals to ride in."[9]

LAYING UP FOR THE WINTER

As the late November days became shorter and shorter and early morning frost appeared more frequently on the deck of his craft, the boat captain began to think about laying up for the winter. Over the long history of the canal there were many seasons when navigation continued into the first and, occasionally, into the second week of December. But there also were years when a hard freeze closed the canal earlier than anticipated. The cautious captain dreaded having his boat caught in an early freeze-up, which meant it had to remain there over the winter, with possible serious damage to the boat.

Latter day boatmen recall the freeze of 1897 which trapped four coal loaded boats in the 9 mile level. "My dad was involved in that," Grant Emery said. "I think two of the boats had tied up at the *Milk House* and the others at Yardley. At first it was decided to leave them there all winter. But then it was felt that these loaded boats would probably be ruined when the water was drained off. So they decided to take them through. I think there were about forty mules involved, and I don't know how many men. It was a couple of weeks before they got through to Bristol. The channel would be opened up for the day and that night it would freeze over again. The ice breakers would be drawn through with fifteen to twenty mules. I remember my dad saying when they got down to the Bristol 2 mile level, the water was very quiet there; they had to saw the channel and drag out the ice cakes. At different times they had to re-iceboard the boats. By iceboarding I mean they would place oak boards around the front of the boat so the ice wouldn't cut through the main siding on the hull. After the boats got in the basin at Bristol, there was no problem in towing them to Philadelphia, where they were unloaded."

Ice formation before the canal officially was closed for the season was a recurring problem that confronted the canal superintendent as well as the individual boatmen. An illustration is a letter addressed to the foreman of the second section, extending between Durham Creek and Erwinna.

New Hope Dec 6th 1842

Thos Gearhart Esqr

Dear Sir

I will come down the line on Monday morning next from Easton. I want to meet you at the upper end of your section you having your check rolls and bills all ready for payment you will make no effort after passing the Ats that left Durham this morning, to keep the navigation open as the ice is entirely to thick and makes to fast to keep it open

Respectfully yours

John Matthews

Sup

I asked Mrs. Mann if her boat ever got stuck in the ice on the Morris Canal. "No, we were never stuck in the ice," she said. "But once mother got stuck the time I was born. My father was trying to get the boat back to Phillipsburg but I arrived too soon and was born in the cabin of our boat. Lots of children were born that way. Mrs. Summers had five girls born on the canal."

By Thanksgiving most of the boatmen living in the Uhlertown area would have tied up their boats along the berm bank near their homes. "We had a small section like a wharf, near our house, where we tied up," Grant Emery said. "We took off practically everything to store on shore. The halters, feed baskets, curry combs and brushes and extra lines we took to the stable. Such things as the blankets, bed ticks, dishes and utensils we took in the house.

Collection of Henry S. Engart
The bank boss drives along the towpath

"One day the bank boss would come down along the line. He usually travelled the towpath with his horse and wagon. He would call along, 'The water is going to be drawn on such and such day. Get your boats out.' He would go all through his section; and, the bank boss of the next section would do likewise. 'Get your boats out' meant, get them out in the middle of the canal. We'd shove the boat over to the towpath side. Then, with some old towline we'd run a line from the bow and stern to a tree or a stake along the towpath. There was enough slack in the lines so the boat would be in the middle of the stream when we pushed it out. We'd have to use the walking plank to get up on the boat again, then put it down on the berm side to get off. With lines to the berm side, we'd have the boat anchored in the center of the canal.

"As the water was drawn off the boat settled to the bottom in the center of the canal. There was always some water left in the canal, not enough to float the boat but enough for good skating. We would then remove the lines from the towpath side, take off any loose materials such as poles and tiller, see that the windows and hatches were closed tight so the snow wouldn't get in, put a pin in the hasp of the feed chest lid so it wouldn't blow open, and then let the boat lay until spring."

The laying-up procedure was the same, whether the boat was privately owned or leased from the Coal Company. Company boats that needed major repairs might be taken to the boatyard at Weissport, where the work would be done during the winter. Otherwise, valuable time would be lost in the spring, or a substitute boat would be used while the repairs were being made.

Occasionally a boatman would live on his boat all winter, usually from necessity. "One time during the depression it was pretty bad," Joe Reed recalled. "So I said to the super, do you care if I live on the boat this winter? 'Sure,' he said, 'I'll send a couple of carpenters down and we'll raise the hatches and put windows in for you, put a floor in for you, whatever you want.' And he did that and we lived on the boat all winter. There was a door from the cabin into the hold where the coal was carried, I call it the stern section, and we had all that for living quarters."

Courtesy, Ernest "Nitro" Schultz
Boats tied in center of channel awaiting removal of water at end of navigation season.

FITTING OUT IN THE SPRING

The approach of Spring was always a welcome time for the boat-men. Their leisurely work around their little farms or small homes was hardly compensation for their busy boating season. Some of the men found work on the canal with the maintenance crews, some did road work or odd jobs while others just sat.

Charley Solomon recalled that one winter he helped rebuild the aqueduct over Durham Creek. During winter evenings Joe Burns, who tended the Durham lock, often entertained the aqueduct work-men with his tall stories. "We had a man, one of the carpenters," Solomon said, "who would sit there and take down all of old Burns' stories. One night Joe was telling how long he had worked here and how long he worked there. The guy said, 'By gosh, Joe, you must be a pretty old man.' 'Oh, I don't know.' 'Well,' he says, 'I've been figuring it up here — you must be well over a hundred years old!'"

By the middle of March the boatmen were beginning to get their equipment in order. "One of my first jobs," Grant Emery said, "was to go up in the woods and pull off some white oak bark and bring down a big basket full. We had a big iron kettle we used for butcher-ing and making soap in, as people did back on the farm. We would fill the kettle about half full of water, put the bark in and cook it over an open fire until it was a strong brown tea. Dad had an oak keg he kept it in. Twice a day — sometimes oftener — we would bathe the mules' shoulders with this tea. We did that for two or three weeks before we pulled out with the boat; bathe those shoulders to harden them up. That was one thing my father was very particular about — having the mules fit when it was time to go to work.

"The harness had to be scrubbed and rubbed with neat's-foot oil; the brass had to be polished; and, of course, the mules had to be shod. The mules would go in the blacksmith shop before we pulled out in the spring and all new shoes put on. If you boated all summer, you would have to get at least two additional sets of shoes. The toe calks were welded on by the blacksmith, and the ends of the shoe were bent over and sharpened for the back calks. Then the clip that came up over the front of the hoof was part of the toe, done by the blacksmith. There were four nails on each side of the shoe, driven up through the hoof, clinched over and rasped off."

It was Joe Lum's recollection that his mules wore out about six pairs of shoes in a season. "If a shoe got loose, you would just have to stop and get it fixed. You didn't dare to run without a shoe on because it would be no time before he wore his hoof off. The next

Courtesy, Horace Sigafoos
Fred Ziegler's blacksmith shop at Erwinna.

Pennsylvania Canal Society
Grant Emery with conch shell a popular instrument for signalling lock keepers.

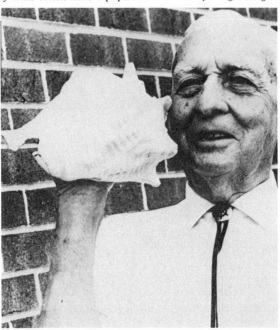

blacksmith shop we came to we would get it fixed. There were quite a few blacksmiths those days — some at the locks or in the towns. About all towns had blacksmiths. They were very common in those days."

As the boating season approached, the bank boss would come along the towpath to announce, "The water is coming in this week and will be here on the 6th," or whatever day. "It was quite a day when the water arrived," Grant Emery remembers. "Everybody would be out looking." Here comes the water! Here comes the water! echoed along the valley. For a day or two the water held at the half way point, then gradually increased to its normal level.

"The lines on our boat would slacken up as the water raised and it could be pulled to the shore and tied up properly," Grant said. "Then, of course, we would start to get things in shape. The inside of the cabin would probably be painted and new oilcloth put on the cabin steps and cabin floor, and mother would make new curtains for the stern windows of the cabin. We would usually make new bed ticks, just wide enough so they could be raised up with the bunks when they were hooked up out of the way. I remember quite well, we always kept a certain amount of rye straw. It had to be flailed out instead of run through the threshing machine, to keep it long, keep it from being tangled up. The bed ticks would be filled with this bright, clean straw, sewed up and put on the boat. Then all the gear had to be put aboard, the lines, the boat poles which had been freshly painted, and all the equipment for the cabin.

"Our boat was leased from the Coal Company so we never did any painting on the outside of the hull. The Company didn't permit any other painting; they were just plain old red skins. Some of the boatmen down in our area owned their own boats. They would probably touch up around the waling, maybe go over the white. Usually the waling planks were green or blue, outside the Company boats, they were all that barn red. They'd paint their dashers and the oats box and the water barrel. The hoops would be painted black and the wood part would be white or blue or green to match the color scheme of the boat."

Boatmen liked to start out in the spring with fresh lines. But that would wait until they got up to the Company store at Mauch Chunk or at Weissport. "They had them big coils up there," Joe Reed said, "and you got just what you ordered, usually 100 or 125 feet for the towline which was ¾ inch in diameter. The snubbing lines were a lot larger. They went from one and a half to two inches. The 1½ was the back-up and the snubbing line was the 2 inch." The life of

Collection of Henry S. Engart
Leedom's coal yard at Bristol, using mechanical unloader.

Collection of Harry L. Rinker
Coal chutes on the Lehigh Canal near Mauch Chunk.

the towline depended a lot upon how it was used. "When you started up, if you let your mules jerk too much, it wouldn't last long," Martha Best said. "I know I would go to the leader and talk to him so he wouldn't jerk into the line too quick."

"It was a big day when you started out with the boat in the spring, with everything fresh and clean and nice," Grant Emery remembers. "The wives would probably go down and give the cabin a final touch up and hope it would remain that way until they joined the crew for a few trips during the summer. Not all the boats started at the same time. Somebody might still have a bit of fence to repair or some other job he hadn't taken care of during the winter. Of course, our first stop was the weigh lock at Mauch Chunk to get our light weight, to be deducted when we came back with a load of coal. In the spring there was usually, quite a collection of boats at Chunk and we had to wait our turn at the chutes.

"A number of the boatmen from our section had regular customers they delivered coal to. My grandad boated to A. T. Perkins at Beverly, New Jersey. The Smith boys ran coal to Leedom at Bristol and Billy Wildes and Billy Smith boated coal to Meliner's at Burlington."

In the early days of canal operation, coal chutes were constructed at various points in the vicinity of Mauch Chunk. Upon completion of the second section of the Lehigh Canal from Mauch Chunk to White Haven, many boats continued up to the latter port to load coal brought by railroad from the coal fields in the vicinity of Wilkes-Barre. After destruction of this second section by the great flood of 1862, the chutes were concentrated at Coalport, frequently called Catfish Pond by the boatmen, about two miles above Mauch Chunk.

The regular spring freshets and periodic floods carried culm and other refuse from the coal mines into the Lehigh River, filling up back of the dams and making navigation difficult to maintain. By 1923 this problem became so bad that facilities were constructed at Siegfried [Laury's Station], about seven miles north of Allentown, for trnsfer of coal from railroad cars to the canal boats.[11] After that time coal shipments from Mauch Chunk ceased.

POTPOURRI OF CANAL LORE

Before clearing the weigh lock at Mauch Chunk, the captain of a loaded boat could draw $10.00 to pay his expenses during the trip down the canals. Upon returning, he could obtain the same amount from the toll office at Bristol. These advances were called "expense money." When the empty boat returned to Mauch Chunk this expense money, together with the 10% "back pay" and any other indebtedness, was deducted from the pay the captain received for the previous load hauled.

A captain's payment was determined by the rate per ton of coal transported. This rate, which depended upon the destination of the cargo, varied from year to year. As the national prosperity improved the Coal Company found it necessary to increase its rates in order to attract a supply of boatmen. In the 1890's the rate from Mauch Chunk to New York City was 70¢ per ton. One boatman said that in the early 1900's he received 42¢ per ton for hauling coal from Mauch Chunk to Bristol. By 1920 this rate had increased to 90¢ per ton.

After Grant Emery had boated with his father for some time, the latter was stricken by serious illness; and, Grant, at the age of sixteen, found himself captain of his own boat. "I remember the first time I came back to the weigh lock and drew my freight," he said, "I was scared to death when I went in and got paid. I didn't know what to do with all the money. At that time the Company paid in gold. I remember as well as it were yesterday. I got two $20 gold pieces, one $10 gold piece, a $5 gold piece, a couple of $1 bills and some change. That was more money than I ever handled at once. There were a lot of boatmen around, a lot of rough necks, a lot you knew and a lot you didn't know. Finally, when I pulled out of the weigh lock, I went down in the cabin; I dumped the sugar out of the sugar bowl into a pan, put the gold in the bottom of the bowl and put the sugar back in again. I left it there until I got back down home. I was scared to death with all that money."

*   *   *   *   *

George Amey of Walnutport, Pennsylvania, captained a boat for the Michael Uhler Line until 1913, after which he started railroading. "Canals are nicer living than railroading," he said. "On the canal you had your meals pretty regular. Sometimes you didn't have anything to eat for 16 hours on the railroad. When I boated for Uhler, I carried everything in back loads, freight, grain, soft coal. I brought soft coal from near Bristol to the Paper Mill at New Hope or sometimes further up the canal. Uhler furnished everything. I only paid and fed the driver. I paid for hay and shoeing and turned it in on an expense account. During the summer I had a stove at the hinge. If it rained I had a big Bush and Bull umbrella over the stove. At Frenchtown there was a big ice house where I used to put a couple of weeks in during the winter. The Delaware was the nicest canal. There weren't so many locks and it was much better boating than up here."

Many boatmen expressed a preference for the Delaware Canal. Topography was, undoubtedly, one reason for this preference. On the Lehigh Canal, between Mauch Chunk and Easton, the locks averaged one every 0.96 mile while on the Delaware they averaged one every 2.6 miles, with numerous levels up to 11 miles long. Then too, the Delaware retained its rural atmosphere throughout its active life with very few industries along its banks. The Lehigh, very early, developed an industrial complex along most of its length, particularly after the iron industry began to expand. Railroads also were installed on both banks of the river from Mauch Chunk to Easton.

As Joe Reed expressed it, "There were long levels on the Delaware where you could let your mules go alone. On the Lehigh the levels were too short and there were too many railroads. If you had a young team, when those engines blew, they would scare the mules. I always liked it when I got on the Delaware. It was easier on that canal. Some places where the road ran close to the canal, there would be people travelling from different states. They would stop their cars and call, 'Hey! who's the boss of this rig? Boy, that's something we'd like to see.' If you want to see it, drive down to the next lock and I'll show it to you. I'd take them aboard and show them everything. Sometimes they'd give me a $10 bill and a good tip to the boy. I thought the people were much nicer on the Delaware."

"But that was only from Easton down," Martha Best said. "From Easton up they thought we were trash. They would stone you and everything; they were real nasty up that way. Up here in Bethlehem, at the lock, I never will forget that. At the bridge I was steering the boat and my husband was down eating lunch. I called to him, 'come up here.' Two big fellows jumped from the bridge on the boat, stark naked — no clothes on at all! My husband said, 'get off!' One fellow said, 'We don't have to get off.' 'You're going to get off,' he said, and threw them overboard. Well, they went up to the lock; and, there they were with stones and stuff. They would have stoned us but my husband was smart, he got his gun out.

"One time right over at the silk mill some swimmers crawled on the rudder. I said, 'don't you have any sense, I've got small children on,' but they acted awful smart, they were students. One climbed up on the rudder. He wanted to reach in the window. My husband had his tobacco hanging there, Dukes Mixture that time. I said to him he should get off and he called me a name. Well, I took the deck poker and hit him right on the head. He fell down into the water and I guess he would have drowned if the other fellows hadn't got him out.

"The worst thing I ever did was in Allentown. You came down around the islands but going up you went along the towpath. It was hard to steer because the water wasn't deep. So there were these two in a canoe who grabbed on my rudder. I said, 'please get off it's hard for me to steer.' They acted awful smart so I said if you don't get off you'll be sorry. You know what I did? I went down and got the chamber potty and threw the whole darned thing on them. You ought to see them dive for water. They took the boat number and from that time on we had no more trouble."

"Most of my trouble was with swimmers," Joe Reed said. "But I would let them get on and dive off and they never bothered me much. Down at Glendon it was bad, maybe there would be 80 to 100 swimmers. They would climb on and it would put you right down on the bottom and you would stop. Well, I would set on the cabin slide and watch them a while, maybe lose 10 to 15 minutes. Then I'd say, 'Come on, boys, you have enjoyed yourselves. Now I want to go.' That way you don't have any trouble."

Sometimes there were characters on the boats who challenged the devilment in small boys. Among these were Rube and Liz Reinhart from up the Lehigh. "Liz was a big, heavy woman," Clinton Kreitz recalled, "who could cuss a blue streak. They called her the Queen of the Canal. Sometimes when she was going through Ground Hog lock I have seen the kids throw pebbles at her and she would cuss the daylights out of them."

*　*　*　*　*

One old boatman remembered an episode at the Catasauqua bridge. Boys used to hang around the bridges and pester the boatmen as they went under. This day there were a number of swimmers on the bridge. "I was at the hinges cooking ham and eggs for my breakfast," he said. "As I went under the bridge one of the boys urinated right down in my drying pan. I was so damned mad I jumped overboard, clothes and all. You know, if it hadn't been for the railroaders I believe those swimmers would have killed me. The next time I come along there one of the railroaders said he could tell me who the boys were if I wanted to do anything about it. But I told him to forget it."

Canal bridges, while sometimes a convenience, were generally considered a nuisance by the boatmen. They were a convenience when the driver, or a captain, wished to board the boat. It was a simple matter to drop on to the boat as it passed under the bridge.

One could also get off that way, particularly if the boat was running light. An alternative in getting on and off was to use the long pole and vault to the towpath or return. This method, however, had its drawback, as Ted Sherman observed. "I saw a fellow vault one time and the pole stuck and left him up in the air. He had to slide down into the water."

A loaded boat had no difficulty passing under the bridges; but, for a light boat the clearance was too tight for comfort. It was always necessary for anyone on deck to crouch while the boat passed under the bridge. At night the driver often called, "Bridge," or "Low Bridge," to warn the steersman. Grant Emery said, "Coming up light you couldn't use a nighthawker, it wouldn't clear under the bridges. You just put a lantern at the bow. It didn't give enough light to steer by. We were guided by the trees that came up from the banks. Sometimes when the levels were high, there was so little clearance under the bridges they might knock the stovepipe off your stove at the hinge. That's why we had a little chain on ours so it wouldn't fall overboard. Sometimes it was even necessary to take out the tiller." Then there were the mischievous youngsters who liked to kick dirt on the boat, particularly if cooking was in progress. The wise captain used covers on his utensils. Even a crossing wagon shook dust and dirt on the boat.

Courtesy, Robert Harmon
A loaded boat has passed a camel back bridge near Bristol.

*   *   *   *   *

Available records give no clear evidence that packet boats ever ran throughout the length of the Delaware Canal. There are, however, indications of wishful thinking and sporadic attempts to operate packets. In a March 16, 1831, letter to the Board of Canal Commissioners. Simpson Torbert reported, "This portion of the canal is now in navigable order from Bristol to New Hope. A daily line of Packet boats have been established to run upon it and all the boats engaged in the river trade will ascend by way of the canal . . ."[12] That prediction was made three years before the canal was in regular service.

In an undated paper on the "Red Line Transportation Company," read before the Northampton County Historical and Genealogical Society, Charles Stewart digressed to say, "Would remark here that a line of Packet Boats was run successfully between Morrisville and Easton. It carried the mail and passengers — had a bar and served meals — had relays of horses every 15 or 20 miles, first change at Monroe about 12 miles down, next at Lower Blacks Eddy and thus equipped, as few boats at that early day plied the canal, they made good time and enjoyed fine patronage."[13] The last sentence suggests these packets evidently ran during the very early years of the canal.

In lieu of packets, most boatmen can tell of passengers they transported over the canals. Joe Lum recalls that, "we occasionally picked up people. Several we had for three or four days. We never charged them; we even fed them. Then, of course, they helped out. I remember a Greek man and his wife. I think we got them somewhere here in Pennsylvania. They wanted to go to New York. He could talk English but she couldn't say a word. So cooking was out but she washed the dishes. They had a couple of what we used to call carpet bags."

"There were no passenger boats on the Morris Canal," Mrs. Mann remembers, "but we used to take people to Newark and Jersey City. They sat on the deck and at night they usually had something to lay on on the deck. We never let them use the cabin."

While on his way with a load of coal, Joe Reed was asked if he would take on a party at Easton. "The superintendent said, 'we picked you out as the guy for this trip.' 'Well,' I said, 'what is it?' 'You're going to take 6 or 7 lawyers and their wives. They want to go with you from Easton to Bristol.' When I come to Easton, there they were. They had beer and all kinds of eats. I don't know whether it was their own women — I didn't care. I had a good time. They had cots and stuff and slept on the top of the boat. At Black Horse Inn, we stopped there, and that hotel at Upper Black Eddy. We stopped all along the line. They were really out for a good time. They rode the mules and how they drank liquor. At the end of the trip they gave me $400."

*   *   *   *   *

The Lehigh Coal and Navigation Company periodically explored the possibility of replacing the mules. As early as 1893 their annual report records that, "Rapid progress in use of electricity for transportation makes it likely we may be able to substitute it for the slow and costly animal power. Generation would be by our water power."[14] A short rail line was installed along the towpath and an electric mining locomotive was used as the motive power. While no tangible results developed from this experiment, the idea apparently persisted in the minds of the management. A final comment appears in their annual report for 1908. "Study of canal traction by electricity justifies its use if canal traffic increased to 450,000-500,000 tons."[15]

For another experiment, at about 1910, the Coal Company procured two power driven tugs for towing canalboats. These boats were designated No. 1 and No. 2. Charles Solomon served for some time as captain of one tug. "There was just two guys on a boat, one ran the engine and I did the steering. They had a bell system just like

Courtesy, Frank Sigafoos
One of two power driven tugs at Uhlertown, used for a time to tow canalboats.

any big tug. The boat I was on was run by producer gas from buckwheat coal. Did you ever throw coal on a fire and pretty soon see a blue flame? That's what this engine ran by. In the morning you would fill up a big hopper on top like a bell hopper, and clamp the lid down. You would push a handle that dropped coal down on the fire to keep it smothered. Around the top were four or five holes which we got in with a slash bar to stir it up. The engine was practically like a gasoline engine.

"Five or six boats were towed, one right after the other. We would go much faster than mules but at the locks we lost a lot of time. When we got to Ground Hog lock, the tug and one boat would go in together. They would go through and hold up until the lock was filled up again and two more would come through. That way you lost too much time. At the single locks it was even worse. One year they had a big flood that filled up the channel at Allentown dam. I spent one whole season with the tug taking boats up and back of Adams Island to the next lock — take the empties up and if there was any loaded ones there, take them down to the next lock. This kept up until they got the thing dredged out."

Mark Wismer remembers these tugs. One of them, which used a diesel engine made by Ingersol-Rand Co., was run by Russel Miller, he said.

*   *   *   *   *

Living conditions on a canalboat were both congested and most primitive. The canal frequently was used for bathing, the water being much cleaner than at present, or a tin basin might be used on deck with water dipped with a pail from the canal. The bushes along the towpath or a pail in the cabin served as toilet facilities. If a woman was aboard there might be chamber pottery. Come wash day, Martha Best brought her wooden tub and wash board up on deck. "I used to put two poles in the pump holes at both ends of the boat and put my line from them," she said.

"I remember people living along the canal had their tubs in the canal — their wooden tubs so they wouldn't dry out," Mrs. Mann recalls. "Had them tied with ropes. Then they had little platforms where they did their washing in the canal. The Morris Canal water was quite clean. The only place it was really dirty was down around Newark and Jersey City."

Courtesy, Frank Swope
Wash day on a boat.

* * * * *

The sounds of music were not uncommon along the Delaware. Of course, the lusty blasts of the tin horn, the conch shell or the bugle, when the boat captain signalled his approach to a lock, were accepted accessories of canal life. There was also instrumental and vocal music. The principal instruments encountered were the accordion, the harmonica and, occasionally, a violin. Clinton Kreitz, who lived at Raubsville, remembers one boatman named Mineo, who was an excellent yodeler. "You could hear him way up around the curve and the echo from across the river. Boy, it sounded good. Then there were some boatmen who were good accordion players. Those were pleasant sounds, especially at night, as the boats came along the canal."

"When I was real young and mother was along," Mrs. Mann recalls, "they would stop where there were mule stables. Where a place could be cleared, someone would play an accordion, a mouth organ and, sometimes, a violin. Then they had a dance—round dances, waltzes, but mostly polkas. My mother played the accordion and my father the violin."

But the sound most affectionately remembered by the river folk was the tinkle of the mules' bells. Many boatmen were careful to select bells that harmonized or sounded chords. This was fortunate for, in the heyday of boating, these sounds must have been continuous. In New Hope, where the mules of the boats crossing the river at the outlet lock had to come back through town and cross the bridge to Lambertville, the sounds of their bells were augmented by those of the mules along the towpath. Joe Lum remembers that, "In towns like Freemansburg, built along the canal, they would say it was music to them. But the bells were good for other things. In the spring and fall when it got so foggy you couldn't see the towpath, how do you think we steered the boat? By the ringing of the bells that the mules carried. Their sound would tell whether they were going around a bend to the right or to the left." Sometimes the fog became so thick that even the bells didn't help. Traffic would stop until the fog lifted.

*   *   *   *   *

Among the problems that confronted the bank bosses, the men who patrolled the canal to observe conditions and anticipate potential trouble, were the muskrats. These animals frequently burrowed into the bank under the waterline. If the burrow extended far enough under the bank on the towpath side, it might break out near the river and allow the canal water to flow through. Unless this condition was quickly discovered and corrected, a break in the bank and a major repair job would result. The bank boss was constantly on the lookout for small whirlpools on the surface of the water, a sure indication of leakage through the bank. The entrance to the burrow must be quickly located and plugged with straw or other available materials until permanent repairs could be made.

Sometimes the muskrats made their nests under the towpath. If these nests were too close to the surface, passing mules sometimes broke through. "It never happened to our team, but I've seen it happen," Grant Emery said. "Mules have broken their legs on occasion. That's one reason why the Coal Company paid you 15¢ for the end of the tail. I ran across a letter recently that accompanied my check from the Lehigh Coal and Navigation Company. You'd take the tail ends to the Squire and get an affidavit which you sent in and they would send you a check."

*   *   *   *   *

One of the tragic events that harrassed the workmen during construction of the early canals was outbreaks of cholera. The Delaware Canal was not spared the ravages of this highly contagious disease. The complete ignorance of the cause of this malady and the primitive medical knowledge of that time were scant solace to the residents along the canal. Strange nostrums were advocated and circulated by the local press. In its July 9, 1832, issue, under the heading, "The Cholera," the *Bucks County Intelligencer* advised its readers, "The following brief but salutary suggestions, which we find published in the *New York Commercial,* on the responsibilities of a respectable physician, deserve attention:

"Let every person protect his body as far as he is able from chillness, by avoiding the night air, by wearing flannel next the skin, by changing his clothing as often as changes in the temperature or moisture of the atmosphere may require, and by avoiding cold bathing when in a state of perspiration. Let every species of ardent spirits be avoided as poison, and the common beverage of the table be water, weak tea or coffee, bread and water, and milk and water. Avoid all iced and acid drinks, and finally, be sparing of all kinds of liquids, particularly if you feel any symptoms of disease."

*   *   *   *   *

From early colonial times until the late nineteenth century burning, or calcining, limestone was an important industry in the Delaware Valley. The remains of a few limekilns may still be seen along the Delaware Canal while old maps locate many others. South of Easton limekilns were operated near the old Kuebler brewery, at the site of the Easton disposal plant, north of Raubsville, opposite Ground Hog lock, at Durham Furnace, at Uhlertown and at Limeport. Several miles below Easton, on the Jersey side of the Delaware, the remains of limekilns may be seen along the river bank.

Among the uses of calcined limestone were farm fertilizer and masonry cement. Clinton Kreitz recalls that, "Lime water was used for whitewashing barns, chicken houses, fences and other farm structures. Some people put salt in it to hold it on better. My dad used to take a couple of chunks of lime and put them in a quart jar of water. After it dissolved, he would pour the water off and drink it. He drank it many a time."

*   *   *   *   *

One of the early independent operators of canalboats was the "Red Line Transportation Company," of Easton.[16] This company was organized about 1836 with Capt. Jacob Able, president. The Red Line boats, which were from 60 to 85 feet long, carried general merchandise between White Haven and Philadelphia, "and after business had been well established, they ran over the Raritan Canal to Jersey City." Depending on the character of the cargo, the capacity of these boats varied from 60 to 80 tons.

About 26 boats comprised the Red Line fleet, many completely covered with a tight deck and openings along the sides through which cargo was admitted and discharged. All the decked boats were painted red with white trimming at top and bottom of the cabin and the boat's name, several feet long, painted on each side. Among the names of the Red Line boats were:

Thomas Bishop	Gray Eagle	Falcon
Henry Clay	John Hancock	Nicholas Biddle
Commerce	Daniel Webster	Robert Morris
Pennsylvania	Susquehanna	Walk in the Water

General merchandise of all kinds was carried in these boats, including grain, stoves, clothing, plaster of Paris, salt, sugar, molasses, groceries, hardware and other merchandise required by the Delaware and Lehigh valley communities. "Rye and corn whiskey, then manufactured so largely on our numerous streams, furnished much freight" to down stream ports.

During the winter season, and when traffic on the canals was interrupted by breaks in the banks, or other delays, Abraham Bercam kept merchandise moving to and from Philadelphia in his fleet of Conestoga wagons.

*   *   *   *   *

Since canal water was not suitable for cooking and drinking, it was necessary to carry a supply of water aboard the boat. The water barrel, which was standard equipment on all boats, was used for that purpose. But it was not merely a case of filling the barrel. Water stored in this manner can deteriorate. The older boatmen knew the secret of keeping a fresh, usable water supply which, if known, was often not utilized by many boatmen. Joe Reed considered one or two springs along the line satisfactory for his purpose but, as he said, after a number of days the water became stale and the barrel had to be emptied. "There were springs all along the canal," Joe Lum said, "but as a rule you never filled the barrel from these springs. I filled my barrel out of the rivers when I crossed."

Grant Emery was even more specific about his water supply. "Our water came from the Delaware River," he said. "Our barrels were filled, and filled only, down on the change of tide, probably between Beverly and Riverside. We used charred oak whiskey barrels. Spring water, well water, city water of any description would last only three or four days in the barrel and would get spoiled; you couldn't use it and would have to pump it out. Different water had been tried from different places but would not keep. How it happened I don't know but somebody, sometime along the line filled his barrel going down the river one time and found that the longer the water was in the barrel the better it got. You could lay up at Mauch Chunk for six weeks with a barrel of that water and it was better than when it was put in. The only answer anyone has been able to give is there was some chemical reaction. You fill that barrel with water from our well at home and in two or three days you would have to throw it out."

FUN AND RECREATION ON THE CANAL

It all began in 1825 when, on October 26th, Governor Dewitt Clinton boarded the *Seneca Chief* and conducted his flotilla of five boats from Buffalo to New York City in a triumphal and festive celebration of the completion of the Erie Canal. From that time the canals of America excited a peculiar fascination in pleasure seekers, from swimming to fishing to pleasure trips on canalboats. Many prominent writers and publicists were attracted to those canals where packet boats operated, either for transportation or for the novelty of travelling on an inland waterway. Such famous writers as Charles Dickens and Harriet Beecher Stowe have left graphic descriptions of travel on the early canals.

The Delaware, however, was basically a freight hauling canal. With the possible exception of one brief interval, no packets with their colorful array of passengers travelled its waters. But this did not deter its use for pleasure and recreation. Whenever a work scow or other suitable craft could be obtained, a picnic party was organized to enjoy a ride behind the slow plodding mules. Prior to 1900 there is a dearth of published material on the use of the Delaware for pleasure. Subsequent to that time numerous colorful articles are available. In its issue of August 26, 1931, the *Philadelphia Bulletin* gives a graphic description of a trip along the canal.

"Canal boats on the old Delaware Division waterway no longer serve the cargoes of commerce. But they have not passed beyond their days of service altogether.

"Motorists have enjoyed the scenic beauty of the Delaware river valley from the road bordering the canal but they have not appreciated the full charm and picturesqueness unless they have left the car and taken a canal boat.

"The Doylestown Nature Club, founded in 1907, made its first canal boat excursion in 1911 and, with few exceptions, the affair has been repeated yearly ever since. Now, such jaunts have become quite a fad with young and old alike, by clubs and private parties, and last summer eighty groups embarked at New Hope on these journeys.

Courtesy, E. Y. Barnes
A day's picnicking on the canal.

Courtesy, David Ennis
A party of canal explorers.

"Some groups made a day of it taking their lunches with them. But by far the most popular times are nights when the calendar promises a moon. Then the crowd sets sail after dark, perhaps with Japanese lanterns swaying from the sides of the boat and ukeleles and banjos aboard. Such a voyage is romantic whether it is taken by day or night. It is the nearest approach to soundless motion imaginable and a trip through the darkness is one of magic.

"There is only the soft thump of the mules plodding along the towpath, drawing the boat at the rate of two or three miles an hour, and the jingle of bells at their collars. You step into a canal boat and you are stepping back into the past, a hundred years or more, travelling as the forefathers did.

"A mule and a horse supplied the pulling power for one of the boats and both ate tobacco and enjoyed it. The captain said it was good for them in small quantities.

"Trees and plants along the banks are of unusual size and luxuriance. There are fine specimens of sycamores, white and slippery elms, locusts, tulip poplars, sour gums, mulberrys, willows, staghorns and upland sumacs. Great vines festoon their way up the trunks.

"In the spring the columbine and rhododendron add lovely touches of color to the green and all summer the landscape is dotted with brightly colored patches of gardens surrounding the dwellings along the shore. It is twice as glorious an experience in autumn when the trees and shrubs are ablaze with the brilliance of many shades."

The termination of freight service on the Delaware Canal in the fall of 1931 did not end its use for canalboat parties. John Winters realized that this pastime was so well established that, if he could procure boats, the service might be continued. "I leased the barges from the state in 1932," he said. "I had 'em when things were tough and I made a living out of it. We used to have a band and I remember when Burns and Allen and Russ Columbo helped entertain."[17] In 1935 he conducted 114 boat parties, carrying people from New York, Philadelphia, New Hope and from other local communities. These parties ended in 1936, the year the flood seriously damaged the canal.[18]

Now, these nostalgic canal trips in mule drawn boats are again being enjoyed by thousands of visitors to New Hope. Inauguration of this service occurred in the fall of 1954 when the first of a fleet of new pleasure boats was launched. The original launching date, however, was delayed by a breach in the towpath which drained out all of the water in that level of the canal. The *New Hope Gazette* for

Thursday, September 9, 1954, announced that, "The grand launching of the Mary P, Pete Pascuzzo's robin's egg blue canal barge, will take place down at the American Legion lot next Saturday [Sept. 11] at 1:30 p.m."

But the following week, September 16, it was necessary to report, "Last Wednesday night at 5:20 just after *Gazette* went to press with the happy news that Pete Pascuzzo's barge would start running on the 11th, a 30 foot section of the canal above Rabbit Run, undermined by the new Texas Eastern gas pipeline, collapsed with a great rush dumping thousands of gallons of water and untold numbers of fish into the river.

"Latest word is that they've started rebuilding—and that Pete Pascuzzo definitely will launch the barge at 1 p.m. next Saturday."

The good news was announced in the following week's issue of the *Gazette* under the heading "The Great Launching."

"Saturday morning [Sept. 18] there wasn't much water in the canal and it looked as though Pete Pascuzzo wouldn't be able to launch his beautiful pea-green barge, the Mary P, after all. But 'arrangements' were made with the Missouri Valley Dredging Company who are rebuilding the big washout at Rabbit Run and by one o'clock the canal was nearly full and some 100 people had gathered at the American Legion grounds for the ceremony.

The mule drawn pleasure boats of New Hope.

"Among those present were Joe Forsyth president of the DVPA and Clint Oblinger of the Washington Crossing Park Commission (who had worked as hard as anyone around for this big improvement). After Mary Pascuzzo smashed a bottle of champagne (covered with a little sweater knitted especially for the occasion by Marie Slack who didn't want anyone to be cut by flying glass) over the barge's prow, the Mary P was snaked down the bank into the water while everyone cheered. . . .

"Then, with 30 grownups, 26 children and one boxer aboard, the barge was hitched up to the mules, John and Pete, and a brief, trial trip was made up the canal. Lloyd Winters, an old bargeman, was at the steering post, old muleskinner John Winters led the mules, Marston Slack rode on the bow with a 2x4 to keep her from hitting posts and rocks and Pep Evans helped with the muleskinning."

The episode of the canal breach produced an interesting legend purporting to illustrate the intelligence of mules. According to the legend, a boat load of children was being taken up the canal. Upon approaching the section where the breach occurred, the mules stopped and could not be induced to proceed. While they were being urged to continue, the breach occurred, causing a mad rush of water into the closely adjacent river. Had the mules not stopped, the boat would have arrived just as the break occurred. Boat and children would have been swept into the river. Only the intelligence of the mules prevented a major catastrophe. Unfortunately for the legend the break occurred more than a week prior to launching the first of Pete Pascuzzo's boats.

*   *   *   *   *

Probably the most unique pleasure trip ever taken on an old American canal occurred in June 1886, when a party of prominent New Yorkers toured from Bristol to Mauch Chunk and back to Easton in an old gravel scow, properly refurbished for the occasion. The annals of history and the pleasure of canal buffs have been enriched by a daily record of this trip, humorously written and later privately printed by one of the party.

Since boats going to Mauch Chunk were called chunkers, "This one," said the writer, "drawn by Molly and Polly is therefore distinguished above all other Chunkers by being the Molly-Polly-Chunker." The record of this voyage is, therefore, called the "Log of the Good Ship Molly-Polly-Chunker."[19]

The roster of the party, together with their colorful titles, as given by the writer of the Log, includes:

Robert W. de Forest, Lord High Admiral, Commissary General and Commander in Chief. (At the time of the trip, de Forest was general counsel for the Central Railroad of New Jersey. From 1913 until his death in 1931, he was president of the Metropolitan Museum of Art. With his wife, he donated the American Wing to the museum.)

Mrs. Robert de Forest, Royal High Chaperon

Miss de Forest, First Honorable Assistant Chaperon. (Sister of Robert.)

Miss Holt, Second Honorable Assistant Chaperon. (Sister of Henry Holt.)

Miss Louise Knox, "Charge" of the chaperons. (Daughter of James Knox, president of Lafayette College.)

Louis C. Tiffany, Honorary Artist of the Expedition. (Son of the founder of Tiffany and Company; an outstanding artist and inventor of the famous Tiffany stained glass.)

Walter C. Tuckerman, Double-Acting Photographer and Lord of the East Wind.

Henry Holt, Scribe (President of Henry Holt & Co., publishers.)

Albert Boyer, Captain and Sailing Master.

John Cosman, Chief Engineer and Superintendent of Motive Power.

William, Butler

David, Officer de Bouche

The stated purposes of the expedition were:

"The Cultivation of the Beautiful and Moral, and the Extension of Human Knowledge. The methods to be followed are:

"First, last and all the time, with occasional intermissions between midnight and 5 A.M., Photography.

"Second, as far as circumstances permit, Pottering, or Keramics.

"Third, the subordination of luxury to necessity: for instance, the Lord High Admiral, having declared champagne and claret to be necessities, while ginger-ale is a luxury, no ginger-ale is to be drunk while champagne and claret can be had. The moral culture of the company is to be constantly promoted by similar exercises of self-denial.

"If, after the performance of the principal functions of the expedition, as just enumerated, any moments remain, they may be devoted, under proper restrictions and the supervision of the Chaperons, to having a good time."

The text of the Log identifies 68 photographs, none of which are included in that volume. Fortunately, the photographs have been located. Copies of the Log and photographs are on file at the library of The Bucks County Historical Society. They may also be seen at the library of the Pennsylvania Canal Society.

When the party stopped at Easton for a visit to Lafayette College, the college paper, the *Critic,* carried the following notice:

"The Rubber Granger people and the Tile Club have found disciples and imitators in a party of New Yorkers who are journeying to Mauch Chunk by way of the raging Pennsylvania Canal. They have had a canal-boat roofed over and fitted up with awnings, curtains, etc., in such a way as to rob it of much of its uncouth appearance; and, with a cook and other servants at command, are prepared for any fate that may befal (sic) them. . . . A newspaper paragraph reports that this new thing in canal-boats 'has made a great commotion among the tow-boys, and has frightened more than one veteran mule.' It is 'moored at night-fall in convenient places along the route, and the evenings are spent as pleasantly as possible . . .' "

In an Epi-log dated November 6, 1886, the scribe announced:

"On this auspicious day, all the company of the Molly-Polly-Chunker assisting, the Artist and the Charge were married, 'and lived happily ever after.' "

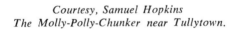

Courtesy, Samuel Hopkins
The Molly-Polly-Chunker near Tullytown.

Some of the M-P-C party, from left, Miss deForest, Louise Knox, Walter Tuckerman, Miss Holt and Robert deForest.

Crew of M-P-C. Butler and chef in cabin, chief engineer on deck and captain at the tiller.

Courtesy, Samuel Hopkins
At Lock No. 4 on Lehigh Canal. Louis Tiffany (right with camera) photo-
graphing the lock tender and his pets.

Courtesy, Samuel Hopkins
The M-P-C draws a group of spectators.

Courtesy, Samuel Hopkins
A scene viewed by the M-P-C crew somewhere between Morrisville and Washington's Crossing.

Courtesy, Samuel Hopkins
The boat building yard at Upper Black Eddy.

Chapter 10

Historic Vignettes of Durham Valley

A (Durham) boat from Easton, containing 400 barrels of whiskey,
equal in weight to 600 barrels of flour, under command of Captain
James Connor, was safely landed at Philadelphia last week. We be-
lieve this is the largest load of whiskey which ever descended the
Delaware from this place.

Easton Centinel, Easton, Pa., March 7, 1828

Throughout the Delaware River valley there exists a great ware-house of historic lore. From the year 1609 when Henry Hudson first saw the river, the Delaware has played a major role in the economic and cultural growth of our country. Overshadowed by the great metro-politan expansion along the lower river, a small mid-river stream and the picturesque valley through which it flows deserves more than a footnote to history.

Here, in northern Bucks County this stream with its numerous tributaries not only provided water to operate one of the first iron furnaces in the American colonies but also an excess of water for use by the Delaware Canal. From its source to Springtown this stream was called Cooks Creek, but from the time of the iron furnaces its lower portion has been called Durham Creek, a name often applied to the whole stream.

With abundant forests to produce charcoal, a liberal supply of limestone throughout the area and huge deposits of iron ore in the hills surrounding the valley, all the ingredients for operating iron furnaces were readily available. Not only did iron production continue here through the first decade of the twentieth century but the Durham furnaces of the 1880's also were rated among the best in the country.

Here, too, the famous Durham boats had their origin, the Durham Cave was a popular attraction for many years and the vicinity of Durham Village proved a popular meeting ground for councils with the Lenni-Lenape Indians. A visitor to the canal will find time spent in exploring Durham Valley a rewarding experience.

DURHAM FURNACES

One of the first iron furnaces in Pennsylvania was located at Durham Village, approximately two miles up Durham Creek from the Delaware River. As early as 1698 iron ore was known to exist in this region on a large tract of land, including all of present Durham township, which William Penn had purchased from the Indians. At his request James Logan, his secretary, contacted various local men who might be interested in developing an iron furnace. The location up Durham Creek was particularly appropriate for such an under-taking due to all necessary ingredients being readily available.

In a paper presented before a meeting of the American Chemical Society, R. D. Billinger recorded that, "In 1726 the Durham Iron Company was organized to erect a blast furnace 'for the manufacture of charcoal pig iron, the casting of pots, pans, bottles, fire-backs and other castings.'

"The partnership agreement between fourteen men in the original association was dated March 4, 1727. . . . The names were those of men prominent in the affairs of the day. Besides Logan, there were William Allen, later chief justice of Pennsylvania and founder of Allentown; George Fitzwater, later a signer of the Declaration of Independence; Clement Plumstead and Charles Read who became mayors of Philadelphia; Anthony Morris (brewer); John Hopkins (mariner); Thomas Lindley (anchor smith); Jeremiah Langhorne (gentleman); Andrew Bradford (colonial printer); Robert Ellis and Joseph Turner. To these were added Gifford Owens and Samuel Powell as trustees."[1]

Collection of author
Remains of the first Durham Furnace, built in 1727.

The original furnace was installed on the side of a hill, as was the custom at that time, so that the iron ore, limestone, charcoal, etc., could be conveyed by wagons and loaded into the top of the furnace. The lower arch of this furnace may still be seen at the site. The products of the furnace were hauled by wagons to the Delaware River where they were transferred to Durham boats for delivery to Philadelphia and other river ports.

During the French and Indian and Revolutionary wars much solid shot and balls was supplied to the Colonial and Continental troops. It is sometimes erroneously stated that one of the great chains that were installed across the Hudson River near West Point during the Revolutionary War was made at Durham Furnace. It was, however, made much nearer the location where it was installed. General Davis records that "Gen. Hugh Hughes, of the Continental army, visited the Stirling Iron Works of Noble, Townsend and Company, Orange county, N. Y., with whom he made a written contract, Feb. 2, 1778, to make an iron chain to be delivered on or before the first day of April, next—each link [being] about two feet long, made of the best Stirling iron two and a half inches square."[2]

For some time after the furnace was constructed, there was a scarcity of laborers in the area. As an inducement wages were necessarily high. According to General Davis, "These facts were stated in a petition to the Legislature, 1737, and permission was asked to import Negroes free of duty to labor at the iorn-works. . . . Negroes were employed at the furnace from its erection to the close of the century. Twelve slaves were at work there in 1780, five making their escape to the British at New York."[3]

The furnace of 1727 passed through many hands, particularly during the Revolutionary War period, and in 1789 ceased operations. What was left of the building structures was torn down in 1819 by William Long, who built a gristmill on the site. This mill was later operated by Backman and Lerch, and in more recent times by the Riegel family. In 1967 the property was sold to the Bucks County Park Foundation, thus ending 147 years of operation as a grist and flour mill. A dam about a mile up Durham Creek from the mill and the present raceway supplied power for the mill as it had previously for Durham Furnace.[4]

From 1789 until 1848 the property of the Durham Iron Co. lay in idleness as far as the production of iron was concerned. In the meantime, important developments were occurring that were to greatly influence the expansion of the iron industry in the Lehigh and Delaware valleys. It had been the dream of Josiah White that anthracite coal was a logical fuel for iron furnaces. But until 1838, when he acquired the British patent rights of George Crane, success had eluded him. At that time David Thomas came from England to construct at Mauch Chunk an experimental furnace for smelting iron with anthracite coal. The Crane furnace met every expectation. In August 1840 David Thomas shipped to Philadelphia "the first boat load of iron made in Lehigh Valley with American anthracite. . . . The *Philadelphia North American* declared: a 'new era has opened.' The governor of Pennsylvania, in his inaugural address, said that 'to foretell the vast import of this new discovery was impossible.' "[5] At Catasauqua, Pennsylvania, the Lehigh Crane Iron Works was established, with David Thomas in charge of operations. This plant thus became the first factory in the New World to make iron with anthracite.[6]

In 1848 the Durham property was acquired by Joseph Whitaker and Company, who built two anthracite furnaces near the mouth of Durham Creek to take advantage of the recently constructed Delaware Canal for transporting coal from the mines up the Lehigh Valley.

Cooper and Hewitt purchased the property in 1874 and completely rebuilt the plant, incorporating many innovations, including a hot blast furnace, the use of coke mixed with the anthracite fuel and a laboratory to control scientifically the operation of the blast furnaces. These innovations made the plant one of the most modern in the country and, together with the other iron furnaces that had been erected in the Lehigh and Delaware valleys, attracted the attention of such national organizations as the American Institute of Mining Engineers.

In May of 1886 the Institute held a series of meetings, with headquarters at the Sun Inn, Bethlehem. A trip to Durham Iron Works is recorded in the *Transactions* of that organization. "Thursday morning, May 20, the members and guests, amounting to about 200 in number, were conveyed by special train of the Lehigh Valley Railroad Company to Glendon Iron Works, Glendon, Pa., and Andover Iron Works, Phillipsburg, N.J., at each of which places they were hospitably received and conducted through the works. From Phillipsburg the train proceeded southward over the Belvidere division of the Pennsylvania Railroad about ten miles to Durham Siding, opposite the Durham Iron Works of Messrs. Cooper and Hewitt. There the party was transferred to open cars, which were ferried across the Delaware to the works. After a luncheon served in the open air, and an inspection of the blast-furnace, a session was held for the reading and discussion of papers in the "Durham Cave," once a famous object of curiosity, and still, although much reduced by quarrying operations,

Bucks County Historical Society
Durham Furnace of the 1880's.

Bucks County Historical Society
Meeting of the American Institute of Mining Engineers in Durham Cave,
May 20, 1886.

large enough to accommodate a considerable audience. During the progress of the session, photographs were taken of the picturesque scene, and a copy was promised as a souvenir to each person present. Upon the adjournment of the meeting, the party embarked in boats upon the Delaware Division of the Lehigh Canal, and enjoyed a pleasant voyage of about seven miles through romantic and varied scenery to Milford, where the river was crossed by the bridge, and the train was reached for return by rail to Bethlehem."[7]

Billinger's paper concludes, "In 1901 the ownership of the furnaces changed, and subsequent operations were less successful. Competition and a change in management caused the final shut-down in 1908, which terminated the production of Durham iron after a span of 181 years. Few industries have been linked to as many important characters and events in our national history. In 1912 the plant was dismantled."[8]

The various Durham furnaces, from the time of Joseph Whitaker and Co., were situated near the mouth of Durham Creek at the approximate location now occupied by Whippany Paper Board Company. After the Delaware Canal was constructed, the water of Durham creek was used for a time to supply additional water to the canal. This was accomplished by building a dam about 1800 feet up the creek and constructing a "feeder" to deliver water into the canal below

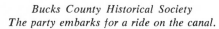

Bucks County Historical Society
The party embarks for a ride on the canal.

Durham lock. The Whitaker Company reopened and enlarged this feeder and built a wharf adjacent to the furnaces. This wharf was used by Joseph Whitaker and Co. and all subsequent owners of the Durham Iron Works for shipping pig iron, castings, safes and other products of the works, and for receiving by boat coal, bricks, sand, lumber and other supplies.[9]

Another means of transportation for the furnaces was a river ferry across the Delaware River, established about 1742. Among the various names of this ferry were Stillwell's and Brinks, but in later years it was called Durham Furnace Ferry. According to B. F. Fackenthal, "When the new and enlarged blast furnace at Durham was put in operation, a more pretentious ferry system was built, with wire rope cables and a large top-deck boat for carrying iron ore and other supplies over the river to the works, and to take back pig iron and castings. The first boat was launched February 16, 1877. . . . On May 10, 1879, a much larger boat was put in commission, with two standard gauge tracks thereon, carrying four large standard railroad cars on each trip. Standard gauge tracks were put down from the river on the New Jersey side, to connect with the Pennsylvania Railroad, where the Railroad Co. had put in sidings to accommodate about 100 cars, and similar standard gauge tracks were put down on the Pennsylvania side from the river to connect with the ramification of tracks through the stock houses and around the plant. This was a primitive way of supplying the furnace with stock and shipping its output, but it served the purpose, although its operation was often interrupted by high water and sometimes by ice. In 1896 the Quakertown and Eastern Railroad was completed as far as the Durham furnaces, when the ferry was no longer required, and it was then abandoned."[10]

Today there is little evidence near the mouth of Durham Creek to indicate the magnitude of activities that existed during the heyday of the iron furnaces. General Davis has recorded that, "In 1873 the furnace buildings comprised 58 dwellings, to accommodate 125 families, two dwellings for superintendents, one stone house, one large stone barn, three smaller barns, foundry building 160 feet by 60 feet, machine shop 300 feet by 50 feet, run by water from Durham Creek, giving 100 horsepower at dryest time, 2 anthracite iron furnaces, with necessary engines and machinery, pattern-shop, case-maker's shop, smith, wheelwright, and saddler's shop, stock-houses, cart-houses, one store, post office and Catholic church. The superintendent and officers were ten in number, with 250 hands."[11]

DURHAM BOATS

On the sloping banks of the Delaware River, just east of Durham Cave, the first Durham boats were constructed. Robert Durham, a skilled woodworker, is generally credited with building these boats. This claim, according to General Davis, "rests mainly on the tradition of families living in the immediate vicinity for several generations and had more or less interest in the furnace. . . . There is no particular date for the building of the first boats, but the general tendency points to 1738-48, while George Taylor was operating the furnace under lease."[12]

The design of this boat was patterned somewhat after the Indian canoe, with pointed bow and stern, and was so well adapted for river navigation that it became the standard for river transportation for over a hundred years, not only on the Delaware, but also on most of the eastern rivers. Large numbers of boats of this design were also built at Schenectady, New York, for use on the Mohawk and adjoining streams.

A letter written from Herkimer County, New York, in 1797 indicates the importance of Durham boats to early inland trade. "And I want you to see the Inland Lock and Navigation Company's canal. Twenty-five hundred feet of it were cut through the solid rock. That's the canal that's doubled the value of my land and every acre of land from here to Lake Erie. You'll see the new Durham boats locked around the falls where in the old days we dragged the bateaux around them with oxen. The Durham boats, Ephraim, carry up to 20 tons of goods! You'll know what that means when you get here and see John Post's store at Old Fort Schuyler outfitting the wagons for the Genesee country. Durham boats can go right on now into Wood Creek through the new canal at Fort Stanwix and on into the Seneca Rivers."[13]

One of the most authentic descriptions of a Durham boat is given by John A. Anderson. "In section the sides of the Durham boat were vertical, for the most part, with slight curvature to meet a like curvature of a part of the bottom which, for most of its width, was flat. Lengthwise, the sides were straight and parallel until they began to curve to the stem and stern posts, at some 12 or 14 feet from the ends, where the decks, fore and aft, began, the rest of the boat being open. The partly rounded form of the hull was preserved at the ends, instead of being hollowed, as was usual in the Indian canoe. Perhaps the craft most like the Durham boat, in general shape, would have been the 'dug-out,' a log hollowed out and pointed at both ends, with the bottom and sides slightly flattened. The ordinary length was 60

feet, although shorter boats were built, and, in some instances, the
length was extended to even 66 feet, with sometimes a foot or two
added to the ordinary width of 8 feet. The usual depth, from top
gunwale to the 12 inch keel plank, was 42 inches with additional
height of some 10 inches at the ends, this and other minor features
depending upon the fancy of the builder. The draft, light, was from
3½ to 5 inches, and loaded, about 28 inches. A boat 60 feet long
would carry 150 barrels of flour or about 600 bushels of shelled corn.
Some of the larger boats would carry 20 tons, although the load for
the ordinary boat was 2 to 5 tons less. The back load upstream was
about 2 tons.

"The movement down stream was by floating with the current,
with the aid, when necessary, of a pair of 18 foot oars. Moving upstream the boat was usually propelled by 'setting poles,' 12 to 18
feet long and shod with iron. On the thwarts was laid, on each side, a
plank 12 inches wide. On these 'walking boards' two members of the
usual crew of three, started at the forward end, with poles on the river
bottom and top ends to shoulders, walked to the stern, pushing the
boat forward. While they rapidly returned to repeat the process, the
captain, who steered, used a pole to hold the boat from going back
with the current, or when necessary pushed it forward by 'setting'
with a pole, in the short distance which the length of the stern deck
permitted.

Collection of author
Model of Durham boat at Washington Crossing State Park.

"The steering oar was 33 feet long, with a blade 12 inches in width. A movable mast, 6 inches in diameter and 33 feet long, with a boom of the same length and a three-cornered sail, enabled the boat to sail up stream, when the wind favored."[14]

In certain areas where upstream navigation was very difficult, "ring rocks" were located for aid of the boatmen. "These ring rocks were located at points in the Delaware River where, owing to shallow water and swift currents, the Durham boats could not be propelled upstream by the use of oars or poles. A rope was fastened to the ring and the boat was pulled by using the capstan. Buoys marked their location."[15] It is still possible to locate some of these ring rocks along the river.

Living aboard a Durham boat was primitive, to say the least. A large iron pot with holes near the bottom for draft, served as a cook stove. A water bucket, a coffeepot and, most important of all, a jug of whiskey, were shared by the crew. They slept under the forward deck, or in the open, on straw when it was available.

For a number of years after completion of the Delaware Canal, Durham boats continued to ply the river. In an 1846 report by the Canal Commissioners, analyzing various methods for transferring boats from the Delaware Canal to the Delaware and Raritan Canal, one of which was an outlet lock at New Hope together with a dam for slack water navigation, it was stated: "Outlet locks at Neely's below the falls, would also be required to allow the ascent or descent of the few Durham boats, which still run the river; but these might be constructed of wood in an economical manner, as it is believed that before a renewal of them would be found necessary, this description of boating on the Delaware would have ceased."[16]

It took nearly 20 years, however, for this prediction to become a reality. "General Davis [in his History of Bucks County] stated that the last trip of a Durham boat to Philadelphia was made by Isaac Van Norman in March 1860. Wilson Lugar of Lambertville, New Jersey, states that he made the last trip to that city with a Durham boat in 1865 with a load of shuttle blocks, and that the boat used on that trip was the last used on the river."[17]

With the Delaware Canal paralleling the river all the way, it was not surprising that the Durham boatmen and operators of other river craft used the canal for the return trip from Bristol to Easton and thus eliminated the arduous passage upstream. To discourage this practice, a double toll was charged for boats making the downstream passage by river and upstream by canal, much to the resentment of the river men.[18]

Courtesy, Elizabeth S. Bellis
Durham cave about 1900.

DURHAM CAVE

Near the Delaware River bank and a little north of Whippany Paper Board Company are the remains of the once famous Durham Cave. According to MacReynolds,[19] this cave was well known to the Lenape Indians and, before the Civil War, attracted visitors from surrounding towns and cities.

The cave, which on T. G. Kennedy's 1817 map of Bucks County was called Devils Hole, projected into an overhanging hill rising 200 to 250 feet above the adjoining land. The entrance to the cave, which was just large enough to admit three men abreast, was about 100 yards from the river. The lofty interior consisted of three huge rooms, one above the other. The lowest room, which contained a large pool of water, was believed to connect with the river, as the water in the pool rose and fell with the river level. A freshet in the river would raise the pool level to the top of the room. The middle room, used in 1886 as a meeting place by the American Institute of Mining Engineers, was at approximate ground level. From this room a stairway was erected to give access to the upper chamber, called Queen Esther's Drawing Room. According to legend this room at one time was used by Queen Esther, whose real name was Catherine Montour, and some of her Indian followers. The overall dimensions of the cave were about 280 feet long by a maximum of 40 feet broad. The height of each chamber varied from 17 to 20 feet.

The cave, unfortunately, was located in a limestone stratum. Burning limestone for use as fertilizer was an extensive industry in that part of the country and every available source was utilized. Destruction of this cave began by 1850 to provide material for the limekilns. The *Doylestown Democrat* of July 9, 1850, reported: "Durham Cave, a resort a few years ago for all persons having business in its vicinity, is really being demolished, and its solid architecture and beautiful stone, broken up, burned and boated off to enrich parts of our state and New Jersey. We suppose that at least one half of it is already gone. . . . The entrance and first rooms are gone, leaving but a small one in the rear. In a few years the history of the cave can be related only by the 'oldest inhabitants.' We very much doubt whether the rest of mankind can then be persuaded that such a cave ever existed in Durham Township."

Upon erection of the iron furnaces near the mouth of Durham Creek, the cave was further demolished to supply limestone for these furnaces. Today only the interior recess of the middle room remains.

Before destruction of the cave had progressed too far, a number of scientific explorations were made for evidences of early man and extinct animals. No evidence of early man was found; but, among the animal remains found by Dr. Joseph Leidy,[20] of the University of Pennsylvania, were the following:

Black Bear	Muskrat	Moose
Raccoon	Gray Squirrel	Wild Turkey
Gray Fox	Gray Rabbit	Snapper
Skunk	Deer	Sturgeon
Porcupine	Elk	Catfish
Beaver		

THE INDIAN WALKING PURCHASE

Since Durham Furnace and the surrounding territory were prominently involved in the sometimes called "infamous" Indian Walking Purchase, it will be of interest to outline briefly some of the features of this historic event.

When William Penn arrived in the New World in 1682, he brought with him a Royal Charter, dated March 4, 1681, which King Charles II of England had presented to him to satisfy a claim of Penn's father to whom the government was indebted in the amount of £ 16,000. This charter granted to Penn the then called "Province of Pennsylvania," a stretch of territory much larger than the present Commonwealth.

Under prevailing custom Penn could have claimed all of this territory regardless of the rights of the aborigines. But being a devout Quaker, he always dealt fairly and honorably with the Indians. As a result Penn retained their friendship and good will throughout his lifetime. When treaties were made and territory purchased, "the consideration paid the Indians for their land was but trifling but there was always a bargain and a sale between them which was satisfactory to both."[21]

The Indians who occupied the Delaware Valley, up to the Pocono Mountains, were a branch of the Algonquian Indians called the Lenni-Lenape. The tribe in Bucks County was known as the Unami, or Turtles. Upon their arrival in this country the British called these valley Indians Delawares.[22] Among the early treaties with these Indians was a transaction made in 1682, called the Neshaminy Purchase, which included lands having a northern boundary up to an east and west line running through Wrightstown in Bucks County. Some years later, on August 30, 1686, another treaty was supposed to have been made between William Penn and the Indians by which the Proprietor purchased the right to certain lands extending northward from the Neshaminy Purchase "as far as a man could walk in a day and a half." No effort, however, was made to carry out this walk until long after Penn's death, which occurred in 1718.

By the time Penn's sons became the Proprietors of Pennsylvania in 1727 more land was needed for settlers. They brought forth what they claimed was a copy of the 1686 treaty and started negotiations with the Indians, first at the original Durham Iron Works in 1734 and later at Pennsbury in 1735, to put it into effect. In April 1735 a preliminary walk was undertaken to explore the northern country and, it was later claimed, to blaze a trail to guide the official walkers. This walk consumed nine days. "John Chapman went along in the capacity of surveyor,"[23] and in the notebook of John Watson, who may have been one of the party, the surveyor's courses and distances are recorded.

It was not until September 19, 1737, that the official walk began. At sunrise on that day the walkers left Wrightstown for their northern journey. Those selected to make the trip were Edward Marshall, Solomon Jennings and James Yeates. Several Indians accompanied the walkers to watch the proceedings. It was soon apparent to the latter that this was no mere walk but an endurance contest; and, they left in disgust. Exhaustion finally caused Jennings and Yeates to drop out but Marshall continued on for the allotted time, covering approximately 65 miles, and concluding the walk about three miles east of Mauch Chunk. The Indians were further incensed when the Proprietors insisted that the line should extend at right angles to the walk which, towards the end of the walk, ran in a northwesterly direction, instead of directly east as specified in the treaty. The projected line struck the Delaware River near the present Lackawaxen: and because of the curves of the river this added to the purchase a great extent of country north of the Blue Mountain,[24] including a large section of the Indians' favorite hunting ground. Despite their complaints about the "Walk" itself, the Indians remained quiet for some time.

"The thing that more than any other gave the 'Walking Purchase' its bad reputation took place twenty years after the event. When, during the French and Indian War, Indian war parties attacked Pennsylvania settlers, groups opposed to the Proprietary government charged that this hostility was a result of the 'Walking Purchase.' This explanation was especially attractive to Quaker politicians who . . . preferred to believe that the real fault lay with William Penn's sons for abandoning their father's Quaker principles. . . .

"It was in consequence of this political quarrel that most of the known accounts of the 'Walking Purchase' were written, to support one or the other of the two contradictory views: and these biased stories are in turn responsible both for a widespread popular interest in the incident and for a great deal of confusion concerning it."[25]

Edward Marshall, the hero of the walk, was 27 years old at the time it occurred. He was the special object of the Indians' hatred and found it necessary to move from place to place. In 1757, while living near Stroudsburg in what was then part of Northampton County, his home was attacked during his absence by a band of Indians who murdered his pregnant wife and eldest daughter. During a subsequent attack his eldest son also was killed. Whether these attacks were due to the Indians' original enmity against Marshall or to the general hostility which the French and Indian War generated is a subject for speculation.

It is generally believed that subsequent to the death of his eldest son, Marshall moved to an island in the Delaware River called Tinicum Island. This island is opposite Lock No. 17 on the Delaware Canal and is now called Marshall Island. Here Marshall lived with his second wife for the remainder of his life, having died in 1789 at the age of 79.[26] This belief, however, is disputed by one of his descendants.

According to MacReynolds, the claim of local historians that Edward Marshall lived on the island may be in error. Mrs. Sarah Ridge, a direct descendant of Marshall, always claimed that the

'Walker' made his home in the stone house in which she lived, located a short distance below Lock No. 17, between the Delaware Canal and the river, and now owned and occupied by Commander Manila D. Barber. Neighbors of Mrs. Ridge recall that she frequently told the following story: "Some men came one day to ask me about Edward Marshall. They said they were writing something in a history book about him. We talked awhile, and then one of the men said, 'Edward lived on the island when he came back from New Jersey.' I told them Edward never lived on the island, but they said he surely did live there and I must be mistaken. I thought, 'Well, if you believe that, you may have it that way,' and did not say anything more about it. But I know Edward never lived on the island. There was no house on it in his time. He owned it and did some farming on it, but he lived right here in this house. He had boats and used them to ferry across to the island whenever he wanted to go there."[27]

Collection of author
Gristmill on site of first iron furnace at Durham village.

Courtesy, Frank Sigafoos
The last boat loads of coal on the Delaware Canal passed through Yardley lock in late September 1931.

Courtesy, Acton J. Shimer
Boats and camel back bridge at Lodi.

Chapter 11

The End – And A New Beginning

As a commercial enterprise its natural beauty was a secondary consideration, while today the commercial value is history and its inherent qualities as a park are primary. For these possibilities to be lost today and lamented tomorrow would be an unforgiveable tragedy which, with the efforts of a combined front, I am sure, can be successfully combated.

Norman Williams of Pittsburgh in *Towpath*, March 1940

By the middle of the nineteenth century the encroachment of the railroads on the state canal business persuaded the Commonwealth to dispose of its canals. By act of April 21, 1858, the Delaware Canal was sold to the Sunbury and Erie Railroad Company. That company, in turn, on July 10, 1858, sold the canal to the newly organized Delaware Division Canal Company, a subsidiary of the Lehigh Coal and Navigation Company. In 1866 the latter company acquired the canal from its subsidiary under a 99 year lease.

With the passage of time the Lehigh Coal and Navigation Company found it expedient to transport more and more of its coal by railroad, with a consequent dropping off of traffic on the Lehigh and Delaware canals. The spring of 1931 saw only 20 boats remaining in operation on these canals. In the fall of that year traffic on the Delaware Canal stopped for good.

No doubt the management of the Lehigh Coal and Navigation Company gave a sigh of relief when the last commercial boat passed into oblivion, for the old canal had been a financial burden for a number of years. But as Flora Henry locked the last boat through Smithtown lock, she realized her tenure as a lock keeper had come to an end. There were others who viewed the occurrence with nostalgia. Dr. B. F. Fackenthal, Jr., recalled that, "It was with a feeling of sadness that I witnessed the last boat (boat No. 181) pass through the canal on the morning of Saturday, October 17, 1931, going north empty." However, there was a ray of encouragement that the old canal would not be lost to posterity. Dr. Fackenthal continued, "During the afternoon of that very day there was a meeting at the Thompson-Neely house in Solebury township, Bucks County, for the formal transfer of that part of the canal between Locks 22 and 23 at Raubsville . . . and Lock No. 5, a short distance below Yardley, a distance of about forty miles. At that meeting, which was largely attended, William Jay Turner, Esq., attorney representing the Lehigh Coal and Navigation Company, presented a deed for that part of the canal to Governor Gifford Pinchot on behalf of the Commonwealth of Pennsylvania."[1]

In the course of his address at that meeting, Governor Pinchot said, "Meanwhile the Delaware Division Canal becomes the property and the charge of the Commonwealth. During my administration it will remain absolutely 'as is'. Not long ago it was suggested to me that its ancient bridges be replaced by earth fills carrying pedestrian or vehicular crossings. I assure you the bridges will stay where they are, during my term of office, at least. They are an integral feature of the canal's beauty. To break the canal with the suggested fills would be not only to destroy that beauty but to do irreparable damage to the canal as a center of recreation.

"I am prouder than I can say that during my administration the Roosevelt State Park becomes public property and I have no slightest doubt that, had he lived to see it, Roosevelt himself would have been proud of it too."[2]

And thus the old canal passed quietly under the jurisdiction of the Commonwealth for use as a public recreational area. Or did it! It is an interesting fact of history that the inception of practically all of the canals built during the nineteenth century was fraught with controversy: as to whether it should be built, where it should be located and how much money should be spent. And in its demise the Delaware Canal met with a similar fate.

In naming the acquired property, "Roosevelt State Park", Governor Pinchot failed to take into consideration the wishes of the people of Bucks County. A local paper of November 13, 1931, editorialized, "Governor Pinchot evidently has no idea how persistent Bucks County's club women can be or he would not have made the reply he did recently to a protest against calling the Delaware Valley State Park, 'Roosevelt Park.'

"Writing in reply to a letter from a former president of the county federation, the governor said, 'I am sorry to have to tell you that your recommendation has come too late for the new park has officially been named after [Theodore] Roosevelt. I think you will agree, however, that it is a fitting tribute to the man who did so much to preserve our national beauty spots and who so loved the out-of-doors.'

"That is just what the Women's Clubs and other Bucks Countians do not agree with—that the name Roosevelt is fitting as the name for a new park.

"Every day some new organization is adopting resolutions protesting against it—many including the comment that it is strange that the new park in Bucks County should be named without any attempt being made to learn the opinions of the residents of the county on the subject.

"The protests, no doubt, will continue to be made—and certainly cannot be ignored in view of the unanimity of objection to naming the park for the late president simply because he was a great outdoor man.

"Roosevelt had nothing to do with Bucks County, ever or in any way. His name attached to the park has no significance. It does not identify it as to its character or location—and for all its name signifies it might be in Kamchatka.

"Delaware Valley State Park, the name unanimously favored, does describe the park and locate it."

Not all voices, however, were unanimous. The Daughters of the American Revolution favored the name "Penn Trail", to which the reply was made that this name might apply to the towpath but was hardly appropriate to the park as a whole.

Regardless of protests, a quarter of a century has elapsed since the park was established; and, its name is still "Roosevelt State Park".

Of far greater significance, however, was a charge of irregularity respecting the Act of June 26, 1931, which stipulated how old canal property might be disposed of. Upon inauguration of the Democratic administration of Governor George H. Earle, the State's Attorney General ruled that the Act of June 26, 1931, was unconstitutional. This opinion was upheld by the Superior Court of Pennsylvania, and so the canal property reverted to the Canal Company.

In the meantime, during March 1936, a disastrous flood did much damage to the canal. It was estimated by the Canal Company that the cost of restoring navigation would approximate $125,000, exclusive of $47,510 already spent by the Canal Company in repairs between the Easton dam and Raubsville.[3] "The Commonwealth having inquired whether the Canal Company intended to restore the canal as a public waterway, the Canal Company, in the circumstances, replied that it was unable to do so . . ."[4] This decision was subjected to litigation but the courts upheld the Canal Company.

Finally, on June 21, 1939, an act was approved authorizing the Secretary of the Department of Forests and Waters to acquire by donation, any part of the property formerly constituting a system of canals, the use of which for transportation has been abandoned, and to utilize such properties for park purposes.

Taking advantage of this act, the Lehigh Coal and Navigation Company recorded in its report for 1940: "The Delaware Division Canal Company during the past ten years has been endeavoring to dispose of its canal property because transportation by canal has become obsolete. These efforts were brought to a conclusion during the year through the donation by the Company to the Commonwealth of Pennsylvania of the entire canal property, in accordance with the provisions of the Act of Assembly approved June 21, 1939."[5]

ROOSEVELT STATE PARK TODAY

When the Delaware Canal finally was accepted by the Commonwealth of Pennsylvania to be used for recreational purposes, it appeared that another beautiful historic and scenic landscape was assured to the people of the state and, in particular, to the residents of the Delaware Valley, for their enjoyment and recreation. But those were serious times for the country. During the 1930's, the decade of dispute regarding ownership of the canal, the United States was struggling through one of its worst depressions. By 1940, when State ownership of the canal was assured, our country's involvement in a world war began to appear inevitable. Government had more pressing problems than thoughts of saving recreational and historic landmarks. Had it not been for the dedicated efforts of a group of Delaware Valley citizens, it is doubtful if the Delaware Canal would have survived that period of stress.

About 1933, shortly after the canal was first returned to the State, "Bill Stover came down from Erwinna," William F. Taylor said, "and told me that the canal was in danger of being drained and lost. I came out here, left New York and came out here, because of the canal. It seemed to me quite impossible. I said, 'Why Bill, surely there will be such a hue and cry from the public; there is no real danger.' But we did organize. We held meetings in different homes and also had the use of Phillips Mill for our early meetings." The hue and cry that Bill Taylor predicted did become a reality and resulted in the organization of the Delaware Valley Protective Association to which Taylor was elected first president.

Many prominent members of the business and political communities joined in the Association's activities. Among these participants were Morris Llewellyn Cook, L. O. Head, Thomas Ross, Senators Edward B. Watson, George Woodward, and Horace G. Prall and representatives Thomas B. Stockham and Wilson Yaekel of Bucks County. The latter two introduced the bills authorizing acceptance by the Commonwealth of old canals for recreational purposes, which were unanimously passed by the Legislature in 1939. The deed for the canal which the Lehigh Coal and Navigation Company presented to the Commonwealth was signed by Secretary Stewart of the Department of Forests and Waters and approved by Governor James on December 18, 1940.

"That was all very well," Bill Taylor said, "but here we had the state in possession of the property with no idea what they would do with it. So it was necessary to go and see the then secretary of the Department of Forests and Waters, G. Albert Stewart. He came from Clearfield and wasn't at all familiar with the canal. Three of us went up to see him, including L. O. Head, president of American Railway Express, who owned Hendricks Island down here in the river, because of the peace and quiet of the valley and the charm of the canal, and Mrs. C. C. Zantzinger of Philadelphia, president of the Council for the Preservation of Natural Beauty in Pennsylvania. Her organization had taken a poll of all the women's groups in the state regarding whether the canal should be retained. When we got into Secretary Stewart's office, I introduced Mr. Head and Mrs. Zantzinger and I said, incidentally, she represents 800,000 women in the State of Pennsylvania who want the canal retained. He said, 'What!' 'That's right', she said, and explained the outcome of her poll. Well, the result was we got him to come down here and really look at the canal."

In view of the critical times then prevalent, the Association was gratified when Secretary Stewart gave assurance that, "If the sponsors of the proposed canal acquisition will not press for any improvements or for any cash outlay beyond bare maintenance during the coming biennium, I am sure we can look with more favor on the proposal that the state acquire it. It is recognized that the canal is worthy of acquisition and our only concern is that we might be able to exercise proper stewardship."[6]

With the status of Roosevelt State Park and the Delaware Canal established, one of the first acts of the Department was to organize a maintenance department to which Russel S. Paetzell was appointed superintendent. This position he held until he retired in 1964. An asset to the successful functioning of this maintenance department was the number of old canal employees who became associated with this activity.

It was recognized early that if the original enthusiasm of the Association's membership was to be maintained, some medium for stimulating continued interest was necessary. The suggestion of one of the members resulted in the publication of the privately owned magazine, *Towpath*. This highly successful monthly magazine was published from December 1939 until mid-summer 1942 when production problems incident to the world war thwarted further publication.

"The start of *Towpath*, like the start of the DVPA, was the result of someone else coming and giving me a poke in the ribs," Bill Taylor said. "Fred Cook of Yardley came up with the idea that a publication would do more to help the Association than anything else. The only reason that I got involved was that Dr. Clarke F. Ansley, editor-in-chief of the Columbia University Press, and a neighbor of mine, talked to me about it and said he would edit the publication. Well, he died before we got the first issue out, and it came out in my name. For better or worse, I remained as editor.

"We started the magazine printed on good stock, with plenty of pictures, a two color cover and enough advertising to just cover expenses. We never made any money out of it. We were fortunate in paying our printer's bills until the war come along. Then I just couldn't keep going."

In spite of its short life, *Towpath* accomplished its purpose of stimulating and cementing the functions of the DVPA as the watchdog of the Delaware Canal and the preservation of the natural beauty of the Delaware Valley. By popular demand *Towpath* was reactivated in July 1951 and continued as a modest eight page publication until October 1966. A perusal of the various issues of this magazine gives one some idea of the problems that confronted the Department of Forests and Waters and its maintenance department not only in rehabilitating the various canal structures but also in keeping a continuous flow of water in the canal.

During the period from 1931 to 1940, when normal maintenance of the canal was practically nonexistent, the destructive flood of 1936 left the waterway in a deplorable condition. It is understandable that, under the unsettled national situation then existing, Secretary Stewart felt constrained to committing his department to mere maintenance of the canal. But work progressed and progress was being made until about 1950, when the old aqueducts over Durham and Tinicum creeks collapsed shutting off water to the southern portion of the canal. Limited by the available funds, the present small aqueducts were installed; water was restored but its restricted flow makes satisfactory water conditions in the lower portion of the canal difficult to maintain. Then came the great flood of 1955 with its devastating effects on the waterway. Undaunted, however, the canal advocates rose to the occasion, emergency funds were made available and most of the damage was repaired.

Continually hampered by inadequate state appropriations, Dr. Maurice K. Goddard has, throughout his tenure as Secretary of the Department of Forests and Waters, rendered yeoman service in the interest of Roosevelt State Park and the Delaware Canal. How tenuous these appropriations are is illustrated by an announcement in the *New Hope Gazette* of May 30, 1957, under the heading "State to Close Canal June 1st."

"Thursday night at approximately 6 P.M. Dr. Wilson McNeary, past president of DVPA and head of its canal committee, was informed by Forests and Waters secretary M. K. Goddard . . . that on June 1, the New Hope Canal was to be closed, its employees discharged and the water drained from its banks.

"The action is blamed on the knife-wielding tactics of the . . . legislature in Harrisburg where many state programs have been slashed in recent days, particularly those having to do with public welfare."

Hal H. Clark, who was elected president of DVPA in 1956 and since that time has courageously guided the activities of that organization, immediately summoned into action its members and other friends of the canal. The *New Hope Gazette* of June 6, 1957, reported that a storm of protests in the form of letters, telegrams and personal contacts flooded the legislators at Harrisburg, many of whom up to that time knew little or nothing about the canal. On July 11, the *Gazette* was able to report that the protests had been effective and that $78,000 had been appropriated by the legislature. Secretary Goddard said this amount urgently was needed for repairs and was not sufficient for fringe operations such as litter and pollution policing. He asked the aid of local communities in supervising these necessary activities.

Due to the actions of thoughtless individuals and to a few disgruntled residents who consider the canal good only as a dumping area, the problems of litter and pollution continually confront the canal maintenance crews. This situation is particularly prevalent in the highly industrialized southern portion of the canal. Periodically, the Boy Scouts and civic groups originate activities to assist the understaffed maintenance department in clearing the debris from the canal and the underbrush from along the banks of the canal.

This 'hit or miss' dependence upon the vagaries of the state legislature in making appropriations has been a source of deep concern to lovers of Roosevelt State Park throughout its existence.

The near miss of 1957 stimulated DVPA to renewed activity. Under the heading, "Let's Get Going," *Towpath*[7] expounded on the frustrations and determination of the DVPA members.

"Starting with Governor Pinchot . . . we have had frequent, sometimes eloquent, expressions of appreciation of the 'Unique and Lovely Park.' This from each and every governor.

"No adequate or consistent appropriation of money for proper maintenance or approved development has been made by the legislature during the term of each and every governor and each and every member of the State Legislature.

"The quarter of a century since the establishment of Roosevelt Park has been one of 'Penny Wise and Pound Foolish' behavior . . ., most of the cost of the park to the state during this time being due to repairs caused by 'less than *bare* maintenance.'

"We can through the DVPA, Fire Companies, Garden Clubs and all other local groups make certain that our legislators know that we want the Department of Forests and Waters to have an adequate appropriation to make the Canal Park popular and usable for Recreation."

There is no question of the increasing popularity of this unique park in terms of public interest and use. According to Department of Forests and Waters records, 140,000 visitors made use of the park's facilities in 1961. This number increased to 361,000 in 1968. Of the latter figure 8,000 were picnickers, 18,000 fishermen, 3,000 hikers, 5,000 boaters, 900 horseback riders, 1,700 water sports, 80,000 canoeists, over 35,000 rode the mule drawn boats and 210,000 enjoyed miscellaneous features of the park.

An encouraging and exciting development in recent years is the interest being displayed by educators in the value of the canal for educational purposes. A trip on one of the mule drawn boats out of New Hope gives one a first hand glimpse of what life was like and how commerce was conducted in the early days of our country. Bus loads of school children from New York, Philadelphia, Baltimore and other surrounding cities are a common sight at the boat dock in New Hope. A state legislator viewing the exuberant, delighted anticipation of these children as they start on their voyage of adventure would find it difficult to vote against any appropriation for the adequate maintenance of this waterway and its adjacent facilities.

An interesting and pertinent item on financing appeared in a 1967 issue of the *Washington Post*. According to a Reuters report from London, "Britain's 2,000 miles of canals are getting a new lease on life. The government recently voted to grant an extra $952,000 *annually* [Italics by author] to clean and turn neglected canals into recreational waterways.

"The government already spends $1.5 million a year to keep them in enough repair to serve as storm-drainage channels, but the restoration of the historic canals will furnish facilities for increasing numbers of weekend sailors, canoe enthusiasts and fishermen."

The article also said that, "The canals pass for much of their length through placid countryside. Their bridges, locks, aqueducts and warehouses are considered to include much good early industrial architecture." In spite of its critical financial and social problems the British government recognized its responsibility to adequately finance the maintenance of its ancient canals for historical and recreational purposes. Should less be expected of the great Commonwealth of Pennsylvania?

An irreparable loss to the lower end of the canal occurred when a group of prominent Bristol citizens petitioned the Department of Forests and Waters to abandon most of the canal in that Borough. By an agreement dated December 7, 1954, the department leased to the Borough of Bristol "all that tract of land comprising the bed and berm banks of the Delaware Division of the Pennsylvania Canal running through said Borough to the Delaware River . . . extending from Adams Hollow Creek . . . to its terminus at the Delaware River." The agreement further permitted the Borough to sublet a portion of the property to the school district of Bristol Borough. On the property thus acquired the school district erected Warren Snyder elementary school.

The abandoned portion of the canal, about a mile in length, included some of its most interesting features, Plate VII. Among these were Locks No. 1, 2 and 3, the tidal basin and the tide lock, all of which have now disappeared. The tidal basin which, had it been retained, undoubtedly would have developed into a useful small boat marina, has been filled in for a parking lot back of the buildings fronting Mill Street.

With the passage of time and the increasing interest in water sports and the allure of old canals, many Bristol residents now feel that a grave error was made in abandoning this portion of the canal. There are local canal enthusiasts who dream that restoration may someday be accomplished, a dream hardly capable of fulfillment.

One of the little known features of the canal is its value to local communities for fire protection. *Towpath*[8] records that, "When fire recently destroyed a quarter of a million dollars worth of the Leedum lumber business in Yardley, Pennsylvania, Lewis C. Leedum, life long volunteer fire fighter and director of the DVPA, watched with satisfaction the efficient work of his fellow firemen.

"He had helped plan and practice Bucks County Fire Fighting for many years and persistently fought to preserve the canal.

"Water from the canal saved Yardley."

In 1958, F. R. White, president of Union Mills Paper Manufacturing Company, expressed appreciation through Hal Clark,[9] "concerning the recent leak in our water supply system which necessitated the use of Eagle Fire Company's pumper and the Delaware Canal for a period of three days to insure adequate fire protection for our plant.

"For your further information similar ocasions have arisen over the past years at both this plant and that of our affiliate . . . also located along the canal at the lower end of the Borough of New Hope.

"I can assure you on behalf of our two companies that it is most reassuring to have a body of water such as this adjacent to our mills for fire protection beyond the capacity of our own storage tanks. In fact, I might point out that for many years we have maintained suction pipes in the canal with necessary fittings for hooking on the pumpers of the New Hope and Lambertville Fire Companies in case of serious fire."

It is no happenstance that visitors walking the towpath or traveling the canal by boat are confronted with many colorful and attractively arranged gardens bordering this waterway. Not only was Mrs. Zantzinger an enthusiastic participant in saving the physical features of the canal; but, she also wanted to preserve and enhance the natural beauty of this picturesque stream. In 1941 *Towpath*[10] announced, "Mrs. C. C. Zantzinger, president of the Council for Promotion of Natural Beauty in Pennsylvania, has appointed Miss Emily Exley, outstanding landscape architect, as chairman of the council's committee to act with other committees and to conduct the 1941 Delaware Canal Garden Competition." The committee was very active in stimulating interest among residents along the canal with the result that the contest covered the area from Riegelsville to Morrisville. In the final judging 44 prizes were awarded. After a lapse of nearly 30 years, the results of this first garden competition still contribute to the pleasure of visitors to the canal.

Nature also has contributed bountifully to enrich the appearance of the landscape. From early spring with its array of dogwood, flowering crab and other flowering shrubs, through June with the rich green foliage of the rhododendron and its masses of colorful bloom, into autumn with its climax of spectacular display, the visitor is confronted with a kaleidoscopic vista of nature's bounty.

In writing this book it has been my goal to trace the origin and function of the Delaware Canal; to describe its operation and the people who made that operation possible and to stress the place this canal deserves in the historic heritage of our country. Public appreciation and encouragement extended to our State legislators and to the Department of Forests and Waters will assist materially in assuring continuing and adequate maintenance of this historic relic.

When Governor Gifford Pinchot accepted the canal for recreational purposes he said, "I sign this bill with keen pleasure because it has resulted in securing for the people of Pennsylvania what is undoubtedly a most unique and lovely park, probably the only park of its kind in the world, namely, forty miles of canal and towpath extending through one of the most beautiful parts of Pennsylvania."[11] To this evaluation the constantly increasing thousands of annual visitors agree.

Courtesy, Roy Creveling
The "Bon Ton Frolic," a summer excursion by workers from an Easton Department Store.

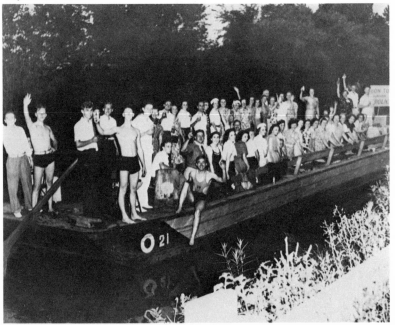

Collection of Henry S. Engart
Tattersall's coal storage at Morrisville

Collection of Henry S. Engart
Lumber and repair yard at New Hope.

APPENDIXES

APPENDIX I–TABLES

TABLE I

LOCK DATA

Number	Lock Dimensions in Feet			Towpath Distance—Miles	
	Length	Width	Drop	Between	Total
Guard Lock	100	22		0	0
22-23	95	22	17.3	5.79	5.79
21	95	11	9	3.88	9.67
20	95	22	8	2.5	12.17
19	95	11	6	5.0	17.17
18	95	11	10	1.6	18.77
17	95	11	6	3.8	22.57
15-16	95	22	12	1.0	23.57
14	95	11	9	2.69	26.26
13	95	11	6	0.13	26.39
12	95	11	5.3	1.36	27.75
11	95	22	8	6.18	33.93
10	95	22	8	0.095	34.025
9	95	22	6.9	0.095	34.12
8	95	22	6.9	0.095	34.215
7	95	11	8	8.62	42.835
6	95	11	6	0.62	43.455
5	95	11	6	1.53	44.985
4	95	11	6	10.75	55.735
3	95	11	6.32	2.16	57.895
2	95	11	6.68	0.095	57.99
1	95	11	7	0.17	58.16
Tide Lock	100	22	-	0.17	58.33
Outlet Lock	100	22	-		

TABLE II

Rapids in Delaware River Between Easton and Trenton

Name of Falls or Rapids	Distance below mouth of Lehigh R. Miles	Length of Each Rapid Feet	Length of Each Rapid Miles	Fall of Rapids Feet	Head of Rapids above lowest tide water Feet
Bixler's Rift	½	2000	.378	7'- 5"	160'- 5"
Clifford's Rift	3½	2000	.378	5'- 1"	150'-10"
Old Sow Rift	5	750	.142	2'- 4"	145'- 7"
Ground Hog Rift	6	1700	.322	1'-11"	138'- 1"
Rocky Falls	7	2000	.378	2'- 9"	136'- 1"
Gravelly Falls	8	1500	.284	1'- 3"	133'- 3"
Durham Falls	9½	350	.066	2'- 9"	130'- 3"
Linn's Falls	12	2300	.435	7'- 4"	127'- 5"
Nockamixon Falls	14	1700	.322	4'-11"	117'- 6"
Furman's Falls	17	700	.133	3'- 7"	110'-11"
Stuhl's Falls	18	350	.066	1'- 8"	107'- 2"
Man-of-War Rift	20	500	.095	1'- 5"	102'- 3"
Marshall's Island Falls	21	1000	.188	11'- 5"	100'- 7"
Tumbling-dam Falls	24	5000	.945	11'- 1"	89'- 1"
Cutsow Rift	25½	1000	.188	3'-10"	85'- 4"
Bull's Falls	27½	800	.151	4'- 5"	72'- 2"
Howell's Rift	31 to 32	1500	.284	7'- 6"	68'- 3"
Galloper's Rift	31 to 32	1500	.284	7'- 6"	68'- 3"
Greenbank Rift	32	500	.095	1'- 9"	58'- 9"
Well's Falls	35½	4780	.905	12'- 1"	49'- 9"
Buck Tail Rift	36½	500	.095	1'- 5"	36'- 5"
Knowle's Point Rift	39½	500	.095	3'- 1"	33'- 6"
Scudder's Rift	44	2500	.473	4'- 2"	24'- 8"
Gould's Rapids	46½	3000	.57	4'- 5"	16'- 8"
Trenton Falls	49	3500	.662	9'- 8"	9'- 8"

From B C H S, Vol. VI, p. 123

TABLE III

COAL SHIPMENTS IN TONS (2240 pounds)

Through Lehigh and Connecting Canals

Year	Lehigh Canal	Delaware Canal	Morris Canal from Lehigh	Delaware & Raritan Via Bristol	Delaware & Raritan via New Hope
1832	75,937		12,000		
1833	122,928	91,824	13,000	Small amount	
1840	225,318	171,210	30,210		
1843	267,793	197,000	30,000	49,160*	
1849	801,246	580,934	103,482		105,000
1855	1,276,367*	755,265	290,730*		156,340
1860	1,091,631	639,323	277,083		341,816
Flood 1862	396,407	217,202	106,431		97,410
1866	1,066,302	792,397*	205,315		526,244*
1870	789,365	648,856	69,939		265,771
1880	431,913	357,299	1,729		90,810
1887	321,239	242,685	Last 359		131,106

		Shipped east by rail from Mauch Chunk
1890	356,639	4,973,275
1900	287,969	5,105,958
1910	203,104	8,210,501
1920	121,495	6,747,125
1930	91,227	
1931	65,566	

*Peak

From annual reports of the Lehigh Coal and Navigation Company.

For 1890 and succeeding years only coal shipments via the Lehigh Canal are given. Most of this coal also passed through the Delaware Canal.

TABLE IV

Freight Transported on the Lehigh Canal in 1855

	Descending Tons	Ascending Tons	Total Tons
Anthracite	1,276,367		1,276,867
Bituminous		456	456
Charcoal		6	6
Grain	195	2,335	2,530
Flour	695	1,358	2,053
Salt	6	1,026	1,032
Salt fish, beef and pork	13	723	737
Other provisions	26	318	344
Beer, porter and cider	1	26	27
Whiskey	1,100	139	1,239
Hay and Straw	40	250	291
Staves, hoop-poles, posts and rails	145	50	195
Lumber	65,965	3,281	69,247
Cordwood	1,369	40	1,409
Brick	109	1,788	1,897
Slate	4,879	378	5,258
Lime and limestone	19,476	8,145	27,621
Other stone and plaster	1,684	2,751	4,435
Iron	64,541	7,465	72,006
Iron ore	7,249	63,488	70,736
Pitch, tar and rosin		94	94
Merchandise	1,631	4,023	5,655
Total	1,445,498	98,147	1,543,646

From Lehigh Coal and Navigation Company annual report dated May 6, 1856, p. 8.

TABLE V

Freight Transported on the Delaware Canal during 1867
(First year reported by LC&N)

	Ascending Tons	Descending Tons	Total Tons
Coal	215	768,792	769,008
Grain	748	125	873
Salt	1,155		1,155
Salt fish and pork	36	11	47
Other provisions	346	51	397
Beer, porter & cider			
Hay and straw	485	284	769
Staves, hoop-poles & rails	3,168	2,119	5,287
Lumber	5,652	1,926	7,578
Brick	2,639	613	3,252
Lime, cement & plaster	7,489	6,447	13,937
Limestone, earth & sand	13,616	47,632	61,248
Iron	12,664	21,736	34,400
Iron ore	255	941	1,197
Merchandise	1,237	258	1,495
Grindstones	1	136	137
Bituminous coal	797		797
Total	50,508	851,076	901,584

From L C & N, May 5, 1868, p. 32.

TABLE VI

Toll Charges on the Delaware Canal

Boat	2.0c per mile
Liquor	0.6c per pound per mile
Tobacco	0.5c per pound per mile
Fish	0.4c per pound per mile
Salt	0.3c per pound per mile
Rope	0.4c per pound per mile
Groceries	0.6c per pound per mile
Dry goods	0.8c per pound per mile
Flour	0.6c per pound per mile
Plaster	0.2c per pound per mile
Furniture	0.8c per pound per mile
Meat	0.3c per pound per mile
Sundries	0.8c per pound per mile
Lime	0.2c per pound per mile
Lead pipe	0.8c per pound per mile
Hardware	0.5c per pound per mile

From "Register of Boats Clearing at Bristol on The Pennsylvania Canal—1849". This volume is in BCHS library.

TABLE VII

STATES HAVING OVER 500 MILES OF CANALS

PENNSYLVANIA		OHIO	
Delaware and Hudson	25*	Ohio and Erie	390
Eastern Div. Main Line	43	inc. Walhanding and	
Juniata Div. Main Line	127	Hocking branches	
Western Div. Main Line	104	Miami and Erie	286
Kittanning Feeder	14	inc. Sidney and St. Mary's	
Susquehanna Div.	41	feeders and Lebanon Br.	
North Branch Div.	169	Wabash and Erie	18
West Branch Div.	73	Sandy and Beaver	74
Bald Eagle Cut	4	Ohio and Pennsylvania	87
Wiconisco Line	12		
Susquehanna and Tidewater	30*	Total	855
Conestoga Navigation	18	NEW YORK	
Codorus Navigation	11	Erie	364
Union	77	Champlain	60
Pine Grove Feeder	22	Cayuga and Seneca	23
Schuylkill Navigation	108	Oswego	38
Lehigh	72	Black River	77
Delaware	60	Crooked Lake	8
Beaver and Erie	135	Chenango	97
French Creek Feeder	25	Chemung	23
Franklin Line	22	Junction	12†
Pennsylvania and Ohio	18*	Genesee Valley	107
Junction	3		
Bald Eagle Navigation	22	Total	809
		INDIANA	
Total	1235	Wabash and Erie	452
		White Water	76
		Total	528

*In Pa.   †In N.Y.

Taken mostly from Noble E. Whitford, "History of the Canal System of the State of New York," Vol. 2, 1905.

APPENDIX II

ITEMS FROM THE AREA NEWSPAPERS

The majority of this material was excerpted by Mr. James Reilly during the summer of 1969 when he was in the employ of the Hugh Moore Parkway, City of Easton.

EASTON CENTINEL, Friday, March 31, 1826

BEAT THIS!

The "Little Belt" of Easton, owned by Captain Jacob Nicholas has performed a trip to Philadelphia in *fifty eight hours;* the quickest trip ever known to be made from Easton.

EASTON CENTINEL, Friday, February 20, 1829

COAL WANTED

The subscriber wishes to purchase from 30 to 40 tons of Mauch Chunk coal, for which he will pay $7.25 per ton. Cash, if delivered before the middle of March at his coal yard near the Point, or place of junction of the Lehigh and Delaware rivers, Easton.

THE WHIG, Tuesday, April 7, 1829

Disturbance—Yesterday afternoon information reached this place that the laborers in the canal fifteen miles above this place had turned out for higher wages, and would neither work themselves or suffer others to do so.

EASTON CENTINEL, Friday, April 10, 1829

The Delaware was higher last week than it has been for a number of years. Mr. Jacob Able's storehouse, on the banks of the Lehigh near its confluence with the Delaware, contained water to the depth of 15 inches on the second floor, the first stories being completely filled. . . . The Delaware was 18 feet above low water mark.

NILES WEEKLY REGISTER, Vol. 36, April 11, 1829, p. 101

About four weeks ago, Isaac Otis, contractor on section sixty-five of the Delaware Canal, a little below Point Pleasant, made a blast with four kegs of gunpowder, about one hundred pounds, blew up four hundred cubic yards of solid rock, which was estimated to weigh upwards of six hundred tons. It was termed a "sand blast", and is believed to be the greatest blast ever made in this country.

THE WHIG, Tuesday, April 21, 1829

If we had only somebody here to make a long story out of the current incidents of the day, the last week would have furnished matter for much amusement to the reading world. The Delaware being in good rafting order, our town was thronged with Raftmen from up the river. These hardy and enterprising pioneers seem, when they descent with their lumber, to give a loose to that fun and frolic which characterises watermen. We have heard of Kentucky boatmen who were "half horse, half alligator, and a little touch of snapping turtle"; —who styled themselves "Steam-boats", "Earthquakes", and dear knows what else. We do not know that any of our Delaware raftmen claim any such great titles, but we have "Roarers from the Lacka-waxen"—"Peelers from Equinunk"—"Ticklers from Ten Mile River", "Snorters from Coshecton", and "Lum Ticklers from The Cook-house" who have descended with thousands of dollars worth of lumber, and have crowded our town to overflowing, enlivening it with their shag dog fights, fiddling, dancing, &c. &c. in the way of their fun and capers. It was like a fair for some days about neighbor Hackett's who spoiled the faces of a good many well cured hams, and cracked the shells of a good many dozen of eggs on the occasion, besides divers quantities of blue rum, gin, brandy, cider royal, &c. used for washing down or keeping the steam up and the fog off. All their fun they kept among themselves, disturbing nobody save each other, and leaving an unusual quantity of oaths and profanity; from which, however, and indeed from all the aforesaid movements many of them are exempt we do not know that any person has a right to find fault with them.

THE WHIG, Tuesday, May 19, 1829

Our town is filled with strangers, drawn here no doubt, by the Canal Letting which takes place tomorrow. There are twelve sections of about one mile each to let, besides two lift locks and a guard lock, a dam across the river Lehigh at this place and the usual quantum of waste weirs, road and farm bridges, fencing, &c. There will be from 200 to 300 contractors here, and there will be in proportion, full as many applicants for contracts disappointed, as there were applicants for office to the presidential election.

THE WHIG, Tuesday, June 9, 1829

About 11 o'clock this morning the packet boat Swan, formerly on the Schuylkill Canal, and intended to ply between this place and Mauch Chunk, arrived at the Point. Her arrival was announced by the discharge of artillery from one of the guns of the Citizen Volunteers.

She belongs to Messrs. Wells, Weiss, Rice, Youngman, and some other enterprising citizens of Bethlehem.

EASTON CENTINEL, Friday, June 19, 1829

Two boats laden with coal, started from Mauch Chunk on the 6th inst. for the Philadelphia market, on the Lehigh Canal, and as we learn from an article in the Mauch Chunk Courier, dated June 10, were expected to arrive at this borough within a few days. Nearly two weeks have elapsed since the boats started from the former place, without being able to reach here, and we apprehend as many more months will go by, ere they can accomplish their object and render the canal navigable throughout the whole line. The boats passed Allentown and Bethlehem and are now within eight or nine miles of Easton, which is as near as they can approach us on the canal at present—we are rather sceptical, and not without just cause, having taken a view of the premises and the amount of work yet to be done, whether this great undertaking can be completed before the beginning of September or October, unless they produce a large additional number of hands. . . . The two boats which are now on the way, may possibly be brought down in the course of a few weeks, but we do not believe the canal will be in good navigable order before next fall.

One of the boats with Mr. J. White, acting manager of the Mauch Chunk Company on board, has, we are informed, since the above article was penned, passed by here, having taken to the river; they were obliged to unload in order to cross the dam which is in an unfinished state.

THE WHIG, June 30, 1829

The water was let into the whole line of the Lehigh Canal on Friday and Saturday last. It reached the outlet lock at this place at half past two o'clock on Saturday afternoon. A great many of our citizens turned out to see it and take a trip up to the dam, three miles above here, in the packet boat Swan. The banks seemed to stand up pretty well or, 'as well as could be expected" for new banks; no breaches occured, nor any material leaks. We may now expect to see lots of coal descending from Mauch Chunk and hundreds of people taking the trip up, on board the packet. By the way, we learn that there is to be an opposition of packets—that a new boat has been purchased to run from this place to Mauch Chunk. If so, we would advise the rival owners to make a daily line of it, one up each day—make hay while the sun shines. The packet travelling on canals don't last long—it may do pretty well while it is new and in fashion. But everything connected with fashion soon changes.

First fruits of the Lehigh Canal—We learn that 10 boats of coal, each carrying 60 tons, arrived from Mauch Chunk by the Canal last evening. The Company contemplate starting five coal boats daily, for some time, when the number will increase, if the Delaware Navigation will render it advisable.

EASTON CENTINEL, Friday, July 3, 1829

THE LEHIGH CANAL—On Friday and Saturday of last week, the water was let into the Lehigh Canal, from Mauch Chunk throughout the whole line. On Saturday afternoon when the water reached here, the banks of the canal were covered with Citizens who were waiting to see the packet boat, Swan, pass the locks, and to make a short excursion on her. The water has been left in the canal since that time, and we have not heard of any break in the embankment. Two boats and a number of arks have arrived and passed this place, within the last few days, destined for the Philadelphia market, and although we stated several weeks ago, our impression that the canal was in a very unfinished state, which undoubtedly was substantially the truth, we are now fully convinced that the coal-trade can and will be briskly and uninterruptedly carried on, during the canalling season, inasmuch as the work that remains to be accomplished can be done without obstructing the navigation. The first trip of the Swan will be made on the 4th of July, (tomorrow) from Easton to Allentown, returning to Easton same day. The public will be apprized in a short time, by advertisement, when the proprietors will be ready to commence running regularly for Mauch Chunk. In the meantime those who are desirous of taking an agreeable jaunt in the canal, will hold themselves prepared as a fine opportunity will be afforded tomorrow for their gratification.

EASTON CENTINEL, Friday, July 10, 1829

A breach in the bank of the Lehigh Canal having occurred in the embankment about a mile above this place, the canal was drained and repairs effected. Eight or ten arks are lying near the locks ready to proceed as soon as navigation is resumed.

ARRIVAL—The packet boat INDEPENDENCE, arrived here from Philadelphia on Sunday last. She is intended for an accommodation boat, to ply on the Lehigh Canal between this place and Mauch Chunk.

THE WHIG, Tuesday, May 4, 1830

We would like to see a cast coal stove that would answer for cooking and warming dwellings. Should our friends in Mauch Chunk furnish us with a model, that would come low, we would insure them that double the quantity of coal that was used here last winter would be consumed by our economical citizens during the ensuing winter.

THE WHIG, Tuesday, September 14, 1830

Our canal (the Delaware) is very near being completed. All the sections for four miles below this place, are entirely done, and so soon as sections No. 111 and 106 are finished the water can be let in to Durham Creek, or indeed to Gallows Run—The outlet lock at Easton and the aqueduct over Gallows Run are not in as great state of forwardness as could be wished, but this is to be attributed to the water continuing so high in the Delaware in the early part of the season as to prevent the foundations being laid as soon as desired.

THE WHIG, Tuesday, October 19, 1830

On Tuesday last, in consequence of closing the dam on the Lehigh, the water was swelled up so as to be let into the Delaware Division of the Pennsylvania Canal opposite this borough. During that day and on Wednesday, the water rose slowly, the dam being but partially gravelled, so as, however, to let in about 18 inches or two feet of water in the canal. . . . (Breaches 2 miles down, being repaired) John Carey Jr. Esq. is appointed Supervisor of the upper section of the canal from Easton to the lock No. 12, below Centre Bridge.

THE WHIG, Tuesday, November 2, 1830

On Tuesday last the water was let into the Delaware Division of the Pennsylvania Canal and made its way down as far as to the vicinity of Daniel Raub, five miles below this place.

EASTON CENTINEL, Friday, November 19, 1830

Messrs. Editors—Permit me to request you to publish for the information of your readers the following accurate statement of the cost of whiskey drank in constructing three quarters of a mile of canal . . .

3425 gallons, at 25 cts. per gallon	$ 856.00
Cost of dealing it out to the men	274.00
Loss of labor of each man in consequence of drinking, six cents per day—27,400 days	1644.00
Cost of whiskey drank on Sabbath and rainy days	244.00
Probable cost of whiskey drank at the shanties	300.00
	$3318.00

Note: The above information was submitted by a member of a prohibition organization.

THE WHIG, Tuesday, December 14, 1830
PACKET BOAT INDEPENDENCE EXCURSION

The packet boat Independence, Capt. John Burt, will leave the first lock of the Lehigh Canal, opposite Easton, on Saturday next the 18th instant, at one o'clock for Bethlehem, to attend the Concert on that evening. The boat will return by leaving Bethlehem at 10 o'clock on Sunday morning. Passage each way 25 cts.

THE WHIG, Tuesday, April 19, 1831
LEHIGH COAL

The subscriber hereby gives notice that he will receive proposals for contracts, to transport in the course of the ensuing two years, fifty thousand tons of Lehigh coal, from Mauch Chunk through the Lehigh and Morris canals to Newark. The subscriber will furnish boats and the contractor will provide every other requisite, and be at every other expense except tolls on the canal.

THE WHIG, Tuesday, May 24, 1831

We have the satisfaction to notice that Nos. 15 and 18 canal boats which arrived at South Easton by the Lehigh Canal on the 17th inst. from Mauch Chunk, carried together 133 tons 4 cwt. of coal which added together the established weights of the boats, makes the enormous load of 173 tons, drawn by two middle sized mules, this we believe to be the largest draft for equal weight of animal power on record, the 2 boats passed the locks side by side, under the care of the usual complement of hands for a canal boat, viz. 2 men and a boy.

THE WHIG, Tuesday, October 25, 1831

Last week several boats left the Delaware for New York, via the Morris Canal. They ascended the first plane very handsomely, and for aught we know, are wending their way just now across the Musconetcong Mountain, to supply our friends of New Amsterdam with a sample of our flour and Mauch Chunk coal, and thus induce them to draw on us for more. They are the articles that Northampton County can furnish of a quality equal to any in the world.

THE WHIG, Tuesday, January 24, 1832
LEHIGH COAL

The Morris Canal and Banking Company will receive proposals for the transportation of 50,000 tons of Lehigh coal, or any part of it, from Mauch Chunk, through the Lehigh and Morris canals. The coal will be laden on board the boats by the Lehigh Company, but is to be delivered from the boat at Newark, or any intermediate place as may be required by the company or their duly authorized agent.

The Company will contract to furnish the boats—the contractor to provide every other requisite, including ropes and tow lines, and be at every other expense.

Or the contractor may furnish his own boat and bear all expense.

Or the Company on good security will advance money, as it may be necessary to enable the contractor to build boats.

Or the Company on like security will sell to the contractor boats, at their cost, which are already built.

Jersey City   Robert Gilcrist, Cashier

THE WHIG, Tuesday, March 13, 1832

We have now a roaring freshet in the Delaware and Lehigh. The Delaware commenced rising the night before last. Yesterday evening it was up to the 18 foot mark on the pier of the bridge—this morning at 8 o'clock it was at (?). The water is now 8 feet over the Lehigh dam; until last evening the Lehigh was highest, during the night the water in the Lehigh fell and the Delaware got the ascendency. The low lands at South Easton below the Lehigh bridge are under water and the Philadelphia stage had to take the hill road this morning. For some distance below this place the water has covered the towpath of the canal.

THE WHIG, Tuesday, May 8, 1832

The Delaware Canal—The works on the Delaware Division of the Pennsylvania Canal is going on with energy. The Lehigh Coal and Navigation Company, with a spirit and liberal (attitude) which characterize all its acts, are furnishing the funds to pay the hands making the repairs, in anticipation of the Commonwealth funds, which are not yet forthcoming.

THE WHIG, Tuesday, June 12, 1832

Collector's Office, Easton, June 11, 1832.

This day the first clearance on the Delaware Division of the Pennsylvania Canal was issued from this office to the Mauch Chunk canal boat No. 30, Capt. William C. Zane, bound to Bristol with 30 tons of coal.

EASTON CENTINEL, Friday, July 27, 1832

The Delaware Canal is now in fine navigable order. From the 16th to the 24th inst. 41 boats passed. . . . Among the boats was the elegant boat "George Wolf" . . . belonging to Capt. Jacob Able of this place.

THE WHIG, July 31, 1832

The Delaware Canal continues in operation. Capt. Able left this place with his boat as we announced in our last, on Monday. He returned with a load of freight on Saturday at noon—performing the trip (160 miles) in a little over five days, including the delays of waiting for the tides.

EASTON CENTINEL, Friday, December 7, 1832

A breach has occurred in the Mauch Chunk Canal during the past week, about two miles above Easton, which has prevented the passage of boats. . . . Several hundred men are at work upon them and it is expected that in a few days the repairs will be complete.

THE WHIG, Tuesday, August 13, 1833

. . . At South Easton, the power of the whole river Lehigh, except what may be necessary for the navigation, with a twenty-two feet fall, is located near the junction of the Lehigh, the Delaware and the Morris canals—in the immediate vicinity of the best iron ore —45 miles from Mauch Chunk—80 miles by the canal from Philadelphia and 96 miles from New York.

EASTON SENTINEL, Friday, August 1, 1834

A noble act—On Wednesday of last week as two boats were passing along the basin above the weigh lock, a boy belonging to one of them fell overboard. The boats continued on their course, and when opposite to the house of Mr. John Snyder at Williamsport, the hands called out that a boy was drowning in the canal. . . . The boy was saved by Mr. Joseph Archer who jumped from a Union Canal boat and effected the rescue.

EASTON SENTINEL, Friday, May 29, 1835

4TH JULY

A meeting of the Boat Builders of the borough of Easton and vicinity, will be held at the Hotel of Melchor Horn, tomorrow evening at early candle light, to adopt measures for celebrating the Anniversary of the Declaration of American Independence.

EASTON SENTINEL, Friday, July 3, 1835

BOAT YARD

The subscriber informs the public that he has taken the Boat Yard recently occupied by Mr. Thomas Bishop in South Easton and immediately at the Lehigh Canal, where he is prepared to Build

CANAL AND OTHER BOATS

Henry M. Smith

THE WHIG, Wednesday, June 15, 1836

NOTICE—To boatmen on the Delaware Canal

It will hereafter be required for every boat navigating the Delaware Division Pennsylvania Canal, to have a Steersman and Bowsman on each boat, either descending or ascending said Canal, and also a boy with the tow horse.

Joseph Hough, Sup.

THE WHIG, Wednesday, September 28, 1836

. . . South Easton now contains 2 grain mills, 2 saw mills and a cotton factory; a rolling and slitting mill, and iron manufactory are partly finished and will soon be in operation, and there is still a large amount of water power for sale. The town has grown with unusual rapidity.

THE WHIG, Wednesday, March 7, 1838

Important Discovery—Hereafter we think the county of Northampton will deservedly rank as the great benefactor of the State. An important discovery, affecting the most solid interests of Pennsylvania, and which promises to prove of the most extraordinary advantage to our vast iron and coal region, has just been effected here. We allude to the fact that Mr. VanBuren of South Easton has succeeded in smelting iron ore with anthracite. He runs his furnaces regularly without one pound of charcoal. The quantity per day averages 1½ tons. He used 1½ tons of anthracite to 1 ton of pig. The iron is said to be of the very best quality. The furnace has been in operation some sixteen or seventeen days. He uses one third rock ore from New Jersey and two thirds of what is called in this neighborhood, Brotzman's ore obtained near Easton.

THE WHIG, Wednesday, March 14, 1838

LEHIGH TRANSPORTATION COMPANY
(Popularly known as the Red Line)

The proprietors of the above company take this method of informing merchants, millers and others having goods, grain, flour, &c. to transport between Philadelphia and White Haven and the intermediate places, viz—Easton, Freemansburg, Bethlehem, Allentown, Mauch Chunk, &c. that they contemplate running a line of boats between the above places. The boats, six in number, viz: Delaware, North America, Lehigh, Nicholas Biddle, Susquehanna and Pennsylvania are nearly all new and are commanded by sober and attentive men. . . .

Goods to be shipped from Philadelphia by the above line, will be stored at Brock's new stores, first wharf below Vine Street, and no charges made for storage.

Flour, Whiskey, Grain, Leather, &c. to be forwarded to Philadelphia and New York, will be received at P. S. Michler's new Storehouse, Easton, and by Selfridge & Wilson and Pretz, Sayer & Co., Allentown.

THE WHIG, Wednesday, February 13, 1839

The Dam—A number of our enterprising Citizens have combined together for the purpose of repairing the dam across the Lehigh at this place, as well as the abutment and basin adjoining, all of which were greatly damaged during the late freshet. The expense it is computed will be from twelve to fifteen thousand dollars, for the indemnification of which the gentlemen alluded to place their trust in the honor of the Commonwealth.

THE WHIG, Wednesday, June 12, 1839

Accident—We are informed that as the deck boat "Delaware" one of the Red Line, was passing under a bridge in the Delaware Canal, about two miles below New Hope, on Thursday last, a barrel lying on the deck, came in contact with the bridge and, by deflecting its course, caused the boat to ground in the opposite bank of the canal. There were three mules attached to the boat, and in endeavoring to get off the ground, by some misstep the hind mule got into the canal and dragged the other two after him . . . all three drowned. The mules were worth about three hundred fifty dollars.

APPENDIX III: WHY NOT ALSO SAVE THE LANGUAGE

As the canal era recedes into history the use of modern language often obscures the words and expressions common to the old boatmen. This is true of the everyday language of the Lehigh and Delaware canals. Unlike the great canals that crossed New York, Pennsylvania, Ohio and Indiana, with their flow of miscellaneous cargoes and hoards of passengers, the Lehigh and Delaware were comparatively isolated. Their chief function was to haul coal from the mines to tidewater markets and the men who operated the boats were plain, simple folk having little contact with the outside world. To them the craft that carried the coal were "boats," the men who operated them were "boatmen." The latter term was general and applied to all members of the crew, which in later years were but two: the man responsible for operating the boat, usually called the captain and his "hand," or driver. Apparently in early canal days there was a third member of the crew, the "bowsman." But he disappeared long before the turn of the century.

As our modern system of inland waterways expanded the cargo boats became larger and larger, often several hundred feet long, capable of carrying thousands of tons of freight. These craft are called barges. This term is often applied indiscriminately to all old canal boats. Nowhere in the reports or other official literature of the Lehigh and Delaware canals are the cargo craft called anything but "boats."

Another type of boat used on these canals by the work crews was called a scow. This was a boat with low freeboard and square ends. In early days of boating on the Lehigh and Delaware canals the regular cargo boats were often called scows.

Such terms as *canallers* or *canawlers, hogies,* a term used on some canals for the mule driver, *mule skinner,* from the great wagon trains of the western plains, and *barges* never were used by the boatmen of the Lehigh and Delaware canals.

Like its people, nothing could be simpler than the language of these canals. The boatmen ran the boats. It was as simple as that!

APPENDIX IV

THE BOATMAN'S HORN

By Lewis Sigafoos

(This poem was read before the Buckwampun Literary Association at the Ringing Rocks meeting on June 10, 1893.)

When the robin and the bluebird return to
    the north,
And the maple buds swell ere its blossoms
    put forth,
When the crocuses peep, and the daisy's
    bright eye
Looks up and behold the cerulean sky,
When the icy-bound rills are unshackled
    and free,
And rush down the hillside in frolicsome
    glee,
Then the boatmen feels sure that the
    moment has come
To bid his adieux to his family and home.
His wife, perhaps, stands, with a tear in
    her eye,
While he kisses the baby and bids them
    good-by.
He hastens aboard, goes to work with a
    will
And arranges things quickly with deftness
    and skill.
Soon his cabin is furnished convenient
    and neat
With household utensils and bedding
    complete,
And he mounts to the deck, casts her
    moorings aside,
Swings her bow from the wharf, and
    floats out on the tide.
With the dexterous move of a well-prac-
    ticed hand,
He heaves forth the line that it reaches
    the land,
Then walks quickly aft — for no time dare
    he lose —

And the "Rainbow" is rigged for her
    first summer cruise.
His team and their driver stand ready in
    place
Awaiting their orders to start off apace;
When he reaches the helm, with a turn
    of his head,
The edict goes forward, "All right! Go
    ahead!"
Her bow cleaves the surface and bright
    ripples break,
And her rudder blade marks out a silvery
    wake
As the "Rainbow" moves onward in
    smooth, even lines,
For a cargo of diamonds from anthracite
    mines.
But hark! hear the sound that rings out
    through the air
And rolls in swift cadence down the
    smooth Delaware!
While the cliffs send the echo in musical
    trills
To bear friendly greeting to Jersey's
    green hills.
But what does it mean? Ah! the lock-
    tender knows;
For the gates of the lock wide open he
    throws,
And the "Rainbow" moves on with the
    aspect of pride
As the captain with helm steers her
    safely inside.
The wickets now open, and the waters
    rush in
With a writhing and foaming and turbu-
    lent din!
The strong-swelling surge, mingling
    frolic with love,
Buoys the boat proudly up to the level
    above,
Then onward the boatman, untrammeled
    with care,

Moves gaily along by the blue Delaware.
Where villages nestled 'mongst hills of
    bright green
Present to the eye a most picturesque
    scene.
He reaches the Lehigh, which winds gently
    through
Hills of exquisite beauty and mountains
    of blue.
His horn gaily winding with notes strong
    and clear,
Re-echoes from cliffs as the "Rainbow"
    draws near.
"America's Switzerland" at length he
    descries,
Where the "Switchback" and "Glen" form
    a real paradise;
Where lovers of Nature and people of
    wealth
Seek a feast of delight — an elixir of
    health.
'Tis here at the chutes with a clattering
    din
The boatman delights to see the crystals
    roll in,
And with diamonds black as his cargo of
    freight
He pursues his slow journey both early
    and late.
On a cliff have I stood by Delaware's side
And watched him below me so noiselessly
    glide,
While with eager ear I would listen to
    hear
The sound of his horn sonorific and
    clear.
When the shadowy mist like a bridal veil
Drapes the face of the sky, and the stars
    grow pale
Ere the light-winged choristers' grand
    matinee
Preludes the approach of the "Lord of
    the day;"

When the "Goddess of night" folds her
    mantle aside,
And the earth stands enrobed like a mod-
    est young bride,
While Nature's sweet choruses mingle in
    sound,
Till echo, enchanted, wafts the music
    around.
When grand and effulgent, the great
    "King of Day,"
Mounts his chariot of fire to haste on his
    way;
When he reaches the zenith and hies to
    the West
Till behind the horizon he sinks down to
    rest,
From the advent of spring till the snow
    clouds appear
Let the sound of the horn ever fall on
    the ear.
Let its musical echoes ring out through
    the sky
Till the last autumn flowers wither and
    die.
Oh! the sound of the horn hath a power-
    ful charm
To lull to sweet rest, or to rouse and
    alarm;
To call forth to battle, to sound a re-
    treat,
To quiet dull care with its melody sweet;
To lift up the soul, to enchant and im-
    press,
To fill hearts with love that they cannot
    express;
To awaken emotions that dormant have
    lain
Like the life-hidden germs in the seed of
    a grain.
Oh, then merry boatman, cease never to
    play,
That the gloom of dull care may be
    driven away.

When the rain of Adversity falls cold and
 chill,
Wake up the heart's music with rapturous
 thrill!
Oh, let not Despondency mark for her
 own
What might be reclaimed by a musical
 tone!
And let sweet inspiration ne'er cease to
 be borne
By the magical tones of the boatman's
 horn.

APPENDIX V

CONTRACT FOR OUTLET LOCK
AT NEW HOPE
Original in Pennsylvania State Archives

Article of Agreement entered into this twentysixth day of August One thousand Eight hundred and forty seven by and Between the Commonwealth of Pennsylvania by W. K. Huffnagle Supervisor of the Delaware Division Penn⁀ Canal of the one part, and Alanson Sumner and Moreau Delano of the other part.

Witnesseth,

That the said parties of the second part do hereby agree to furnish the material and construct in a permanent and workmanlike manner, and according to the plan and specification exhibited at the letting, which are to be considered as forming a part of this contract, All that Canal, Locks, and fixtures, necessary to form the connection between the feeder Level of the Delaware Division of the Pennsylvania Canal and the Delaware River at Wells' Falls, authorized to be constructed by the act of the 20ᵗʰ of April 1846, and all its appurtenances Complete, and to finish the same on or before the Thirtieth day of November next.

It is Further Agreed that the said parties of the second part will conform to the directions of the Supervisor of the Line, and that the workmanship and Materials shall at all times be subject to his inspection and approval. And the said Sumner & Delano are to be paid for completing this Contract the sum of Eighteen thousand dollars as compensation in full. Payments to be made on the Estimates of the President of the Board of Canal Commissioners as the work progresses.

This Contract not to be binding on the Commonwealth, until approved by the Board of Canal Commissioners.

In Witness Whereof, the said parties have hereunto set their hands and seals the day and year aforesaid.

Witness.
Andrew J. Beaumont

W. K. Huffnagle {Seal}
Sup. Del. Div. Pa Canal
Alanson Sumner {Seal}
Moreau Delano {Seal}

NOTES

Abbreviations used in notes

PSA— Collections of the Pennsylvania State Archives, Harrisburg.

BCHS— Bucks County Historical Society, Doylestown, Pennsylvania.

Hazard—The Register of Pennsylvania, Devoted to the Preservation of Facts and Documents, and every other kind of Useful Information Respecting the State of Pennsylvania, Edited by Samuel Hazard, Philadelphia.

LC&N— Lehigh Coal and Navigation Company, Annual Reports.

CHAPTER 1 The Delaware River Before Canals

1. Harry Emerson Wildes, *The Delaware* (New York: Rinehart and Co., 1940), Chap. 1.

2. A paper presented at the second Annual New Jersey Historical Congress at Atlantic City, as reported in the *Philadelphia Public Ledger* of Apr. 7, 1934.

3. Leslie C. Wood, *Rafting on the Delaware River* (Livingston Manor, N.Y.: Livingston Manor Times, 1934), Chap. 1.

4. *Ibid.,* p. 22.

5. *Ibid.,* p. 26

6. *Ibid.,* pp. 47-55.

7. *Ibid.,* p. 67.

8. *Ibid.,* p. 82.

9. B. F. Fackenthal, Jr., "Improving Navigation on the Delaware River with Some Account of Its Ferries, Bridges, Canals and Floods," BCHS, Vol. VI (1932), p. 113.

10. Wood, *op cit.,* p. 112.

11. Fackenthal, *op cit.,* p. 122.

12. Wood, *op cit.,* p. 189.

13. *Ibid.,* p. 38.

14. *Ibid.,* p. 41.

15. This series of articles appears as "A Rafting Story of the Delaware River," BCHS, Vol. VI (1932), pp. 467-524.

16. Thaddeus S. Kinderdine, "Lumbering Days on the Delaware River," BCHS, Vol. IV (1917), pp. 239-252.

CHAPTER 2 Building the Canal

1. Washington not only favored inland navigation but also took every opportunity to stimulate interest in this means of transportation. When the Patowmack and James River companies were organized, he was made president of each, *Old Towpaths,* pp. 11 and 12.

In a 1785 letter to James Madison, Washington said, "It appears to me that no country in the Universe is better calculated to derive the benefits from inland Navigation than this is, and certain am I, that the conveniences to the Citizens individually, and the sources of wealth to the Country generally, which will be opened thereby will be found to exceed the most sanguine imagination." *The Writings of George Washington from the Original Manuscript Sources, 1745-1799.* (Washington: U.S. Government Printing Office, 1932), Vol. 28, p. 336.

2. Hazard, Vol. I, (Jan. 12, 1828), p. 23.

3. Hazard, Vol. III, (Feb. 14, 1829), p. 101.

4. William J. Foster, Jr., *Communication from the Canal Commissioners Relative to the Construction of an Outlet Lock, Delaware Division, Pennsylvania Canal* (J. M. G. Lessure, Printer to the State, 1846), p. 3.

5. Doran Green, *A History of Bristol Boro* (Camden, N.J.: C. S. Magrath, 1911), p. 144.

6. *Ibid.,* p. 144.

7. Hazard, Vol. IV, (Aug. 1, 1829), p. 69.

8. Canvass White, *Papers,* Cornell University Collection of Regional History, Box 609.

9. PSA, R. G. No. 17, Box 1, p. 100.

10. *Ibid.,* p. 61.

11. Hazard, Vol. V, (May 8, 1830), p. 302.

12. Hazard, Vol. VII (Jan. 1831), pp. 12 and 24.

13. Josiah White, *Josiah White's History, given by himself.* Privately printed.

14. LC&N, (Jan. 14, 1833), p. 3.

15. White, *op cit.,* p. 61.

16. Fackenthal, *op cit.,* p. 202.

CHAPTER 3 Tour Guide to the Canal

1. The Indians gave the name Lech-au-we-kink to the area now comprising Easton.

2. William H. Shank, *Historic Bridges in Pennsylvania,* (York: Buchart-Horn, 1966), p. 4.

3. W. W. H. Davis, *History of Doylestown, Old and New.* (Doylestown: Doylestown Intelligencer Print, 1904), p. 199.

4. *Wayside Scenes Along the Philadelphia and Easton Electric Railway,* a brochure in BCHS library.

5. Information on Raubsville Hydroelectric Station was supplied through the courtesy of Don Worthington of Pennsylvania Power and Light Corporation.

6. Fackenthal, *op cit.,* p. 154.

7. Alvin F. Harlow, *Old Towpaths* (New York: D. Appleton and Co., 1926), p. 382.

8. *Fifty Years of Paper Making—A Brief History of the Origin, Development and Present Status of the Warren Manufacturing Company, 1873-1923.* Privately printed. (Boston: Walton Advertising and Printing Co., 1923).

9. B. F. Fackenthal, Jr., "Manufacture of Hydraulic Cement in Bucks County." BCHS, Vol. VI (1932), p. 346.

10. A blicky was a container holding about one quart, usually a tin pail.

11. James H. Fitzgerald, "River Boulders and Cobblestones Used for Paving." BCHS, Vol. VI (1932), p. 91.

12. See *Map of the Delaware Division of the Pennsylvania Canal,* by A. W. Kennedy, circa 1828-30, 23 plates. Pennsylvania State Archives.

13. George MacReynolds, *Place Names in Bucks County Pennsylvania.* (Doylestown: The Bucks County Historical Society, Sec. Ed., 1955), p. 385.

14. F. Francis Rapp, "Lehigh and Delaware Division Canal Notes." BCHS, Vol. IV (1917), pp. 600-606.

15. Alice Eastburn Smith, "The Smith Plow." *Towpath* (New Hope, Pa.: The Towpath Pub. Co.), No. 4, p. 12.

16. John Richardson, *Solebury Township* (Philadelphia: Offset Service Co. 1958), p. 23.

17. This story, somewhat fictionized, is related by John P. Rogers in *The New Doane Book* (Doylestown: the Bucks County Historical Society, 1952), p. 170.

18. W. W. H. Davis, *History of Bucks County* (Sec. Ed. 2 Vol., New York: The Lewis Pub. Co., 1905), Vol. I, p. 291.

19. Richardson, *op cit.,* p. 22.

20. Artist McClellan authored *The Delaware Canal a picture story,* (New Brunswick: Rutgers University Press, 1967.)

21. PSA, *R. G. 17, Delaware Canal, Reports and Misc. Documents, Box 1,* p. 11.

22. By Act of Assembly dated July 25, 1917.

23. Richardson, *op cit.*, p. 30.

24. George MacReynolds, ed., *The New Doane Book* (Doylestown: The Bucks County Historical Society, 1952), p. 227.

CHAPTER 4   Locks, Aqueducts and Other Engineering Features

1. Lieut. Harry F. Hodges, Corps of Engineers, *Notes on Mitering Lock Gates* (Washington: Government Printing Office, 1892).

2. LC&N, May 5, 1863, p. 43.

3. Rapp, *op cit.*, pp. 600-606.

4. Hazard, "Canal Commissioners' Report of 1830," Vol. VII, p. 24.

CHAPTER 5   Canal Boats

1. PSA, *R. G. 17, Delaware Canal, Reports and Misc. Documents, Box 4*, p. 60.

2. Jesse L. Hartman, "John Dougherty and the Rise of the Section Boat System." *Pennsylvania Magazine of History and Biography.* (1945), Vol. 69, pp. 294-314.

3. David G. Williams, "The Lehigh Canal System." Plate VII of Supplement. *Proceedings Lehigh County Historical Society* (1958).

4. Fackenthal, "Improving Navigation . . .," p. 114.

CHAPTER 6   Canal Maintenance and Improvement

1. Hazard, "Canal Commissioners' Report for 1833," Vol. XII, p. 388.

2. PSA, *R. G. No. 17, Delaware Canal, . . . Box 4*, p. 149.

3. *Ibid.*

4. LC&N, Feb. 24, 1880, p.

5. Ralph D. Gray, *The National Waterway—A History of the Chesapeake and Delaware Canal, 1769-1965* (Urbana: University of Illinois Press, 1967), p. 82.

6. *Ibid.* pp. 124-125.

7. *Ibid*, p. 264.

8. LC&N, Jan. 9, 1832, p. 13.

9. "Delaware Canal, Early History of Waterway from Original Sources." Anon. *Internal Affairs*, Vol. 21, Nos. 9-10 (1953).

10. PSA, *R. G. No. 17, Delaware Canal . . . Box 1*, p. 59.

11. PSA, *R. G. No. 17, Delaware Canal . . . Box 4*, p. 72.

12. *Ibid.*, p. 6.

13. *Bucks County Intelligencer*, July 15, 1832.

14. William Strickland, *Reports on Canals, Railroads, Roads and Other Subjects made to The Pennsylvania Society for the Promotion of Internal Improvements* (Philadelphia: H. C. Carey & I. Lea, 1826).

Strickland reported, p. 10, "After a careful examination of the canals in this country [England] I am induced to draw a conclusion unfavorable to the construction of wide lock chambers, on any canals intended for the general purposes of coasting or internal trade. . . . The extreme width of the locks of canals in the interior of the country, is from eight to twelve feet. . . . Narrow lock chambers are expeditiously and conveniently filled; they are less expensive; they require but little water; they save time; and in this country, where they have been practically tested, they are now approved and adopted."

15. LC&N, Jan. 12, 1835, p. 7.

16. LC&N, Jan. 14, 1839, p. 28.

17. Foster, *op cit.*, p. 3.

18. PSA, *R. G. No. 17, Box 1*, p. 83.

19. LC&N, May 7, 1850, p. 8.
20. LC&N, May 7, 1867, p. 7.
21. LC&N, May 6, 1856, p. 10.
22. LC&N, May 4, 1852, p. 9.
23. PSA, *op cit.,* p. 92.
24. LC&N, May 3, 1852, p. 12.
25. LC&N, May 2, 1854, p. 10.
26. LC&N, May 1, 1855, p. 13.
27. LC&N, May 5, 1857, p. 11.
28. LC&N, May 7, 1867, p. 25.
29. LC&N, May 3, 1870, p. 8.
30. LC&N, Feb. 28, 1878, p. 26.
31. Kennedy, *Map of the Delaware* . . .
32. PSA, *R. G. No. 17, Box 2,* p. 1003.
33. PSA, *R. G. No. 17, Box 4,* p. 156.
34. LC&N, Jan. 9, 1843, p. 19.
35. W. H. Gausler, "Reminiscences of the Lehigh and Delaware Canals from 1840 to 1856" (*The Penn Germania,* Vol. XIII, No. 6, Old Series, June 1912), pp. 452-456.
36. LC&N, May 3, 1853, p. 7.
37. LC&N, May 5, 1863, pp. 31-32.
38. *Ibid.,* pp. 44-45.
39. Gausler, *op cit.*
40. Fackenthal, "Improving Navigation . . .", p. 215.
41. LC&N, May 3, 1870, p. 27.
42. LC&N, Feb. 26, 1878, p. 26.
43. *Towpath,* Vol. 8, No. 1, (Feb. 1956).
44. *Towpath,* Vol. 8, No. 2, (Oct. 1956).

CHAPTER 7   The Coal Trade and Other Commodities

1. George Korson, *Black Rock—Mining Folklore of the Pennsylvania Dutch* (Baltimore: The Johns Hopkins Press, 1960), pp. 14-16.
The origin of this legend was a paper titled, "A Brief Account of the discovery of Anthracite Coal on the Lehigh," presented on April 19, 1826, by a Quaker physician, Dr. Thomas C. James, before the *Council of the Historical Society of Pennsylvania.* The Doctor said he felt no objection to committing his little narration to paper "although the circumstances detailed occurred at such a distance of time as must plead an excuse for imperfect recollection."
2. Korson, *op cit.,* Chap. 1.
3. Eleanor Morton, *Josiah White, Prince of Pioneers* (New York: Stephen Daye Press, 1946), p. 103.
4. *Ibid.,* p. 105.
5. *Ibid.,* pp. 109 and 118.
6. *Ibid.,* p. 158.
7. *Ibid.,* p. 163.
8. Korson, *op cit.,* p. 44.
9. *Ibid.,* p. 57.
10. Frederick M. Binder, "Anthracite Enters the American Home" (*The Pennsylvania Magazine of History and Biography,* Jan. 1958), pp. 82-99.
11. Morton, *op cit.,* p. 163.
12. Hazard, Vol. XIV, Oct. 25, 1834, p. 267.
13. All Data on the transportation of coal was taken from the annual reports of the Lehigh Coal and Navigation Co.

14. LC&N, Dec. 31, 1911.

15. PSA, *R. G. 17, Delaware Canal . . . Box 1*, p. 42.

16. Green, *op cit.,* p. 147.

17. MacReynolds, *op cit.,* p. 34.

18. LC&N, Jan. 14, 1833, p. 4.

19. LC&N, Jan. 14, 1834, p. 5.

20. BCHS, in archives.

21. Harlow, *op cit.,* p. 183.

22. This volume is in the library of BCHS.

23. The opening and closing dates for navigation on the Delaware Canal varied greatly from year to year. A reasonably average year would be from Apr. 1 to Nov. 30, or, less Sundays, 212 operating days.

24. LC&N, Feb. 28, 1882, p. 20.

25. Interesting information on the boat situation is contained in the *Annual Report of the Secretary of Internal Affairs of the Commonwealth of Pennsylvania* for the year 1875. Part IV of that report contains technical and operating data of the various canals in the Commonwealth. In reporting on the Delaware Canal, The Delaware Division Canal Company stated that about 1000 boats were owned and run by private parties. The Lehigh Coal and Navigation Company reporting for the Lehigh Canal, stated that no boats were owned by the Company but that 884 boats were owned by Private parties.

26. Morton, *op cit.,* p. 243.

27. Gausler, *op cit.*

28. LC&N, Jan. 8, 1844, p. 6.

29. *Ibid.,* p. 7.

30. LC&N, Feb. 24, 1874, p. 7.

31. LC&N, Feb. 28, 1878, p. 7.

32. The daily reports of the *Pinkerton's National Detective Agency* are on file at the library of BCHS. Sections of the reports that give names of suspected individuals have been omitted from this book in consideration of descendents who may still be living.

33. LC&N, Feb. 12, 1907, p. 14.

34. List of quantities which are estimated as a ton in collecting tolls: Flour— 10½ barrels; Whiskey—8 barrels or 2 hogsheads; Wheat, Rye, Indian corn and Flaxseed—40 barrels; Oats—80 bushels; Barley—50 bushels; Stone—four fifths of a perch; Salt fish— 7½ barrels; Lumber—1000 feet board measure; 1000 barrel staves and headings; 100 rails or posts; 1000 hoop-poles; Cordwood —half a cord; Bricks—500; Salt—Liverpool fine, 45 bushels, all other descriptions, 32 bushels; Tar—7 barrels; Rosin—8 barrels; Oysters—4000; Lime—28 bushels; Window glass—2800 feet. From John N. Hoffman, *Anthracite in the Lehigh Region of Pennsylvania, 1820-45* (Washington: U.S. National Museum Bulletin 252, U.S. Government Printing Office, 1968), p. 96.

35. LC&N, Feb. 12, 1907, p. 15.

36. LC&N, Feb. 10, 1908, p. 11.

37. From a portion of Church's diary discovered by Grant Emery.

CHAPTER 8   Others Canals in the Upper Delaware Valley

1. Williams, *op cit.,* p. 99.

2. Morton, *op cit.,* p. 204.

3. Richard F. Veit, *The Old Canals of New Jersey* (Little Falls, N.J.: New Jersey Geographical Press).

4. Manville B. Wakefield, *Coal Boats to Tidewater* (South Fallsburg, N.Y.; Steingart Associates, Inc. 1965).

5. Fackenthal, *op cit.,* p. 170 fn.

CHAPTER 9   Life and Times Along the Canal

1. Thomas Fall, *Canalboat to Freedom* (New York: The Dial Press, 1966).
2. Gausler, *op cit.*
3. LC&N, Jan. 11, 1830, p. 4.
4. LC&N, Jan. 8, 1838, p. 12.
5. *Delaware Canal, Early History of Waterway from Original Documents* (Internal Affairs, Vol. 21, No. 9-10, Aug.-Sept., 1953).
6. PSA, *R. G. No. 17, Minute Book of Canal Commissioners, Box 1,* June 13, 1833.
7. Willis M. Rivinus, *Early Taverns in Bucks County* (New Hope, 1965), p. 53. Rivinus calls this building the "Beer and Cake House" and states it was "a solitary residence that at one time sold beer and cakes to canal boatmen." The cakes were somewhat similar to pretzels.
8. Harlow, *op cit.,* p. 382.
9. LC&N, Jan. 12, 1829, p. 7.
10. Pennsylvania Canal Society library.
11. LC&N, Dec. 31, 1923, p. 9.
12. PSA, *R. G. No. 17, Delaware Canal Reports . . . Box 4,* p. 116.
13. Charles Stewart, "Red Line Transportation Company" *Northampton County Historical and Genealogical Society,* Library No. 386, S849.
114. LC&N, Feb. 28, 1893, p. 8.
15. LC&N, Feb. 10, 1908, p. 11.
16. Stewart, *op cit.*
17. The *New Hope Gazette,* July 29, 1954.
18. The *New Hope Gazette,* Aug. 19, 1954.
19. While doing research at the library of The Bucks County Historical Society, it was my good fortune to locate long forgotten copy of this log.

CHAPTER 10   Historic Vignettes of Durham Valley

1. R. D. Billinger, "The Durham Furnace" *Industrial and Engineering Chemistry,* Vol. 30, April 1938, p. 428.
2. W. W. H. Davis, *op cit.,* Vol. II, p. 140.
3. *Ibid.,* p. 140.
4. *Easton Express,* Mar. 3, 1967.
5. Morton, *op cit.,* p. 226.
6. *Ibid.,* p. 246.
7. "Proceedings of the Forty-fifth Meeting," *Transactions of the American Institute of Mining Engineers,* (May 1886 to Feb. 1887), Vol. XV, p. lxiii.
8. Billinger, *op cit.,* p. 8.
9. Fackenthal, *Collections,* Folder 34, BCHS.
10. Fackenthal, "Improving Navigation . . . " p. 149.
111. W. W. H. Davis, *The History of Bucks County, Pennsylvania* (Doylestown: Democrat Book and Job Office Print, 1876).
12. Davis, *History . . .,* Vol. II, p. 141.
13. Codman Hislop, *The Mohawk* (Holt, Rinehart and Winston, Inc. 1948).
14. John A. Anderson, "Navigation on the Delaware and Lehigh Rivers," BCHS, Vol. IV, p. 282.
15. Fitzgerald, *op cit.,* Vol. VI, p. 90.
16. Foster, *op cit.,* p. 4.
17. Anderson, *op cit.,* p. 296.
18. "Delaware Canal, . . . *op cit.,*
19. MacReynolds, *op cit.,* pp. 140-145.

20. *Pennsylvania Geological Survey* (1877).

21. Fackenthal, "The Indian Walking Purchase of September 19 and 20, 1737, and the Lunching Place of the Walkers at Noon on the First Day of the Walk." BCHS, Vol. VI, pp. 7-24.

22. Willis M. Rivinus, *The Red Men in Bucks County* (New Hope, 1965).

23. John R. Connelly, *A Study of the Surveys Confirming the Walking Purchase—1737* (Palmerton, Pa. 1962). This highly technical analysis consists of 66 typed pages together with numerous maps and tables. For private circulation. A copy of this report is in the library of the Pennsylvania Canal Society.

24. *The Walking Purchase,* Historic Pennsylvania Leaflet No. 24. (Harrisburg: Pennsylvania Historical and Museum Commission, 1961).

25. *Ibid.,* p. 4.

26. Fackenthal, *op cit.,* p. 23.

27. MacReynolds, *op cit.,* p. 121.

CHAPTER 11   The End—and a New Beginning

1. Fackenthal, "Address of Welcome to Glacialdrift at Riegelsville," BCHS, Vol. VI, p. 331.

2. *Doylestown Daily Intelligencer,* Oct. 19, 1931.

3. LC&N, Feb. 17, 1937.

4. *Ibid.*

5. LC&N, Feb. 27, 1941.

6. *Towpath,* Vol. 1, No. 1, Dec. 1939, p. 7.

7. *Towpath,* Vol. 10, No. 1, Mar. 1959.

8. *Towpath,* Vol. 8, No. 3, Nov. 1957.

9. *Towpath,* Vol. 9, No. 3, Sept. 1958.

10. *Towpath,* Vol. 2, No. 11, Nov. 1941, p. 17.

11. *Towpath,* Vol. 10, No. 1, Mar. 1959.

BIBLIOGRAPHY

American Institute of Mining Engineers. "Proceedings of the Forty-fifth Meeting." *Transactions* . . ., Vol. XV, May 1886 to Feb. 1887, p. lxiii.

Anderson, John A. "Navigation on the Delaware and Lehigh Rivers." *The Bucks County Historical Society,* Vol. IV, 1917, pp. 282-312.

Andrist, Ralph K. "The Erie Canal." *American Heritage,* Vol. XIX, No. 6, Oct. 1968, pp. 22-77.

Billinger, R. D. "The Durham Furnace." *Industrial and Engineering Chemistry,* Vol. 30, Apr. 1938, pp. 428+.

Binder, Frederick M. "Anthracite Enters the American Home." *The Pennsylvania Magazine of History and Biography,* Jan. 1958, pp. 82-99.

Brandt, Francis Burke. *The Majestic Delaware—The Nation's Foremost Historic River.* Philadelphia: 1920.

Brzyski [Bryski] Anthony J. "The Lehigh Canal and its Effect on the Economic Development of the Region Through Which it Passed—1818-1873." Unpublished dissertation for Ph.D., New York University, June 1957.

Calhoun, Daniel H. *The American Civil Engineer. Origins and Conflict.* Cambridge: Harvard University Press, 1960.

Chalmers, Harvey II. *The Birth of the Erie Canal.* New York: Bookman Associates, •1960.

Connelly, John R. *A Study of the Surveys Confirming the Walking Purchase.* Palmerton, Pa.: 1962. Unpublished work.

Cummings, Hubertis M. *Pennsylvania Board of Canal Commissioners' Records with Allied Records of Canal Companies Chartered by the Commonwealth, Descriptive Index.* Harrisburg: Bureau of Land Records, 1959.

Davis, William W. H. *History of Bucks County, Pennsylvania,* 2d. 2 Vols. New York: The Lewis Pub., Co., 1905.

———. *The History of Bucks County, Pennsylvania.* Doylestown, Pa.: Democrat Book and Job Office Print, 1876.

———. *History of Doylestown, Old and New.* Doylestown: Intelligencer Print, 1904.

"Delaware Canal, Early History of Waterway from Original Sources." *Internal Affairs,* Vol. 21, No. 9-10, 1953.

Fackenthal, B. F., Jr., "Address of Welcome to 'Glacialdrift' at Riegelsville." *The Bucks County Historical Society,* Vol. VI, 1932, p. 331 fn.

———. "Improving Navigation on the Delaware River with Some Account of Ferries, Bridges, Canals and Floods." *The Bucks County Historical Society,* Vol. VI, 1932, pp. 103-230.

———. "Manufacture of Hydraulic Cement in Bucks County." *The Bucks County Historical Society,* Vol. VI, 1932, pp. 346-355.

Fackenthal Collection. The Bucks County Historical Society, Folder 34.

Fifty Years of Paper Making—A Brief History of the Origin, Development and Present Status of the Warren Manufacturing Company, 1873-1923. Boston: Walton Advertising and Printing Co., 1923. Privately printed.

Fitzgerald, James H. "River Boulders and Cobblestones Used for Paving." *The Bucks County Historical Society,* Vol. VI, 1923, pp. 88-95.

Flory, Jane. *A Tune for the Towpath.* Boston: Houghton Mifflin Co., 1962.

Foster, William J., Jr., *Communication from the Canal Commissioners, Relative to the Construction of an Out-Let Lock. The Delaware Division, Pennsylvania Canal.* Harrisburg: J. M. G. Lescure, Printer to the State, 1846.

Gausler, W. H. "Reminiscences of the Lehigh and Delaware Canals from 1840 to 1856." *The Penn Germania,* Vol. XIII, No. 6, Old Series, June 1912, pp. 452-456.

Gray, Ralph D. *The National Waterway—A History of the Chesapeake and Delaware Canal, 1769-1965.* Urbana: University of Illinois Press, 1967.

Green, Doran. *A History of Bristol Boro.* Camden, N.J.: C. S. Magrath, 1911.

Harlow, Alvin F. *Old Towpaths.* New York: D. Appleton and Co., 1926. New ed., Port Washington, N.Y.: Kennikat Press, Inc., 1964.

Hartman, Jesse L. "John Dougherty and the Rise of the Section Boat System." *Pennsylvania Magazine of History and Biography,* Vol. 69, 1945, pp. 294-314.

Hazard, Samuel, ed. *The Register of Pennsylvania, Devoted to the Preservation of Facts and Documents, and Every Other Kind of Useful Information Respecting the State of Pennsylvania.* Philadelphia: Wm. F. Geddes, 16 vols. 1828-1835.

Hislop, Codman. *The Mohawk,* New York: Holt, Rinehart and Winston, 1948.

History of Northampton County, Pennsylvania, Philadelphia and Reading; 1877.

Hodges, Harry F., 1st Lieut. Corps of Engineers. *Notes on Mitering Lock Gates,* No. 26, Professional Papers of the Corps of Engineers of U.S. Army. Washington: Government Printing Office, 1892.

Hoffman, John N. *Anthracite in the Lehigh Region of Pennsylvania, 1820-45.* U.S. National Museum Bulletin 252. Washington: Smithsonian Institution Press, 1968.

Hunter, Henry W. *Dock and Lock Machinery.* (English). New York: D. Van-Nostrand Co., 1922.

Jacobs, David and Neville, Anthony E. *Bridges, Canals and Tunnels.* New Brunswick: D. VanNostrand Co., 1968.

Kenderdine, Thaddeus S. "Lumbering Days on the Delaware River." *The Bucks County Historical Society,* Vol. IV, 1917, pp. 239-252.

Kennedy, A. W. *Map of the Delaware Division of the Pennsylvania Canal, 1828-30.* 23 plates, Harrisburg: Pennsylvania State Archives.

Korson, George. *Black Rock, Mining Folklore of the Pennsylvania Dutch.* Baltimore: The Johns Hopkins Press, 1960.

———. ed. *Pennsylvania Songs and Legends.* Baltimore: The Johns Hopkins Press, 1949.

Lane, Wheaton J. Paper presented at Second Annual New Jersey Historical Congress at Atlantic City as reported in *Philadelphia Public Ledger* of Apr. 7, 1934.

Lehigh Coal and Navigation Company, Annual Reports. Complete file from 1828 to 1956 in library of Lehigh University. Consecutive reports from 1826 to 1876 in library of Pennsylvania Canal Society.

Livingood, James Weston. *The Philadelphia-Baltimore Trade Rivalry, 1780-1860.* Harrisburg: The Pennsylvania Historical and Museum Commission, 1947.

MacReynolds, George. *Place Names in Bucks County,* 2d ed. Doylestown: The Bucks County Historical Society, 1955.

———. ed. *The New Doane Book,* 2d ed. rev. Doylestown: The Bucks County Historical Society, 1952.

McClellan, Robert J. *The Delaware Canal, a picture story,* New Brunswick: Rutgers University Press, 1967.

McNair, Thomas S. *Map of Delaware Division Canal from Surveys Made in April and May 1868 for the Delaware Division Canal Co. . . . and the Lehigh Coal and Navigation Co. . . .,* 50 plates. In Pennsylvania State Archives, Harrisburg.

Morton, Eleanor, [pseud]. *Josiah White—Prince of Pioneers.* New York: Stephen Daye Press, 1946.

Payne, Robert. *The Canal Builders; The Story of Canal Engineers Through the Ages.* New York: The Macmillan Co., 1959.

Pennsylvania State Archives. *Delaware Canal, Reports and Misc. Documents, R. G. No. 17.*

———. *Minute Book of Canal Commissioners, R. G. No. 17.*

Pine, Joshua, III. A series of articles that appeared in the Walton, N. Y., *Chronicle* from June 21 to Oct. 4, 1883, and recorded as "A Rafting Story of the Delaware River." In *The Bucks County Historical Society,* Vol. VI, 1932, pp. 467-524.

Rapp, Francis F. "Lehigh and Delaware Division Canal Notes." *The Bucks County Historical Society,* Vol. IV, 1917, pp. 600-606.

Register of Boats Clearing at Bristol on the Pennsylvania Canal, 1849. In library of The Bucks County Historical Society.

Richardson, John. *Solebury Township, Bucks County, Pennsylvania,* Philadelphia: Offset Service Co., 1958.

Rivinus, Willis M. *The Red Man in Bucks County,* New Hope, Pa., 1965.

_____. *Early Taverns of Bucks County,* New Hope: 1965.

Sanderson, Dorothy Hurlbut. *The Delaware and Hudson Canalway, Carrying Coal to Rondout,* Ellenville, N.Y.: The Rondout Valley Publishing Co., 1965.

Shank, William H. *The Amazing Pennsylvania Canals,* York, Pa.: Printing Plate Craftsmen, 1965.

_____. *Great Floods of Pennsylvania,* York: 1968.

_____. *Historic Bridges of Pennsylvania,* York: 1966.

Simonetti, Martha L. *Inventory of Canal Commissioners' Maps in the Pennsylvania State Archives,* Harrisburg: Bureau of Archives and History, Pennsylvania Historical and Museum Commission, 1968.

Smith, Alice Eastburn. "The Smith Plow," *Towpath,* Vol. II, No. 4, Apr. 1941, p. 12.

Stephenson, Clarence D. *Pennsylvania Canal, Indiana and Westmoreland Counties,* Marion Center, Pa.: Pub. by the author, 1961.

Stewart, Charles. "Red Line Transportation Company." *Northampton County Historical and Genealogical Society,* unpublished MS. Library No. 386, S849.

Tyler, David Budlong. *The Bay and River Delaware, A Pictorial History.* Cambridge, Md.; Cornell Maritime Press, 1955.

Veit, Richard F. *The Old Canals of New Jersey.* Little Falls, N.J.: New Jersey Geographical Press, 1963.

Wakefield, Manville B. *Coal Boats to Tidewater. The Story of the Delaware and Hudson Canal.* Fallsburg, N.Y.: Steingart Associates, 1965.

Washington, George. *The Writings of George Washington from the Original Manuscript Sources, 1745-1799.* Washington: U.S. Government Printing Office, 1932.

Wayside Scenes Along the Philadelphia and Easton Electric Railway. A brochure in The Bucks County Historical Society library.

Williams, David G. "The Lehigh Canal System." *Proceedings Lehigh County Historical Society,* Vol. 22, 1958, pp. 99-135.

White, Canvass. *Papers.* Cornell University Collection of Regional History, Box 609.

White, Josiah. *Josiah White's History given by himself.* Privately printed.

Whitford, Noble E. *History of the Canal System of the State of New York Together with Brief Histories of the Canals of the United States and Canada.* 2 vols. Albany: Brandow Printing Co., 1906.

Wildes, Harry Emerson. *The Delaware.* The Rivers of America Series. New York: Rinehart and Co. 1940.

Wood, Leslie C. *Rafting on the Delaware River.* Livingston Manor, N.Y.: Livingston Manor Times, 1934.

Wyld, Lionel D. *Low Bridge, Folklore of the Erie Canal.* Syracuse: Syracuse University Press, 1962.

INDEX

(Italicized page numbers indicate illustrations or maps)

Buck Creek 78, 124
Bucks County Historical Society,
  The 9, 31, 40, 85, 207, *215*, *216*
Bucks County Intelligencer 112, 199
Bucks County Park Foundation 213
Bucks County Playhouse (Parry
  Gristmill) 70
Bucks County Women's Club 228
Buffalo 201
Burlington 189
Burns, James 118
Burns, Joseph 185
Burns and Allen 203
Busick, Joseph 66

C

Cable Ferry or Rope Ferry
  (Easton) 28, 93, 169
Cable Ferry (New Hope) 74, 93,
  94, 124, *172*
Cable Ferry, operation of 93-4
Cake and Beer House 163-4, 171
Calkings, Blake 3
Camden 176
Camden and Amboy Rail Road and
  Transportation Co. 152
Canalboats, 18, 21, 22, 32, *84*, 95,
  96, 97, *98*, 99, 100, 101, 103, 114,
  132, *132*, 133-37, 146, 152, 153,
  155, 171, 182, 199, 200, 201, *202*,
  203, 207, 218-220
Canalboats, cabin 100, 101, 187
Canalboats, construction 102-03,
  133-34
Canalboats, poles 103
Canalboats, weighing of 90, 91
Canal Commissioners 14, 15, 16, 17,
  18, 45, 95, 107, 108, 112, 115, 116,
  117, 120, 166, 194, 220
Canal Dimensions (Prism) 18, 19,
  148, 149, 150, 152, 153, 154, 155
Canal Maintenance 19, 21, 107, 108,
  109, 110, 111, 112, 113, 114, 115,
  116, 117, 118, 119, 120, 121, 122,
  123, 124, 125, 126, 136, 203, 204,
  233
Canal Museum at the Forks of the
  Delaware 25, *25*, 27
Canal Society of New York State
  12, *129*
Capstan *84*, 103, 220
Captain (Canalboat) 87, 99, 101,
  138, 140, 141, 142, 161, 162, 163,
  164, *164*, 166, 168, 169, 170, 172,
  176, 179, 180, 181, 184, 185, 189,
  190, 192, 196, 203, 206, *208*
Carbondale 154
Carpenterville 9
Catfish Pond, see Coalport
Cat and Fiddle, The 60
Catasauqua 159, 192, 214
Cement, hydraulic 43, 45, 84
Central Rail Road of New Jersey
  137, 206

Centre Bridge 9, 66, 121, 171
Centre Bridge Inn 67
Chain Bridge (Lehigh Gap) 121
Chain Dam (Glendon) 143, 160
Chapman, John 223
Charles F. Howell 139
Chemung Canal 130
Chesapeake City 109
Chesapeake and Delaware Canal 109
Chez Odette 72
Cholera 21, 198, 199
Chunkers 95, 205
Church, I. M. 142, 143, 146
Clark, Hall H. 233, 236
Clark, James 108
Clearfield (Pa.) 231
Cleveland, Grover 64
Clinton, DeWitt 201
Clymer, Lee S. 35
Clymer Power Co., The 35, 37
Coal, anthracite 127, 128, 129, 130,
  131, 132, 133, 134, 135, 136, 137,
  138, 139, 140, 141, 142, 143, 144,
  146, 154
Coal Company, see Lehigh Coal and
  Navigation Company
Coalport 171, 189
Cobblestones 47, 48
Coffeetown 158
Colligan's Inn 66
Columbia University 151
Columbia University Press 232
Columbo, Russ 203
Colvin, Anderson 48
Commerce 157, 200
Commercial Herald 130
Company Boats 135, 184
Composite Lock 84
Connelly, John *89*
Connor, James 211
Construction (section contracts)
  13, 16, 17
Construction 18, 19
Cook, Fred 232
Cook, Morris Llewellyn 230
Cooks Creek 211
Cooper, Lewis S. 107, 108
Cooper, Hewitt & Co. 155, 214
Cooper Creek 176
Coryell's Ferry 67, 70
Council for the Preservation of
  Natural Beauty 231, 236
Cramp Ship Yard 176
Crane, George 214
Crane Iron Furnace Co. 159, 214
Creveling, Roy *237*
Critic 207
Crosman, John 206, *208*
Culverts 19, 92
Culvert (Cuttalossa Creek) 125
Culvert (Primrose Creek) 67
Cuttalossa Creek 64, 125
Cuttalossa Inn 65
Cuttalossa Road 65, 66

281

Martin, David 23
Mary Ann Furnance 129
Mary P 204, 205
Mathews, Jackson 55, *56*
Mauch Chunk 15, 21, 22, 23, 95, 118, 121, 122, 123, 127, *129*, 130, 131, 135, 136, 137, 139, 147, 148, 149, 150, 159, 165, 171, 172, 181, 187, *188*, 190, 191, 201, 205, 207, 214, 224
M'Calla & Co. 23
M'Culloch, George P. 150
Meliner's 189
Menninghoffs 168
Metropolitan Museum of Art 76, 206
Mexico, see Uhlertown
Michael Uhler Line 52, 139, 140, 190
Michaels, Ralph *33*
Milford (N.J.) 40, 46, 139, 141, 216
Milk House 164, 173, 181
Miller, Russel 196
Millers 168
Milton Creek, see Paunaucussing Creek
Minder, William A. 142, 143
Mineo 197
Minisink Ford 1
Mitchell boys of Callicoon 3
Missouri Valley Dredging Co. 204
Mitre Gates 84, 85
Mohawk River (N.Y.) 218
Molly McGuires 137
Molly-Polly-Chunker, see Log of . . .
Monongahela Navigation 146
Monroe 9, 158, 194
Moore, Capt. James 75
Morgan 140
Morris, Anthony 212
Morris, James H. 35
Morris Canal 14, 16, *24* (Map), *28*, 88, 95, 96, 97, 99, 114, 130, 131, 135, 144, 146, 150, 151, *151*, 152, 159, 160, 169, 183, 194, 196
Morris Canal and Banking Co. 150, 151
Morrisville 9, 15, 78, 79, 80, 111, 116, 173, 194, 210, 236, *238*
Mountainside Restaurant 62
Mules *30*, 126, 128, 132, 153, *158*, 161, 162, *162*, 163, 164, 165, 166, 169, 170, 171, 175, 176-181, *178*, 182, 185, 191, 195, 197, 198, 201, 203, 205, 206
Mules, substitution for 32, 195, *195*, 196
Musconetcong River 40
Mutz, Larry 175
Myrtil, Madame Odette 72

N

Narrows Hotel 46

Narrowsville 9, 10, 44, 45
Narrowsville Grist Mill 44, 45
Narrowsville Lock, see Lock No. 20
Neshaminy Purchase 223
Neversink River 1
Neversink Valley 154
New Brunswick 14, 152, 153, 171, 172
New Hope 19, 57, 66, 67, *68* (Map), *69* (Map), 70, 72, 74, 77, 88, 107, 108, 110, 111, *115*, 116, 118, 119, 121, 124, 125, 131, 138, 140, 143, 145, 170, 171, 173, 180, 181, 190, 194, 198, 201, 203, 234, 236
New Hope Historical Society 70
New Hope Fire Company 236
New Hope Gazette 203, 204, 233
New Hope Mills 67
New Jersey State Archives *153*
New York 14, 115, 116, 132, 133, 135, 150, 153, 154, 165, 170, 171, 172, 190, 194, 201, 203, 230, 234
New York Commercial 199
Newark 130, 150, 152, 160, 194, 196
Newtown 112
Neyer, Joseph 128
Nice, John, Jr., 141
Nicholas Biddle 200
Nighthawker *84*, 101, *156*, 158, 193
Nockamixon Palisades 42
Northampton 112
Northampton County 225
Northampton County Historical and Genealogical Society *26*, 194
Nott, Rev. Dr. Eliphalet 129
Notzer, Peter 170

O

Oberacker, Jacob *12*
Oblinger, Clint 205
Old Ferry Inn 76
Orr, Painter and Co. 101
Outlet Lock 88
Outlet Lock (Easton) 16, 17, 18, *24* (Map), 28, *28*, 47, 88, 169
Outlet Lock (New Hope) 47, *68* (Map), *73*, 74, 88, 116, 117, 124, 131, 133, 171, 198, 220
Overflow 30, *30*, 75, 93, 170
Overpeck, William *56*
Owens, Gifford 212

P

P. & R. R.R. Co. 138
Packer, Asa 136
Packets 95, 106, 152, 154, 155, 194, 201
Paetzell, Russell 142, 143, 231
Palmer, Timothy 23
Palmerton Camera Club *145*
Panic of 1873 131, 137
Parry, Benjamin 67

283

284

285

286

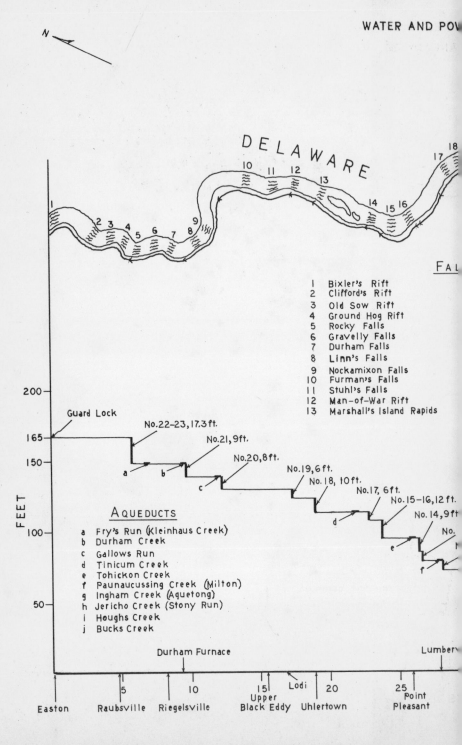

DELAWARE

18
17

10 11 12
13
14 15 16

1
2 3 4 5 6 7 8 9

Fal

1 Bixler's Rift
2 Clifford's Rift
3 Old Sow Rift
4 Ground Hog Rift
5 Rocky Falls
6 Gravelly Falls
7 Durham Falls
8 Linn's Falls
9 Nockamixon Falls
10 Furman's Falls
11 Stuhl's Falls
12 Man-of-War Rift
13 Marshall's Island Rapids

Guard Lock

No.22-23, 17.3 ft.

No.21, 9ft.

No.20, 8ft.

No.19, 6ft.

No.18, 10ft.

No.17, 6ft.

No.15-16, 12ft.

No.14, 9ft

No.

No.

200

165

150

FEET

100

50

a
b
c
d
e
f

AQUEDUCTS

a Fry's Run (Kleinhaus Creek)
b Durham Creek
c Gallows Run
d Tinicum Creek
e Tohickon Creek
f Paunaucussing Creek (Milton)
g Ingham Creek (Aquetong)
h Jericho Creek (Stony Run)
i Houghs Creek
j Bucks Creek

Durham Furnace

Lumber

5
10
15
Lodi
20
25

Easton   Raubsville   Riegelsville   Upper   Uhlertown   Point
                                       Black Eddy   Pleasant